To Frances Bell, with all
best wishes and thanking you
for attending my lecture!
Richard W. Ruth
May, 1975

Investments
You Can Live With
and Enjoy

Investments You Can Live With and Enjoy

by Richard H. Rush and
the Editors of U.S.News & World Report Books

Joseph Newman — Directing Editor

U.S.NEWS & WORLD REPORT BOOKS

A division of U.S.News & World Report, Inc.
WASHINGTON, D.C.

Book Trade Distribution by Simon and Schuster
Simon and Schuster Order Number 21855

Library of Congress Catalog Card Number 74-81185
Printed in the United States of America

Contents

Illustrations

Tables and Charts

Acknowledgments

Richard H. Rush, the author of the manuscript, and the Editors of *U.S.News & World Report Books* express their appreciation to the following for their valuable assistance in gathering material for this book:

Department heads at Sotheby Parke Bernet, New York: Armin B. Allen, European porcelain; Gabriel Austin, books; Mary-Anne Berman, modern paintings and drawings; Barbara Deisroth, Art Nouveau and Art Deco; James R. Fack, old master paintings; Kirk A. Igler, European furniture and rugs; Joseph J. Kuntz, European works of art; James J. Lally, Chinese art; Judy Landrigan, nineteenth-century European paintings; Marc E. Rosen, prints; Dennis J. Scioli, jewelry; Kevin L. Tierney, silver and antique jewelry; and David Tripp, coins.

Department heads at Christie, Manson & Woods, London: J.M. Broadbent, wines, Gregory Martin, old master paintings, and Douglas Massey, rare book and manuscript authority.

Auctioneers Charles Hamilton, New York, and Bernard D. Harmer, of H.R. Harmer, New York, and dealers Vojtech Blau,

New York; Edmund Dring, managing director of Bernard Quaritch, Ltd., London; Lucien Goldschmidt, New York; Martin Zimet and Robert Samuels of French and Company, New York; Alan Hartman, Rare Art, Inc., New York; Mary A. Benjamin, New York; Jack Tanzer, M. Knoedler and Company, New York; Spencer Samuels, New York; Messrs. Vose of the Vose Galleries, Boston; Harold Leger and Stuart Leger, Leger Galleries, London; Clyde Newhouse, Newhouse Galleries, New York; and Alfio Moriconi, Calvert Wine and Cheese Shop, Washington, D.C.

Collector J. Paul Getty and art authorities and collectors Robert and Bertina Suida Manning and the late Dr. William E. Suida.

The librarians of the Frick Art Reference Library, New York; the National Gallery of Art, Washington, D.C.; the Metropolitan Museum of Art, New York; the Netherlands Royal Art Archives, The Hague; and the Arnold Witt Library of the Courtauld Institute, the University of London.

John Herbert of Christie, Manson & Woods, London; Liz Robbins Walley, Peggy Shannon, and Martin Stansfeld of Clark, Nelson, Ltd., New York, for Sotheby Parke Bernet, New York; and Richard A. Holman, publisher of the *Wall Street Transcript*, New York.

Julie Rush, who assisted her husband in his research by taping interviews with leading authorities on the various types of collectibles, and who assisted in the selection of photographs.

Roslyn Grant of *U.S.News & World Report Books* edited the manuscript and coordinated the editorial work on the book, assisted by Judith Gersten.

PART ONE

The Boom in Collectibles

Prices are reaching new highs in the fields of art, antiques, and antiquities as the boom in collectibles continues. This Dutch silver-gilt nautilus cup, 11½ inches high, made by Jan Jacobsz van Royesteyn in 1596, was purchased for $800 in 1938. In 1973 it was sold for $55,000.

CHAPTER 1

Unique Investments

Almost every area of collectibles—from twentieth-century American paintings to antique English furniture to Oriental objects—is booming in sales volume and in price.

The main causes of this boom have been the general prosperity of the industrial nations of the world and inflation, which in many industrialized countries is approaching 10 percent per year and in some countries exceeds 10 percent. One of the principal objectives in collecting is to purchase items which will increase in value each year more than the rate of inflation.

The decline in the value of currency, including the dollar, has been another important factor in the collectibles boom. Many collectors have been motivated by the wish to rid themselves of weak currency and acquire objects which will not only retain their value but possibly increase in worth.

From a pure investment point of view, the stock market has been the main competitor of the collectibles market. Throughout the 1950s and up to the late 1960s, the stock market competed well with collectibles. Stocks rose rapidly in this period. Although a number of collectibles rose too, it was not until after 1968 that the contrast between collectibles and the stock market became sharp. Following the recession of 1969-1970, the stock market did not recover, but collectibles rose steadily and some skyrocketed. For this reason many collectibles have proved to be a better investment by far than the stock market since 1968.

In the early part of 1974 trouble struck on various fronts. The boom in the national economy was petering out. Inflation was rampant and growing. Washington was filled with scandal. Oil imports were cut. Fuel prices rose, and so did utility bills. The automobile industry was hard hit. In response, the stock market was in the doldrums. However, the prices of collectibles did not decrease. Thus, if a collector-investor did not like what he saw on the economic horizon, he had sufficient time to liquidate his investment in collectibles at auction.

While it is reasonable to believe that a serious worldwide recession would reduce the values of collectibles, a recession in the United States alone would not have this effect as collectibles have a worldwide market, which is not dependent on the state of the economy in the United States.

The investor in art, antiques, and other collectibles can enjoy his investments apart from any consideration of their rising value. If the investor is interested in what he is collecting, his collection brings him tremendous "psychic income." The stock market cannot supply this satisfaction. Neither can part-ownership of a piece of commercial real estate, nor a mortgage, nor a certificate of deposit.

Price movements studied

Almost all paintings traded on the international art market on the average doubled in price between 1950 and 1955. They tripled in the years 1955 to 1960 so that in the decade between 1950 and 1960 they went up six times in value. In the next decade they tripled again, so that in twenty years they went up eighteen times, and they better than doubled between 1970 and the end of 1973.

This appeared to be a great performance until the price movements in other fields of collectibles were studied. The general tendency was for items other than paintings to be bought as painting prices rose. The collector who had bought old masters began to purchase classic automobiles instead, as an example. This movement from a high-priced field to lesser-known areas pushed up the prices of virtually all collectibles. It even affected some items that until the past few years were considered entirely out of the field of collectibles and not worthy of collector interest, such as British fairings, little objects given away or sold for a penny or two at fairs. Some fairings are now selling for over $1,000. This move-

Art Prices vs. the Stock Market

Comparison of Rise, 1960-73
Base: 1960 = 100%

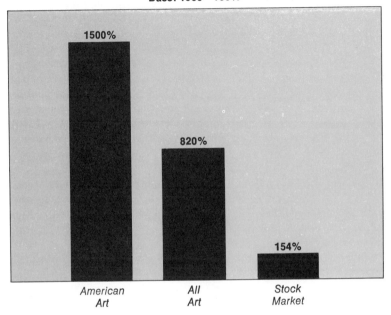

Comparison of Rise in 1973
Base: 100%

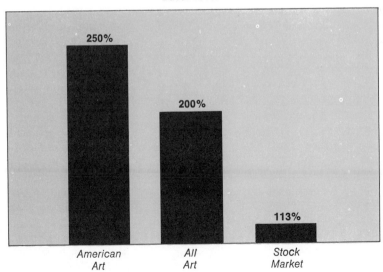

ment to new collectibles can be expected to continue indefinitely.

The price of anything results from the interaction of supply and demand. In the case of collectibles, there is usually an absolutely fixed supply, since most collectibles have an antique rarity. There are, for example, about thirty-six known paintings by Vermeer in existence. Over the years all but six of these paintings have found their way into museums. Six Vermeers were in private hands in 1945. There are still six in private hands, and if a collector wants a Vermeer, he can buy only from among these six, provided any private owner wants to sell. In 1961 a London dealer made an offer of $1 million for a Vermeer owned by an American, who refused to sell it at that price. In 1968 an offer of $2 million was transmitted to the American owner, who promptly replied, "I think my Vermeer is worth $10 million."

Investment capital is enormous as compared with the volume of available collectibles, and this fact is of key importance in forecasting prices. Investment capital is being organized into "financial funds," such as Modarco in Switzerland and Artemis in Belgium—organizations which buy paintings and other art objects solely as investments looking to future appreciation.

Private capital in the hands of collectors and funds organized as investment trusts will increase in the future, while the supply of paintings, antiques, and other collectibles diminishes, and while more and more of these items move into museums in response to governmental tax policy. The price level over the long run is thus likely to be up. However, ridiculous price heights are being reached by certain collectibles, such as Georgian flatware at $70 an ounce and Chinese tureens at $140,000 a pair as of the spring of 1974. This indicates that there will be a movement of collectors out of sky-high price areas and into areas of lower price levels.

At some point there must be a halt in the price rise of collectibles in general. Otherwise a projection of present price trends would lead to $10,000 for a Georgian coffee pot of ordinary quality and $10 million for a Jackson Pollock painting as of the year 1980.

Home furnishings favored

Most of the collecting that is booming now consists of elegant things for the home—clocks, Oriental carpets, Georgian silver, modern and old master paintings. To a considerable extent today, the up-to-date home—even the small house or the compact apartment—contains art, antiques, and antiquities. No longer are the pictures with gilt frames and the Oriental rugs exclusively for palaces and mansions. While the home with entirely new furnishings is not by any means out of style, the home furnished with antiques is decidedly emphasized in the 1970s.

Vory raro underglaze copper-red wine ewer sold in London in late 1973 for
$400,000.

If elegant decor is also a good investment, the lid flies off the buying of art, antiques, and antiquities. It does not seem such an extravagance to purchase an item for $2,500 if, soon after the buyer gets it home, he is offered $15,000 for it. This happened recently to a collector who acquired an eighteenth-century Chinese red lacquer table for $2,500 and a few months later was offered $15,000 for it.

Pleasure and profit combined

The purpose of this book is to tell you how to combine pleasurable collecting with profitable investment. You need not sell your collectibles if you prefer to keep them, but this book will try to help you to collect items which are likely to rise in value, whether or not you intend to take advantage of the increase in value by selling.

Even if the collector has absolutely no intention of investing for future sale, the fact that he can sell at a profit goes a long way toward quieting his conscience after he has spent $5,700 for a set of four Venetian armchairs.

Perhaps this book will be of value to the affluent collector, but it is intended primarily for the person who has enough income and enough savings to invest only modest sums in collectibles. Most investments discussed are in the range of, say, $100 for an English watercolor to perhaps $10,000 for an old master painting, a classic car, or a set of eighteenth-century chairs. Within this price range many investment collectibles will be explored and indications given of what to look for, where to find such items, and how to judge value. Price trends of the past will be analyzed so that an idea may be formed of future values.

The collectibles discussed in this book have been included because they meet three standards: They are for the most part not too expensive to purchase; they are available in sufficient quantity to make them relatively easy to acquire; and they are likely to repay the collector most handsomely from both the aesthetic and the financial viewpoints.

To get some idea of the magnitude of demand for these collectibles, we can look at the sales figures of America's largest auction house for just two seasons: the 1972-1973 season versus the previous season, 1971-1972.

- In just one year the entire category of American paintings rose in sales volume from $2,991,700 to $7,985,320.
- In the same period, contemporary art, mainly American art of recent origin, rose from $950,000 to $2,035,025. Minor paintings rose from $600,000 to $1,577,000.
- The sales of jewelry increased from $3,946,000 to $7,387,000.
- The sales of prints increased from $1,213,000 to $2,816,000.

- American furniture and decorations rose from $1,924,000 to $2,520,000, while antique silver rose from $1,430,000 to $1,712,000.
- The catch-all category of porcelain, bronzes, tapestries, glass paperweights, and some other items rose from $1,979,000 to $3,218,000.
- Chinese art rose from $1,367,000 to $2,509,000 and Japanese art skyrocketed from $187,350 to $1,504,730.

If only a fraction of this rate of increase is maintained each year during the next decade, collectibles would prove to be one of the greatest "growth investments" of the century.

The knowledgeable investor will pick areas which have not experienced a great price rise to date and where artistic value seems great in relation to cost. If collectibles are invested in wisely and with knowledge of both the items and their price history, they can be both a prime investment and a life-enriching experience.

T'ang dynasty glazed figure of a mounted drummer, 16¼ inches high, sold for $113,000 in mid-1973. This is a superb piece, but there are fake T'ang horses on the market which cannot easily be distinguished by the nonexpert.

CHAPTER 2

How
to
Collect

Luck of course plays a part in collecting, as it does in other human endeavors. The good luck to be in the right place at the right time has enabled many collectors to acquire remarkable bargains. But knowledge, not luck, is the essential ingredient for successful collecting. Knowledge enables the collector to recognize a great buy when he sees one. Knowledge can also help him to avoid the fakes and copies which abound in many fields of collectibles. Sometimes collectors are even more knowledgeable than those who earn their living by buying and selling the rare and valuable accouterments of civilization.

Not very long ago a collector spied a pair of antique urn-shaped knife boxes in a shop on Third Avenue in New York. He examined them very carefully to make sure they were from the eighteenth century. When he was convinced that they were of that period, he asked the price. The clerk said that he was not sure about the price but asked the collector to return in two hours when the shop owner would be there.

The collector proceeded to the nearest lunch counter and there drank coffee until the two hours were up. He then went back to the shop, where the dealer informed him that the price of the two knife boxes was $150.

The money was virtually out of the collector's pocket and paid before the dealer had finished stating the price. The dealer then looked around and added, "You know, I have another matching box, a smaller one, for spoons." It was all the collector could do to conceal his feelings. Finally he said, "Well, now that I have paid $150, I don't have much money left. How much will the third box cost me?"

A price of $20 for the third box was decided on. Just as the collector was about to leave with his purchases, the dealer raised the lid of one of the boxes and remarked, "I didn't see that label on the inside of the top!"

The label read, "Art Treasures Exhibition of 1928—Number 129."

The collector's heart sank. The label looked like a perfect "plant." He could visualize the dealer affixing hundreds of these labels to fake antiques. Nevertheless, the deal was done and the collector took his purchases away somewhat anxiously.

The collector's next job was to try to locate the "Art Treasures Exhibition of 1928." He searched for a mention of it in the antique magazines of the period and in the newspapers, but found nothing— which confirmed his opinion that the label was probably a fake.

Still, he decided to make one more try. He went to the Metropolitan Museum of Art and examined the card catalog. There he found it: "Art Treasures Exhibition of 1928—London."

He quickly secured the catalog of the exhibition and looked for Number 129. There it was: "Three Urn-Shaped Adam Knife Boxes, Circa 1775." They were placed on exhibition by M. Harris and Company, leading London antique dealers.

From the Metropolitan the collector went immediately to the Madison Avenue firm of Ginsburg and Levy, specialists in this particular field of antiques, and, as casually as possible, asked Mr. Ginsburg his estimate of the value of a pair of Adam urn-shaped knife boxes, circa 1775. Mr. Ginsburg answered, "About $2,500."

The collector then asked, "How about a third box for spoons?" Mr. Ginsburg replied, "I don't know. I haven't seen a set of three urn-shaped knife boxes in years."

Some time later the collector discussed the boxes with the Third Avenue dealer who had sold them, in order to learn more about the background of the boxes. The dealer did not seem to be particularly dismayed that he had let three rare antique knife boxes go for $170. In fact, he volunteered the story about how he had acquired the boxes. He said, "Those boxes were brought to me by the garbage man. He wanted to know whether I wanted to buy them. I paid him $50 for the three!"

Although such finds are certainly still possible, the novice collector should bear in mind that more and more people are learning about more and more collectibles. As they learn quality and values, they buy, and there are therefore fewer and fewer collectibles for sale at bargain prices that turn out to be rare works worth many times what they cost.

How to begin collecting

When you are ready to begin collecting, you might follow these steps:

1. *Take a "self-taught" course in your chosen collectible.* If you want to collect French modern paintings, for example, borrow or buy all the books you can on the subject and study them. Also visit museums and familiarize yourself with the various artists in the school.

2. *Visit dealers.* The obvious source of many, if not most, collectibles is dealers, and you should begin by visiting them whether you are considering Gallé glass, French paperweights, classic cars, paintings, ceramics, coins, stamps, or any other collectible. The dealer has a selection you can inspect, and the more dealers you visit the more collectibles you will see—to get an idea of what is available and at what prices.

One of the primary reasons for visiting dealers and buying from them is to learn more about your collectible. The antique dealer, for example, will show you what to look for in order to determine the authenticity and age of a piece of furniture, how to spot a restoration that may diminish an item's value, and how to distinguish a fine piece from a poor one.

The better dealers handle better items, so buying from a reputable dealer is also some assurance of authenticity, originality of the piece, and overall quality.

In the case of some collectibles, it is best to buy from the dealer as a general policy. The dealer in classic automobiles, as an example, can put the car into good condition without difficulty and at relatively low cost. He is not likely to offer for sale a car in need of extensive repairs, and if the car develops faults shortly after purchase, he may make repairs at little or no cost. He is also likely to give preference to the purchaser whenever the car needs repairs in the future—a point to remember when, as at the present time, it is not unusual to have to leave a car in a repair shop for six weeks for a job that requires only two days of concentrated repair work.

In the present rising market for many collectibles, including boom markets for art, antiques, Rolls-Royce cars, and other items, the dealer often has old stock which he purchased months or even years ago when prices were lower, and these items may sometimes be bought at less than auction prices.

3. *Get auction catalogs and price lists and attend auctions.* In an auction house, authenticity of an item and its condition are generally not so important as they are to the dealer. An auction house is simply an agent and a warehouse for selling items that belong to others. Therefore, an auction house can warrant authenticity and condition only up to a point.

Still, for the expert buyer, auctions are a must, and with present scarcities in a number of collectibles, auction houses perform a real service for collectors by gathering together collectibles for sale. In the case of eminent collections, very often the auction house has a virtual monopoly. The seller of a fine collection knows that the auction house will definitely sell his entire collection, that he will receive a lump-sum payment within a specific time, and that the auction house will advertise and publicize the items he is selling if they are to any extent outstanding.

The auction house is a gold mine for knowledgeable collectors who want to make such discoveries as paintings labeled "English School" that turn out to be genuine Romneys. The more knowledgeable the collector the safer it is for him to buy at auction.

Auction house officials are not only knowledgeable in their fields, but they stand ready to advise the collector about the authenticity, condition, and general desirability of items offered for sale.

4. *Set up an acquisition budget.* Determine in advance about how much you want to spend for any one piece or, better still, how much you want to invest over a period of, say, a year. At the end of the year an assessment can be made to determine your budget for the next year.

5. *Decide whether your collecting is to be done out of income or out of capital.* Should purchases be made from current savings or should a security or other investment be sold and replaced with a collectible? This decision is extremely important, because it will determine whether you will be a serious and substantial investor.

6. *Place an absolute limit on the amount you will pay for any one purchase.* Purchases at first might be limited to $1,000 a painting, for example. Then mistakes, which occasionally are made, are not so difficult to take, and losses are not unbearable. As time goes on and you gain knowledge and self-confidence, your arbitrary dollar limit, whatever it is, might be raised.

7. *Locate experts in the field of your chosen collectible.* Such persons are usually the ultimate judges of authenticity and condi-

Woody River Landscape by the seventeenth-century Dutch painter Aelbert Cuyp was auctioned in June, 1973, for $1,400,000.

tion. If you decide to collect Dutch paintings, for example, you should have the paintings authenticated by the Netherlands Art Archives in The Hague. If you collect stamps, you should make sure you have not purchased fakes by showing them to such experts as New York auctioneer H. R. Harmer. The same applies to auction specialist Charles Hamilton if you collect autographs. In each field there is at least one expert whose opinion is of great value when acquiring a collectible, whether it is George Washington's signature or a four-dollar gold piece or a Rembrandt.

8. *Buy quality.* Quality items hold up the best in value over the years. In a rising market they also tend to rise the most in value. Buy a coin in good condition, a good example of an artist's painting, a fine Penny Black stamp.

9. *Do not necessarily buy the most expensive items.* The most expensive collectible is not necessarily the best investment. The most sought after of all recent vintage wines is Lafite-Rothschild 1961. Yet this wine, which sells for well over $100 a bottle, did not necessarily rise faster in price than a good château-bottled 1961 Bordeaux that sold for $2.50 a bottle in 1971.

If you buy less expensive items of quality you may find a readier market when you wish to sell them, since the higher the price the fewer the persons who can afford to purchase a collectible.

In the December 6, 1973, auction sale of old masters held at the

Sotheby Parke Bernet Galleries in New York, the lowest-priced paintings of one collector sold at enormous multiples over their cost, while his finer paintings had a hard time finding buyers.

10. *Locate all organizations that may be of assistance to you in your collecting.* If you collect antique cars, for example, subscribe to the antique car magazines and join the antique car clubs. They and their members can be of great assistance to you. If you live in or near New York and you collect old master or even later paintings, use the Frick Art Reference Library and its extensive files to "prove out" paintings and to learn the history of paintings already in your collection.

11. *Try to document each collectible.* If the item is subject to documentation, list such information as where you bought it, when you bought it, from whom you bought it, how much you paid for it, changes you made in it and when, and what its background was prior to your purchase. Information regarding a collectible's history often adds tremendously to its value. You might maintain a file on each major purchase. Some collectors have found such files of great value when their collections were finally good enough to go on public display. Public display, incidentally, often increases value considerably—a Jaguar XK150 roadster that won the Jaguar Award three times was for sale for twice the price of similar cars with a less illustrious background.

Investment guidelines

If you wish to collect for investment, you should:

• Concentrate on objects that have the best prospect of increasing in value—in the not-too-distant future. These are items which at the present time are showing a definite rise in value, not those which may in the future possibly rise in value.

• Concentrate on collecting objects which have definite market prices so that values are easily determinable. Prices paid at auctions are your best guide in determining values. Supplement these with dealer prices, whenever possible, to confirm trends and values.

• Keep a close watch on the market for collectibles by checking the value-guide publications and the priced catalogs of Sotheby Parke Bernet in New York and Christie's and Sotheby's auctions in London. These large, general auction houses sell catalogs with price lists for ceramics, glassware, American twentieth-century paintings, French antiques, American antique silver, and pre-Columbian art, among many collectibles. And bear in mind that England is the most important art, antique, and antiquity market in the world.

• Concentrate on items which are readily purchasable. You could

Those seeking to invest in collectibles have a wide range from which to choose, including items such as these: from top to bottom and left to right, French Art Deco bracelet set with diamonds and jade, William III coin, Penny Black stamp, Bordeaux wine, Sèvres porcelain tray, walnut slant-front desk made in New England circa 1760-80, and a 1930 Bugatti supercharged two-seater.

very likely look in vain all of your life if you want to buy a painting by Leonardo da Vinci, a jewel by Cellini, or a statue by Michelangelo. Suitable collectibles must quite often appear on the market at prices within your means.

• Concentrate on items which are hard to fake and on items whose condition is not extremely difficult to determine. T'ang dynasty horses, for example, are not very easy for the nonexpert to distinguish from fakes, and elaborate restorations on genuine T'ang pieces are often almost impossible for the amateur collector to spot.

• Concentrate on items which will form a collection. The collection should grow in time and become more nearly perfect. It should have some unity in order to provide the collector with satisfaction.

• Concentrate on items which are not too plentiful, so that as demand goes up and prices rise, the market is not flooded with such items.

• Be wary of collecting fad items. As an example, prices of certain minor abstract expressionist paintings, particularly of the Greek school, crashed in Paris in the early 1960s. A collector who had invested heavily in such paintings might well have sustained large losses.

• Seek out undervalued items or those whose values seem to be lagging, such as eighteenth-century British portraits and British watercolors by the minor masters.

• Collect items which are of interest to other collectors, so that you can exchange information, views, and market news.

• Concentrate on collectibles for which there is a trade paper providing information on the items and their prices.

• Find out if there is a club of collectors of your collectible. Such clubs exist for sports cars, antique cars, watches, coins, stamps, and many other collectibles. Clubs put out publications of value to collectors and facilitate the exchange of information among members.

• Consider carefully whether you want to collect items which require much storage space, such as classic cars; items which require much restoration and maintenance, such as antique cars; items which require special storage conditions and which may deteriorate, such as vintage wines; or items, such as old master paintings, which are very expensive to insure and protect.

• When you profit from selling an item, consider using the sales price—or a portion of it—to acquire other items for your collection. One collector of vintage wines determined to take out all of his sales proceeds until this amount covered his entire investment. The wine left in his inventory then was, in a sense, "for free" and he could drink it or let it age and increase in value. He had recouped

Portrait of Anne Pole-Carew painted by George Romney, a leading eighteenth-century British portraitist, was sold in 1973 for $6,000.

his investment in the wine, and could use the money to add to his collection.

• Do not hesitate to sell. If you are investing you must occasionally sell. Otherwise the Internal Revenue Service may conclude wisely that you are not an investor but rather collect simply to beautify your home or for other reasons. You will then be unable to deduct expenses connected with your collecting for tax purposes.

The government's position in such matters has a great deal of logic to it. How can you invest if you never receive a return on your investment? It is also a logical position from the viewpoint of the collector, who should sell for a reason in addition to the wish to realize profits: to get rid of items that the collection has "outgrown" because better examples of the collectible have been found as the collector's taste has improved.

Collect for investment—but collect the things you like, because if you collect what pleases you, it will sustain your interest in making wise investments.

PART TWO

Investing
in Art

Rembrandt's *Aristotle Contemplating the Bust of Homer* was purchased in 1961 by the Metropolitan Museum of Art, with special funds and gifts of friends of the museum, for $2,300,000. While Rembrandts bring top prices, fine paintings by artists of his school can be bought for $5,000.

CHAPTER 3

European Old Master Paintings

In many ways old masters are the most undervalued of all paintings. It is entirely possible for an astute collector today to begin acquiring gradually a very fine collection of old master paintings, without spending a fortune. In fact, a painting budget of $5,000 to $15,000 a year is sufficient.

Such a collection might well include a portrait of a man by George Romney, a landscape by Daubigny and one by Diaz de la Peña, and possibly a seventeenth-century Dutch portrait by Mierevelt or Nicolaes Maes—all museum-quality paintings. It also would be possible to include an excellent seventeenth-century Dutch landscape by an artist such as Jan Griffier or a hunting scene by the very good seventeenth-century painter of dogs, Adriaen Beeldemaker.

Fine paintings of the Italian school of the eighteenth century and earlier, such as a Pietro della Vecchia, could be included. It might also be possible to buy a masterpiece by Luca Giordano or Corrado Giaquinto.

Such a collection does not have to be secured all at once. In fact, no great collection assembled by any person, no matter how wealthy, was acquired en bloc. One of the great joys of collecting is building the collection. This process usually takes not just years but decades. In some years two, three, or more pictures may be purchased. In other years perhaps only one picture is acquired. And in some years the collector may not purchase any pictures—although this is rarely the case after one has been bitten by the "collecting bug." In the recession year of 1970, a collector found on the London art market two masterpieces a little above his ability to purchase. He therefore purchased them on the time-payment plan. There was no problem in using this method because the paintings were left with the dealers until payment was completed. Thus, the dealers ran no risk.

Old masters abound

More old master paintings by far are sold at auction than are those of any other school of art. In an analysis of its operations in connection with its issuance of stock to the public, Christie's—one of the two largest auction houses either in England or the United States—found that 29 percent of its sales consisted of old master paintings. The remaining 71 percent of sales included other schools of painting, silver, glassware, Oriental ceramics, antique and classic cars, wines, and furniture.

For two decades, impressionists have attracted enormous attention at auctions and in the press. Yet the impressionist artists are not many—Renoir, Monet, Manet, Pissarro, Sisley, Degas, Cassatt, and a very few lesser names. The postimpressionists are even fewer —Gauguin, van Gogh, Cézanne, Signac, and Seurat, and the last two are better known as pointillists than postimpressionists.

In sharp contrast to the impressionists and postimpressionists, there are about 2,000 seventeenth-century Dutch artists represented by possibly 200,000 paintings which appear on the market from time to time. There is a similar number of seventeenth-century Flemish artists whose comparable number of paintings appear in the shops of dealers or in auction salesrooms.

The Italian baroque school of art which flourished in the late sixteenth and seventeenth centuries consisted of perhaps the same number of artists as the seventeenth-century Dutch or Flemish, and baroque paintings that come onto the market number in the hundreds of thousands.

The collector who visits the art dealers and auction houses of London will find at any one time literally thousands of old master paintings for sale.

A visit to Paris can also be fruitful for the collector. The Galerie Marcus, for example, stocks several thousand old masters. Located in a back alley, the Galerie Marcus is primarily a wholesaler, specializing in sales to dealers. The collector who visits the shop indicates the school of art in which he is interested—only old masters, of course. If he says he is interested in seventeenth-century Dutch paintings, for example, the gallery attendant indicates a desk where he may sit. The attendant then hands the prospective buyer a large file of photographs of every seventeenth-century Dutch painting in the enormous stock. The collector examines each photograph until he comes to a photo of a painting he might be interested in examining further. He gives the photo to the gallery attendant, who gives it to a porter. All paintings are carefully classified and stored in numbered bins. When the prospective purchaser has selected all of the photos of paintings which might interest him, he gets up from the desk—and there are the paintings waiting for him to examine.

The Galerie Marcus is visited by leading art dealers and museum curators. The Metropolitan Museum of Art of New York City, as an example, has bought at least one masterpiece from the Galerie Marcus—a magnificent flower painting by the French artist Desportes.

A collector could put together an excellent collection over the years simply by buying from this one dealer. In late 1973, the Galerie Marcus offered a splendid pair of large paintings featuring female figures by Charles Michel-Ange Challe—certainly an artist not very inferior to Fragonard or Boucher of the eighteenth-century French school. The pair was offered for $2,500.

What are old masters?

Old master is a flexible term. It most certainly includes thirteenth-century Flemish and Italian primitives through eighteenth-century paintings. It also includes paintings of the early nineteenth century, such as those by the Spanish master Goya. The term also is sometimes extended to include the later nineteenth-century schools of art, but here we run into those treated by most art historians as separate and distinct schools, such as the impressionists who painted in the 1860s to 1880s, the postimpressionists who painted in the 1880s and 1890s, and a few other very specialized schools not generally considered as old masters.

The nineteenth-century realistic or academic schools of art are generally not considered to be old masters, whether they are English painters such as Cox and Watts, Dutch painters such as Israels and Jacob Maris, or French painters such as Tissot and Bouguereau. In the last decade the nineteenth-century Italian school, the realistic painters, has developed into a tremendously popular and high-priced group of artists, but traded for the most part only in Italy. These traditional, realistic, nineteenth-century schools of art are enormous in size and will not be treated here as old masters. Still, paintings by artists of these schools are rising in price rapidly, whereas a decade ago they were in relatively little demand.

On the other hand, paintings of good quality from any country that were produced earlier than in the late sixteenth century are very rare and very high in price. There are not enough of these paintings on the market to make them available to the collector of modest means.

The following list is of old master schools of art which offer good possibilities for the collector who has $5,000 or $10,000 to invest. Listed are the well-known painters of the various schools, but more often than not it will be the followers and the lesser old masters of these schools who will have to be selected—unless the collector is fortunate enough to make a major discovery for little money.

- *Seventeenth-century Dutch school,* of which the highly valued leaders are Rembrandt, Hals, and Vermeer.
- *Seventeenth-century Flemish school,* of which the leaders are Rubens and Van Dyck.
- *Eighteenth-century and baroque Italian school,* which includes Giovanni Battista Tiepolo, Guardi, Antonio Canale (known as Canaletto), the Carracci family, Luca Giordano, Pittoni, and Sebastiano Ricci.
- *Eighteenth-century French school,* led by Fragonard and Boucher.
- *Eighteenth-century British portraitists,* most especially Gainsborough, Romney, Reynolds, Lawrence, Hoppner, and Raeburn.

Obviously it is not likely that a Rembrandt can be purchased for $5,000 or $10,000, but you might acquire a fine painting from the school of Rembrandt by, say, Govaert Flinck, for $5,000. You might not be able to purchase a Vermeer for any sum of money, but a somewhat similar painting by Jakob van Loo might be available for $5,000.

No known Rubens can be purchased for $5,000, but a fine drawing or even a monochromatic oil sketch by a member of Rubens's school, such as Abraham van Diepenbeeck, may well be purchased for a maximum of $5,000.

As recently as 1972, a fine Luca Giordano—one of museum quality—in the Italian school of art was for sale for about $10,000. It had been in the stock of a dealer in Rome for many years.

To date, the eighteenth-century French school of art has not risen as far in price as its quality might seem to warrant. At times, even Boucher and Fragonard can be purchased for as little as $25,000, and lesser masters in the school can still be obtained for sums under $5,000.

Occasionally excellent pictures in other old master schools of art

How Major Paintings Have Increased in Price
On the International Art Market

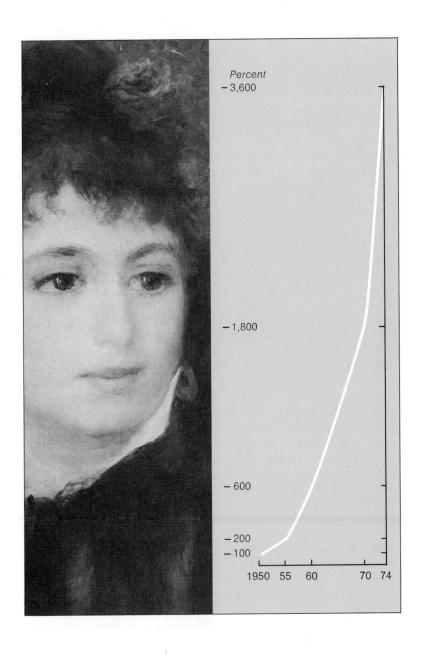

Percent
- 3,600

- 1,800

- 600

- 200
- 100

1950 55 60 70 74

are offered for sale. Sometimes these paintings sell for under $10,000, but they are few and far between on the American market.

The increase in prices

Between 1950 and 1955 the entire art market doubled in value. In other words, a painting that sold for $1,000 in 1950 would have sold for $2,000 in 1955. This market index was based on prices of 125 major artists whose paintings were traded on the international art market during the period.

The work of the approximately 2,000 Dutch painters and the 2,000 Flemish painters of the seventeenth century—primarily painters of small landscapes and seascapes, but who also turned out a number of highly competent portraits—lagged behind the overall art market and rose only about 35 percent between 1950 and 1955. The average landscape by one of the lesser artists of the school might have brought at most $250 on the market in 1950. In 1955 it might have brought $300 to $350.

In the next five-year period, 1955 to 1960, the art market tripled, but not the seventeenth-century Dutch artists, who rose only 68 percent—perhaps to $500 a painting.

By 1970, a decade later, the prices of seventeenth-century Dutch art had doubled, but the art market overall had increased threefold. Dutch art, as well as Flemish art of the seventeenth century, still lagged behind the more active schools of art in price increases.

Then Dutch and Flemish art took off. Between 1970 and late 1973, Dutch and Flemish art tripled in price. Now the simple, but competently done, little landscape was at the $3,000 level at least, and many ordinary landscapes sold for much more. At the beginning of 1974 there was still no diminution in the rate of price increase of this school of art.

Italian baroque art and Italian painting of the eighteenth century may be considered together, as their price movements are somewhat similar. Between 1950 and 1955, the prices of baroque and eighteenth-century Italian art rose only 19 percent, much less than seventeenth-century Dutch and Flemish art increased in price.

In the next five-year period—to 1960—baroque art rose even less. Its increase was 16 percent. Yet, in the ten-year period from 1950 to 1960 the art market, taken as a whole, increased sixfold.

In the next decade—to 1970—baroque and eighteenth-century Italian art rose to 280 percent of the 1960 level, compared with a 200 percent figure for Dutch art.

Between 1970 and the end of 1973, Italian baroque painting rose to 250 percent of its 1970 base. It had, in other words, increased two and a half times in about three years, while seventeenth-century Dutch paintings had risen 300 percent. In general, by early

The Price Rise for Dutch and Flemish Paintings of the Seventeenth Century

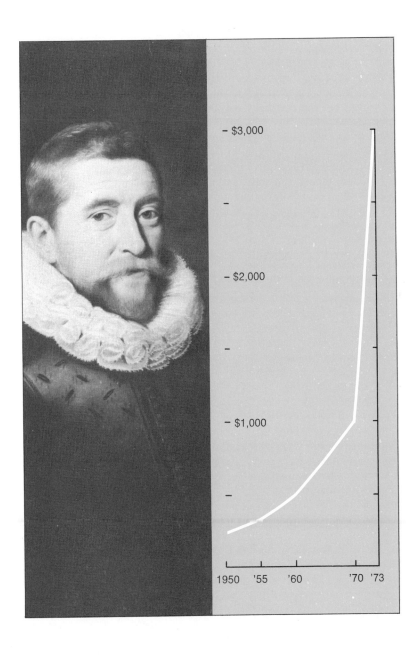

$3,000

$2,000

$1,000

1950 '55 '60 '70 '73

1974, baroque art was less expensive than seventeenth-century Dutch and Flemish art. Certainly the collector could get more picture for the same money in Italian paintings than he could in Dutch —the "cost per square inch" of Italian paintings was much less than for Dutch. Despite the price increases, $3,000 to $5,000 would buy a very good Italian baroque painting in early 1974.

The prospective collector should bear in mind that much of baroque and eighteenth-century Italian art has a religious theme, a good deal of it of an unhappy nature, and some art buyers do not care to hang such pictures in their homes. Then, too, the paintings are often quite large and not suited by size to the smaller house or city apartment. There is a great deal of pictorial action in many of the Italian paintings, whereas the Dutch paintings impart a feeling of tranquillity. The Dutch paintings have a definite decorative quality, but many of the Italian baroque paintings do not.

The eighteenth-century French school of art is a peculiar one in some ways, as compared with these Italian and Dutch paintings. The leaders, Boucher and Fragonard, are in tremendous demand at high prices. From these two greats, the drop in price to most of the other French artists of the same period is steep. A Fragonard or Boucher landscape with figures—a simple one measuring, say, eighteen by twenty-four inches—may well bring $50,000. A Lagrenée might bring under $10,000, and paintings by Challe, Noel Hallé, and many other competent artists can still be bought for a few thousand dollars each.

The price rise in this school of art has been anything but spectacular in the period from 1960 to 1974. Only highly important works have brought extraordinary prices.

Bargains in portraits

The "greatest art for the least money" is almost certainly the work of the eighteenth-century British portraitists. At the end of the 1920s this school hit a peak. It was sought out by the great collectors of the era—Frick, Morgan, Mellon, Huntington—and it represented the height of elegance, refinement, and wealth. An "average" portrait that sold for, say, $135,000 in 1929 dropped steadily to about $30,000 by 1950. In that year, a Hoppner portrait of a lady—a very attractive painting—could be purchased for well under $5,000. A Gainsborough portrait of a man was available for $10,000.

Then, in the early 1950s, the market began to turn. By 1955 there was a definite upswing in prices, and by 1960 prices were up to a level of 148 percent of the 1955 base. In the next ten years price rises lagged for this school, and rose by perhaps only 25 percent. Then they increased rapidly, and by 1973 they had risen to a level

The Price Rise for Italian Baroque
And Eighteenth-Century Paintings

of 200 percent of their 1970 base. Still, if a prospective buyer watched the market he could often purchase a masterpiece by Romney or Hoppner or Raeburn for under $5,000.

In the summer of 1973, the fine Norton Simon collection of eighteenth-century British portraits came onto the market in London. One of the masterpieces was Romney's *Lady Hamilton as a Bacchante,* a large painting, 40 by 50 inches, fluid of brushstroke and colorful. The painting sold at auction for less than $5,000. However, in mid-1974 this painting was priced at $45,000.

Tips for the would-be collector

If you are interested in the possibility of collecting old master paintings for pleasure and profit, you might take these steps:

1. Study the entire field of old masters to see what schools of art may be of most interest to you. Each of the major British artists of the eighteenth century, for example, has a definitive work written about him, together with a list of his portraits. Such books include Ward and Roberts's *Romney* and Sir Walter Armstrong's *Raeburn* and *Lawrence.* In the case of French artists, as another example, a number of specialist works have been published, such as Georges Wildenstein's *The Paintings of Fragonard.*

2. Look at paintings in museums to get a firsthand idea of the characteristics of each school of art.

3. Visit art reference libraries such as the National Gallery Library in Washington, D.C., and the Frick Art Reference Library in New York City, which have extensive files of photographs of paintings by a large number of artists in each school of art. These files will not only familiarize you with the painting styles of various artists in the school or schools in which you might be interested, but also sharpen your eye for determining whether a particular painting is actually by the master himself.

When you begin collecting

When you are ready to begin your collection, you might keep these points in mind:

• It is important to patronize reputable dealers and major auction houses that spend time and energy "proving paintings out." In old masters, the main problem often is to locate paintings which are definitely by a particular artist. Many paintings offered on the market are doubtfully attributed to masters.

In seventeenth-century Dutch art, the artist's signature is often found on the painting. This signature may, of course, be forged, but if genuine, it solves the problem of correct attribution of

The Price Rise in British Portraits
Of the Eighteenth Century

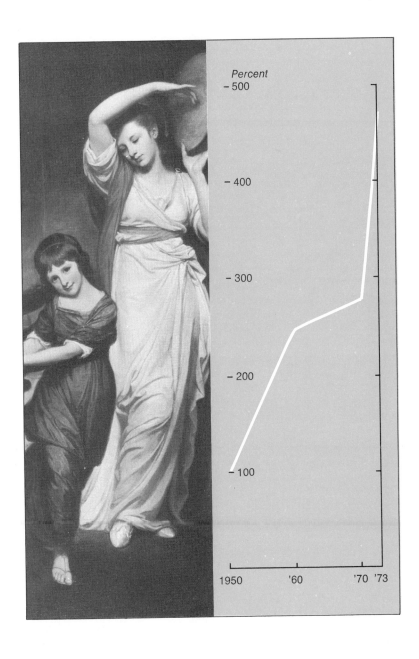

Percent

- 500

- 400

- 300

- 200

- 100

1950   '60   '70 '73

the painting. Eighteenth-century French paintings are often not signed. Italian paintings of the baroque period and of the eighteenth century are seldom signed, and the eighteenth-century British portraitists almost never signed their work. Thus the job of attribution of an unsigned painting is usually more difficult than if the painting bears a signature.

• The condition of a painting is very important. The older the painting the poorer its condition is likely to be. An ultraviolet light is very useful when looking for overpainting or restoration, which stands out from the rest of the painting as a heavy black. The more "black" the less desirable the painting is as a purchase. In time, a collector can sharpen his eye so as to detect overpainting, thinness, and restoration.

• All other things being equal, the better the provenance of a painting, the more desirable it is to own. A painting is a better buy if it has ever been sold by a large and important dealer such as M. Knoedler, Wildenstein, Agnew, Colnaghi, the Leger Galleries, or some other prestigious firm, for the reason that a major dealer thought it was good enough to purchase and resell.

To have a painting listed, and particularly illustrated, in a major work on the artist helps to prove the painting and raises its value. If a Luca Giordano is listed and illustrated in Ferrari and Scavizzi's *Luca Giordano*, the painting is to a great extent "proven."

If a prominent collector such as Norton Simon has owned the painting, it tends to assume a greater authenticity and a greater value—the reason being that if a prominent collector owned it, presumably he approved of it, and if he is prominent he very likely knows authenticity and quality.

Finally, if a painting ever was on display in London's National Gallery, or the Metropolitan in New York, or in another important museum, it tends to be regarded as more authentic and more valuable.

• The painting preferably should be beautiful. The brushwork should be well done and the subject should be pleasant for the painting to have a good value and be resalable. Beauty is becoming very important as a value determinant, and the question is often asked, "Does the painting have decorative value for a home?"

• A tiny painting usually has less value than a larger painting of equal quality, but after a particular size is reached, the painting becomes unsalable to a number of private collectors. If the artist is a great one, the work may be an excellent museum painting, but a mediocre nineteenth-century Dutch painting eight feet high and ten feet wide may have a very limited market and bring a low price at auction.

• The period of the painter's life in which the painting was produced is an important factor. A Luca Giordano painted by the artist in Venice tends to be more valuable than one painted while he was in Naples, in the same way that an American Gilbert Stuart is worth more than an English Gilbert Stuart and certainly more than an Irish Gilbert Stuart.

• The price of a painting should be in line with the market. To determine the market for a particular artist, you should consult the painting sales catalogs of the major auction houses, including Christie's and Sotheby's in London and Sotheby Parke Bernet in New York. A review of recent sales which contained pictures by the artist being considered will give a clear idea of present values—as well as price trends, to make certain that the trend is up and not down.

• Auction house officials are extremely frank in discussing paintings they have for sale, including each painting's correct attribution, history, and condition. Dealers specializing in particular artists or schools of art also can be of immense help; some of them charge a well-earned fee for assisting the purchaser.

Some collectors rely on the advice of dealers. There is one collector, for example, who owns five George Romney portraits but would never think of putting a substantial sum of money into a Romney without first consulting the Newhouse Galleries in New York, the largest dealers in eighteenth-century British portraits in this country.

Recent market prices

To give the prospective collector some idea of what is available on the market, following is a list of old masters offered for sale in just one auction—at Sotheby Parke Bernet in New York, America's largest art auction house—at the end of 1973:

Italian paintings

• Corrado Giaquinto, *A Shepherdess*, 15 by 18¾ inches; a beautiful girl holding a shepherd's crook, with lambs and cows. This is probably the loveliest of all Neapolitan artists of the period. The painting—a museum piece—sold for $4,500.

• Luca Giordano, *Saint Anne and the Virgin Adored by Saints*, 52¾ by 27⅝ inches. This is the model for the altarpiece now hanging in the Church of Santa Maria in Campitelli, in Rome, with figures of the donors added. It is by a great painter, and is beautiful as well as being in perfect condition. The price paid at the sale was $12,000.

• Luigi Garzi, *Venus at the Forge of Vulcan*, 19¾ by 25¼ inches. This painting was once in the inventory of a leading London dealer. It realized $1,700 in the auction.

A Shepherdess by Corrado Giaquinto sold at auction in New York for $4,500 at the end of 1973.

Dutch paintings

• Nicolaes Maes, *Portrait of a Lady*, 24 by 19¼ inches, signed. This is a brilliant portrait, dominated by the red dress of the sitter, by one of seventeenth-century Holland's best portraitists, examples of whose work can be found in many leading museums, including the Metropolitan Museum of Art in New York City. The painting, which came from a first-rate gallery in London, sold for $3,000.

• Wallerant Vaillant, *Portrait of a Gentleman*, 10¼ by 9 inches, signed. The price was $1,700.

• J.S. Mancadan, *A Landscape With Ruins*, 10½ by 13¾ inches. This painting, by one of the most remarkable and rare Dutch artists of the seventeenth century, sold for $4,000.

• Dirck van Deelen and Jacob de Wet, *The Liberation of Saint Peter*, 17½ by 22½ inches. A typical church interior by van Deelen with figures by de Wet, it sold for $4,000.

• Michiel Mierevelt, *Portrait of a Gentleman Said to Be Meindert Lasden*, 44½ by 33 inches. A large, brilliant, half-length portrait by one of the most popular and most competent portrait artists of seventeenth-century Holland. The picture brought $8,000.

English portraits

• George Romney, *Lady Ducie*, 92 by 57 inches. This is a full-length portrait by one of the best portrait artists of eighteenth-century England. The only deficiency in this painting is that the subject is not a particularly attractive woman. The painting was sold for $6,000. In the 1920s, it might have brought $50,000 or more.

• Sir Henry Raeburn, *Lt. Col. Shirriff*, 92 by 57 inches. This is also a full-length portrait—by the foremost Scottish artist of the eighteenth century. It was bought for $7,000 by the leading English dealer in this school of art, Harold Leger.

• Sir Thomas Lawrence, *Portrait of Francis North, Earl of Guildford*, 29½ by 24½ inches. Lawrence was one of the greatest eighteenth-century British portraitists. This painting sold for $3,500.

• Benjamin West, *Mythological Study With Many Figures*, 19 by 24¼ inches. West was an American artist who painted extensively in England. This painting realized $5,500.

• Joseph Highmore, a pair of portraits of Felix and Christianna Calvert, 35 by 38 inches, competently done and colorful, unlike a number of somber British portraits of the eighteenth century. The pair sold for $4,250.

How one collector fared

One collector sold fourteen paintings in this sale. There is absolutely accurate information available on when this collector purchased each of these paintings and how much he paid for each:

Lot 78 was the portrait by Mierevelt listed above. This painting was purchased in 1966 from Herman Galka, the New York dealer, for $700. It realized $8,000 in the sale.

Lot 79 was the Luca Giordano model for an altarpiece. This painting was purchased in 1963 from the Rome dealer Paolo Lucano for $1,000. In the 1973 sale, it brought $12,000.

Lot 80 was a landscape, 16½ by 27¼ inches, by seventeenth-century Dutch landscapist Jan Griffier. It was purchased—cleaned and framed—in The Hague in 1963 for $100. In this sale it brought $4,250.

The next lot in the sale was a 29½-by-23⅜-inch portrait of a young man by seventeenth-century Dutch artist Jan Westerbaen the Elder. It was purchased in 1965, as having been painted by an unknown artist, from New York dealer Walter F. Altschul for $200. It realized $1,500 in the sale.

The Mancadan landscape described earlier was purchased from London dealer Dennis Vanderkar in 1963 for $550. In the 1973 sale it brought $4,000. Mr. Vanderkar attended this sale, buying for his stock. It is possible that he repurchased this painting—for very much more money than he sold it for ten years before.

Lot 83 was a landscape by Dutch artist Willem Verboom, 32¼ by 44¾ inches. It was purchased privately in 1969 by the collector for $450. The owner had left it with a museum to try to find a buyer. At the 1973 auction this painting brought $3,550.

Lot 86 was the small portrait by Wallerant Vaillant listed earlier. This painting was in a sense a fake. It contained the false signature of van der Werff and was bought from the Moroney Galleries in Washington in the late 1950s for $90. After the painting was cleaned, the original signature of Wallerant Vaillant appeared under the false van der Werff signature. Perhaps 100 years ago, when the fake signature was placed over the genuine one, van der Werff was more valuable than Vaillant, but not in 1973. The Vaillant realized $1,700 at the auction.

In 1967 a dealer selling antiques at the 34th Street Armory Exhibition in New York City offered this collector a painting of fish, represented by the dealer as being "old," at least "eighteenth century." The painting contained an indecipherable signature.

The price the dealer asked for the painting seemed high to the collector. The exhibition and sale closed. But the collector could not forget the painting. He called the dealer in New Jersey and asked whether the painting had been sold at the fair. It had not. The collector then got into his car and drove to New Jersey, where a sale was concluded for $125. On the way home the collector parted with another $125 for a secondhand power lawn mower that was also for sale. The signature on the painting was later positively identified as being that of Pieter de Putter, a leading seventeenth-century Dutch artist who specialized in the portrayal of fish. In the December, 1973, auction the painting realized $2,400. A few months before the auction the lawn mower, too, was sold. It realized $150.

In 1956 an auctioneer at the Savoy Art and Auction Galleries in New York knocked down to this same collector a small painting of a church interior by Dirck van Deelen and Jacob de Wet—the former the painter of the church interior, the latter the painter of the figures of Peter and the angels. The price the collector paid was $55. In the 1973 auction he received $4,000 for this painting.

In 1963, when the collector was in London, he bought a fine Dutch landscape of a hunting party, 18 by 23½ inches, by the eminent painter of dogs, Adriaen Beeldemaker. He purchased it from Sotheby's auction house for $90. When he returned to New York a few weeks later, he found a smaller hunting scene by the same artist in the shop of Walter Altschul and purchased it for $45. At the 1973 auction, the collector refused to take two bids on these pictures—$1,500 for the first painting and $650 for the second.

Detail of a seventeenth-century Dutch painting by Pieter de Putter which was purchased for $125 in 1967 and sold in December, 1973, for $2,400.

This collector also refused the top bid of $1,750 for a Flemish seventeenth-century painting, *The Burning of Antwerp*, which he had purchased in 1961 for $180 in an art dealer's shop in Rome.

At the same auction the collector also refused a dealer's bid of $12,000 for both an early Flemish picture that had cost him $3,600 in 1967 and another painting that he had bought for $600.

Finally, he turned down $6,500 at the same auction for a fine Dutch landscape that had cost him $1,000 in 1961.

When the collector made his final tally, he found that the pictures which he had sold brought him $51,750. They had cost him a total of $6,245, and he had held the paintings an average of about eight years. The selling price turned out to be about eight and one-quarter times his purchase price for this eight-year average investment. He could have realized $22,000 more for the five paintings that did not reach his minimum prices. These paintings had cost him a little under $5,000.

He had to pay the auction house a total of $9,350 in commission, so that his net return was $45,505—over seven times his original investment. His net profit after total costs and commissions was $36,155. All of the paintings had been purchased by the collector out of his income and not out of his capital, and only two of them cost as much as $1,000. One cost over $1,000, and four cost $100 or less.

The paintings were gone, to be sure, but for many years they had added immensely to the attractiveness of his home. The collector, taking inventory after the sale of these paintings, calculated that he had parted with exactly 5 percent of his collection. The other 95 percent remained both as an investment and as an adornment for his home.

Perhaps the collector should have resented the fact that he was required to pay the auction house a commission of almost $10,000 for selling his pictures, but he did not feel resentful, since how otherwise could he have so quickly reached buyers who would take all of his paintings? Perhaps he should have resented the fact that the auction house placed reserves on his paintings at prices dealers would pay, recognizing the fact that dealers want a 100 percent markup. Perhaps he should have resented the fact that dealers bought his paintings in order to double their prices when reselling them. But he did not resent these facts either.

After considering everything about his investment in the paintings, the collector felt quite fortunate to have done so well, in view of the fact that during the morning of the auction the stock market had hit a low of under 800—after a precipitous decline of 198 points in a relatively few weeks. He also concluded that the paintings had been a unique investment—one which had held up well during a financial slide and had allowed him ample time to earn good profits before the economy of the country began a cyclical decline.

Still, it is quite possible that most of the paintings this collector sold at the auction, and also most of those remaining in his collection, may be worth even more, and some of them far more, in years to come, because art can be an excellent investment.

Nineteenth-century landscapist Thomas Moran's *Canyon Mists: Zoroaster Peak (Grand Canyon, Arizona)* brought $80,000 when auctioned in 1973, but lesser paintings by leading American landscapists of his era are available for well under $5,000.

CHAPTER 4

American Paintings

The late art dealer Edith Halpert was staunchly opposed to the idea of art as an investment and stated more than once that she would never sell a painting to any prospective purchaser who wanted to "invest in art."

In 1973, Mrs. Halpert's stock of paintings, consisting almost entirely of American art, was sold at auction in New York. She had purchased one of the paintings some years before for $2,000. At the auction this painting sold for exactly $175,000.

On October 18, 1973, the Robert C. Scull collection of American paintings was sold in the same auction house—Sotheby Parke Bernet. Mr. Scull had purchased his collection during the previous thirteen years.

As far as can be determined, the fifty works of art auctioned in this sale by Mr. Scull cost him less than $150,000. They realized at auction a total of $2,242,900.

These are his purchase prices for some of these American paintings compared with what he realized at the 1973 auction:

	Purchase Price	Auction Price
Jasper Johns—*Painted Bronze* [*Ale Cans*]	$ 960	$ 90,000
Jasper Johns—*Bronze Flag*	720	21,000
Jasper Johns—*Target*	5,000	125,000
Jasper Johns—*Double White Map*	10,200	240,000
Robert Rauschenberg—*Double Feature*	2,500	90,000
Robert Rauschenberg—*Thaw*	900	85,000
Cy Twombly—*"A"*	750	40,000

As recently as ten years ago, American art, with the exception of some of the abstracts, was generally not in demand. It was more or less traditional, "has-been" art.

Describing the work of Thomas Moran, who painted scenes of Yellowstone National Park, the Grand Canyon, and Yosemite National Park, the *Encyclopedia of Painting* states: "His later huge canvases . . . achieved, like those of Bierstadt, a monumental dullness." It should be remembered that this is a definition contained in an encyclopedia, not a critic's review of an exhibition of paintings by Thomas Moran.

In the fall of 1973, Thomas Moran's *Canyon Mists: Zoroaster Peak (Grand Canyon, Arizona)* brought $80,000. It was not quite one of his "later huge canvases [that] achieved . . . a monumental dullness." Had it been one of these, it might have sold in the 1970s for $250,000 or more.

Even as late as 1965, most American art had not risen spectacularly in price. A very large canvas attributed to Thomas Moran was offered for sale in Washington that year by a doctor's widow. It was not a Moran for a certainty, but a photograph of the painting looked very good to a New York dealer in nineteenth-century American art. Still, he did not feel the painting justified a trip to Washington to examine the picture closely. The widow finally, in desperation, sold the painting to a Washington dealer for $1,000 less commission. Today, on the basis of the photograph and without examining the painting itself, at least one collector would offer ten times the price realized by the widow.

It might appear that because prices of American art are so high, the time to buy it for investment has passed. However, there are most certainly paintings on the market that are within the reach of almost everyone, and that might reasonably be expected to increase in value in the future.

The nineteenth-century landscapists

This is a beautiful, highly decorative, and well-executed school of art which had been long out of favor but is now very much an "in"

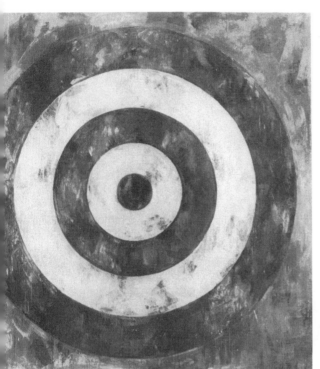

Two of the American paintings from the Robert C. Scull collection auctioned in 1973. *Target,* left, by Jasper Johns had been purchased by Mr. Scull for $5,000. It brought $125,000 at the auction. Robert Rauschenberg's *Double Feature,* right, which had been purchased for $2,500, sold for $90,000.

school. An important George Inness landscape cannot at present be purchased for little money. Nor can an important Thomas Moran, nor a Winslow Homer. However, lesser paintings by some of the leading artists of this era can still be purchased at reasonable figures. This group was sold at auction in the fall of 1973:

• A small George Inness, *Landscape With Figures,* 15¼ by 18¼ inches, painted in 1872 and signed, brought $5,750. The painting is typical of the artist and contains a plain, a mountain in the distance, and a large and typical Inness tree.

• An Edward Lamson Henry flat landscape, *Vespers,* 15 by 25 inches, with two figures and with hills in the distance, signed and dated '98, was sold for $2,400.

• A typical A.F. Tait painting of sheep in a meadow, entitled *The Broken Fence,* 16 by 21, signed, and dated 1902, brought $3,000.

• A painting, 13¾ by 19½, of a fine horse with a landscape background, signed Albert Bierstadt—the painter who achieved "monumental dullness," according to the *Encyclopedia of Painting*—was sold for $3,000. Another Bierstadt brought $7,500. This is a little painting of a mountain lakeside scene, 9½ by 13, on millboard, signed with initials, and dated 1895.

• Edward Moran does not bring the high prices of Thomas Moran. Nevertheless he, too, is an attractive, competent artist. His painting entitled *The Distant Horizon,* a picture of a boy sitting with his dog on a pier watching sailing boats, 22 by 36 inches, signed, brought $4,000.

• Another significant artist of the late nineteenth and early twentieth century who specialized in landscapes was Jasper Cropsey. His *Autumn Landscape,* signed, and dated 1897, 12 by 20 inches, was sold for $3,250.

• Still another prominent landscapist of the period was A.H. Wyant. In the decade of the 1960s his paintings could be found easily and at most modest prices—in the hundreds of dollars. His prices are even now not high. In the auction, Wyant's *Woodland Glade,* signed, 20 by 16 inches, brought $2,250.

• A large Bruce Crane, 24 by 36 inches, signed and inscribed *New York*—a country scene with a pond, a boat tied to the shore, and trees—brought only $1,600.

• Two paintings by the highly individualistic artist, Ralph Albert Blakelock, whose work is almost instantly recognizable because of his unique style, were sold in the sale. Blakelock used extremely heavy paint and his pictures are generally woodland scenes with sunshine. His *Landscape at Sunset,* 7 by 10¾ inches, a typical Blakelock, signed and on a wood panel, and his *Wooded Landscape,*

The Broken Fence by Arthur F. Tait, signed and dated 1902, sold for $3,000 in 1973 at auction in New York.

Albert Bierstadt's *Carmel Mission* was sold in 1970 for $3,200. In 1974 it was valued at $12,000.

12 by 18 inches, a lighter and larger picture, signed, each sold for $1,800.

• *The Alps,* signed, 12 by 16 inches, of snow-covered mountains, by Edward Potthast, brought $950.

• An extremely attractive "upright" landscape with a waterfall by Homer Martin, a good-sized painting, 36 by 22 inches, and signed, sold for $1,200.

Finally, a very fine Frederick Waugh brought $2,750. The painting is *The Cove,* a typical coast scene by this artist. It is large—25 by 30 inches—and signed. Another Waugh of the same size and same subject, *Seascape With Rock Formation,* also signed, was sold for $4,250. Waugh might appear to be very much underpriced in the present market, considering the quality of his painting, his pleasant scenes, his bright colors, and his reputation as a competent artist.

The above fifteen beautiful and well-recognized paintings could have been purchased for $45,500—a little over $3,000 a painting. They would have formed a very acceptable collection of American art that would adorn any home.

The portraitists

This is another school of American art that is within the reach of many collector-investors. Yet the group includes what is probably the most celebrated name in the entire field of American painting—Gilbert Stuart—famous for his paintings of George Washington. The quality of these portraits rivals that of the great eighteenth-century English portraitists, such as Romney, Lawrence, Hoppner, and Reynolds. Stuart has given his own explanation as to why he was so anxious to paint Washington's portrait:

"It was whispered about," Stuart explained, "that I fixed on Washington because I needed the money. How true! I was as broke as last year's bird's nest, but that isn't all. I believed that Washington was the greatest man in history, and I'm not too modest to say that I was the only artist capable of doing him justice."

In the autumn of 1973 a very typical portrait by Gilbert Stuart of *The Honorable John Heard, Judge of Probate* was auctioned in New York. Judge Heard had lived in Boston and was a member of the Massachusetts senate. The painting, 28 by 23 inches, was done in about 1810. It was handed down in the Heard family; was recorded and illustrated in Lawrence Park's authoritative *Gilbert Stuart;* and was twice exhibited in the Boston Museum of Fine Arts, an excellent means of authenticating a Gilbert Stuart. The portrait sold for $6,750 in the 1973 sale.

What is of great importance is that this portrait is an American Gilbert Stuart. The portraits Stuart painted in England are worth

The Cove, a fine painting by Frederick Waugh, sold at auction in New York for $2,750 in 1973.

far less than those painted in America, and the portraits he painted in Ireland are worth least of all his work. A few years ago London art dealer Harold Leger offered for sale an English Gilbert Stuart of a woman for $1,500. At the same time, New York dealer Herbert Roman offered the same type of Stuart portrait of a woman, painted in England, for exactly the same price. It is expected that the work of this most celebrated of all American portraitists will climb steeply in value.

In the same autumn of 1973 sale in New York, another American portrait was sold for just $550—John Neagle's *Portrait of a Gentleman,* 30 by 25, done in 1840. As in the case of Stuart's portrait of Judge Heard, this is a portrait of a man in a dark coat. Had these two portraits been of women colorfully dressed and attractive looking, the prices would have been considerably higher.

In another New York auction held at about the same time, a painting by another significant American portrait artist, John Wollaston, was sold. His *Portrait of Alexander McNutt,* 30 by 25, brought $4,250.

In the same sale, a pair of 29½-by-25 portraits by Christian Gullager, of Caleb and Nancy Dorr Clapp, brought $4,500 for both. This artist is very well known in American portrait circles and is represented in museums in this country. These particular paintings had been on loan to Blair House in Washington, D.C.

A prime portrait of George Washington by Gilbert Stuart will bring upwards of $100,000. A good large portrait by the most valuable of all American portraitists, John Singleton Copley, will bring $250,000. Still, paintings by important artists in this school can often be purchased for relatively small sums, and in many ways they form a "bargain school of art."

The twentieth-century schools

Up to the late nineteenth century, portraitists and landscapists predominated. At the turn of the century and into the twentieth century, new and experimental art began to develop in the United States. The Halpert collection and the Scull collection represent the most sought after and most highly valued paintings in these later schools. Most of the works of these schools are not within the means of the average collector, but some of them are.

There is a large group of artists who might be called the American scene painters. This school to a considerable extent specialized in depicting America during the Great Depression, and some of these artists are consequently known as the depression painters. They emphasized drabness and poverty in their work. The artists who are typical of this group include Gladys Rockmore Davis, John McCrady, Aaron Bohrod, Edward Hopper, Georgia O'Keeffe,

Charles Sheeler, Charles Burchfield, Charles Demuth, and George Biddle.

The next group of twentieth-century American painters might be known as the modern French-American school, since, to a considerable extent, their art seems based on French modern art, the school that began to appear in 1905. Some of these colorful, strong American artists are Maurice Sterne, Max Weber, and Yasuo Kuniyoshi (of Japanese ancestry).

A third group is what might be known as expressionists—realistic expressionists and, to a degree, abstract expressionists. They try to get across to the viewer a "great idea" or a "great emotion." This intent is known as expressionism. If naturalism and realism give way to pure design, expressionism becomes abstract expressionism. The painters in this group are not pure abstract expressionists; they are expressionists who use abstract elements at times, at least to a degree. They include Kenneth Callahan, Philip Evergood, Stuart Davis, George Grosz, Marsden Hartley, and Ben Shahn.

Prices of paintings by twentieth-century artists were generally sky-high in 1973. Still, some of their works were still selling at reasonable figures, at least within the price range of a large group of collectors. A good-sized Max Weber sold for $4,500, another brought $3,250, and two small Webers went for $1,600 and $800. A Charles Demuth brought $5,250. A fine Stuart Davis went for $6,000. A small mixed-media Kuniyoshi—an artist in absolutely top demand—went for $5,500. An excellent portrait by Walt Kuhn —the painter of clowns—brought only $1,500.

Even in the Scull sale, for $4,500 one could buy an extremely large abstract by Peter Young, entitled #6, measuring 84 by 84 inches. It had been exhibited in the Solomon R. Guggenheim Museum in New York. For $1,400, a pure abstract urethane foam figure by John Chamberlain entitled Shan, 40 by 45 by 34 inches, could be bought.

The collector with $9,000 to spend at the Scull sale could have his choice of an extremely colorful, untitled abstract by Philip Guston, signed, on masonite, 25 by 36 inches, or a painted aluminum work, 84 by 85 by 12, by Robert Morris, with the title Square Doughnut, or a piece by Claes Oldenburg—a big name in this school of art—entitled Souvenir: Woman Figure with Salt and Pepper Shaker Breasts (Times Square Figure), 13¾ by 6 by 9¾ inches.

While strict abstracts may not be to everyone's taste, their prices have risen tremendously over a very short period of time.

American art leads in price rise

A review of price trends of all schools of art traded on the major art markets of the Western world—from the latest abstract expressionists back to Italian and Flemish primitives—shows that American art, overall, is in the forefront on the basis of degree of price rise, and this price rise has been particularly extreme in the past decade.

How an artist or school of art performs pricewise depends on the base, or basic year, from which the rise is computed. If we compare prices of American paintings with Italian Renaissance paintings, we get quite different results by using 1962 instead of 1972 as the base, because the rise in American art between 1962 and 1972 was enormous as compared with Italian Renaissance art. The rise in American art between 1972 and 1973 was less startling. It had risen so far by 1972 that further increases in price became harder to achieve. Prices for major American works had become so high that fewer and fewer people could purchase them.

If we use 1960 as the base year and make it equal to 100 or 100 percent for each major school of art, so that we can make price comparisons to the present time, we find nineteenth-century British art and all American art running very close, with American art overall performing a little better than nineteenth-century British art.

Then if we take just nineteenth-century American art and compare it with nineteenth-century British art, we find that both schools of art rose enormously in price level between 1960 and 1973. They rose to about 1500 percent—fifteen times their 1960 level. In other words, if a painting cost $100 in 1960, in 1973 the same painting would have sold for $1,500. All other schools of art used for comparison purposes in this price study showed smaller increases.

The next significant comparison in price between 1960 and 1973 is between all American art and all art. While American art rose to 1500 percent of its 1960 base, all art rose to only 820 percent—about half as much. Still, the "about half as much" compares with a 54 percent rise in the stock market—to a level of 154 percent of the 1960 base. The degree of rise in the stock market is nowhere near the degree of rise in the overall art market and certainly nowhere near the degree of rise in the American segment of the art market.

The "era of the abstracts" was the 1950s. Then, for many years they were under something of a cloud, and in the 1960s they did not turn in a brilliant price performance. In the 1970s they again began to post new price records.

If we compare segments of the American art market from 1960 to 1973, we find the new American abstracts rising from a price level of about $2,000 to about $50,000. This is an average figure combining the work of various artists and is thus somewhat ficti-

How British and American Art
Of the Nineteenth Century
Has Soared in Price

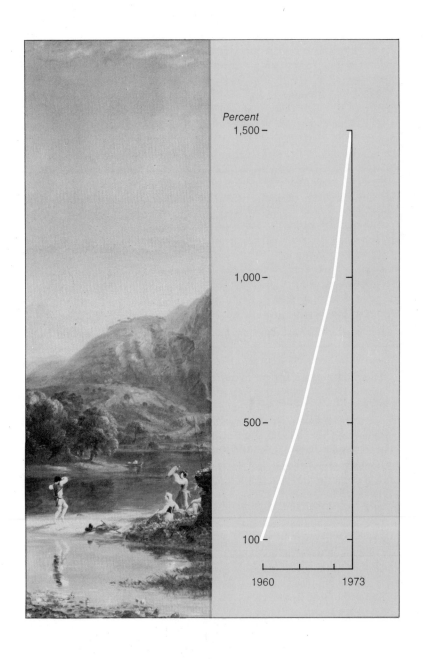

tious, but it does show fairly accurately the degree of price rise in the period. The artists included in the index are Mark Rothko, Clyfford Still, Josef Albers, Robert Motherwell, and Robert Rauschenberg. These artists are very difficult to secure at low prices on the present market. Thus they are not being considered here as possibilities for the collector of moderate income.

Prime Gilbert Stuarts of the American period rose from about $5,000 to about $75,000 between 1960 and 1973, and the price would include a good example of Stuart's many portraits of George Washington although one superb example brought over $200,000. The celebrated American portraitist John Singleton Copley rose from perhaps $5,000 to about $100,000 in the period.

The art market was in something of a slump in 1969 and 1970, particularly in the latter year. From this low point it rose rapidly until it reached the boom years of 1972 and 1973.

Between 1970 and 1973, American art—ranging from eighteenth-century portraits to abstracts—rose to a level of over 250 percent. Italian baroque art rose about the same amount. Only seventeenth-century Dutch and nineteenth-century British art did better price-wise.

While American paintings rose to a level of better than 250 percent in 1973, the overall art market rose to only 200 percent. The stock market rose to 113 percent.

Good buys in landscapes

The nineteenth-century American landscapists did better than the overall American school of art—and this is the part of the American school which offers good possibilities of purchase for the more modest collector. These landscapists rose to 250 percent in the period 1970-73. The price index includes Winslow Homer, George Inness, Thomas Moran, Albert Bierstadt, Jasper Cropsey, William Bradford, F.E. Church, A.F. Tait, A.H. Wyant, Martin Heade, and Homer Martin.

To move to the later schools of American art, in that same three-year period the American scene painters—Gladys Rockmore Davis, John McCrady, Aaron Bohrod, Edward Hopper, Georgia O'Keeffe, Charles Sheeler, Charles Burchfield, Charles Demuth, and George Biddle—rose to a level of 300 percent.

The so-called American expressionists—Stuart Davis, Marsden Hartley, and Ben Shahn—also tripled in value in the three years.

The modern French-American school, exemplified by Maurice Sterne, Max Weber, and Yasuo Kuniyoshi, rose to 250 percent.

Tremendous rise in American art

To summarize, in 1960 the American school of art was almost of

How American Abstract Art
Has Skyrocketed in Price

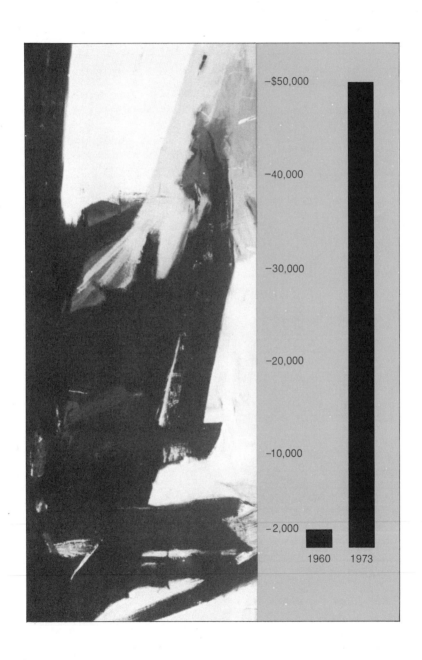

no consequence in the art market, except for a few "in" artists such as Maurice Prendergast and the strict abstract expressionist Jackson Pollock. Even the first half of the decade of the 1960s did not show an outstanding rise in price for the American school.

After 1965 a tremendous rise took place. In the years 1972 and 1973, this rise turned into a boom, with prices often running into six figures, particularly for the later expressionist schools, the French-American artists, pop art, and the strict abstract expressionists as typified by Jackson Pollock. A large Pollock was sold to an Australian museum in 1973 for $2 million.

If any of the entire American school of art remains in a bargain category it is the nineteenth-century and early-twentieth-century traditional landscapists. These artists are not so subject to fad buying as some of the later, less realistic schools.

There is hardly a week that goes by in New York when a number of American paintings of the nineteenth and twentieth centuries are not sold at low prices. These are attractive, well-executed paintings, many of them by recognized artists and many of them signed and dated. They are simply not by "in" artists. Many of the paintings are good-sized landscapes. Many are scenes of New York done, say, fifty or sixty years ago. These paintings are available in New York at many galleries, including the Plaza Art Galleries, P.B. 84, Astor Galleries, Manhattan Galleries, Fischer Auction Galleries, and the Hartman Galleries. A large group of Hayley Levers, a well-recognized name in art, was sold at the Plaza Galleries in 1973 for a few hundred dollars a painting.

In 1959 many signed landscapes by seventeenth-century Dutch artists could be bought in the smaller auction houses in New York for prices under $100. Today they would be worth an average of $1,500, and they are seldom found in the smaller auctions.

What will happen to the good and very numerous American landscapes that appear in many auctions in New York, Philadelphia, Baltimore, Washington, and in other major cities? In 1974 it seems as though these paintings will be in the salesrooms forever, and at near giveaway prices. But fifteen years ago this was the attitude toward the seventeenth-century Dutch landscapes. If one does not wish to invest thousands of dollars in paintings, it might be a good idea to purchase a number of these very attractive, very decorative works of art while they are available for $100 or less, and just see what happens to their prices over the years. In the meantime, the paintings would beautifully decorate the collector's home.

John Sell Cotman's signed watercolor, *West View of Saint Clement's Church, Tilney,* sold for $7,728 in March, 1974. Cotman is one of the high-priced English watercolorists. Many attractive English watercolors by lesser-known artists are available for under $100 each.

CHAPTER 5

English Watercolors

English watercolors are probably the most suitable of all paintings for home decoration. Most of them are extremely pleasant landscapes with muted colors; a number are seascapes. They are harmonious with most interior decors, whether contemporary, ultramodern, or antique, and they are usually small enough to fit well on the walls of modern houses and apartments.

Probably the appeal of English watercolors when they were first painted was that they brought into the home the beauty of the English countryside. Some of these pictures were of places that at the time they were painted were inaccessible to most people. The wealthier watercolor buyers commissioned artists to paint their manor houses and their gardens and grounds. Surprisingly enough, there are very few poorly done English watercolors.

Since these watercolors are usually executed in delicate, fresh, translucent washes, they are unobtrusive and light. Perhaps this unobtrusive quality is not entirely suited to America, where the picture often must stand out as a striking piece of culture and as something which represents the investment of a good many dollars.

The English watercolor market is enormous in relation to almost every other kind of painting. Probably over 10,000 watercolors are sold each year in London alone. Together the two leading English auction houses, Sotheby's and Christie's, sell about 500 watercolors every month and issue special catalogs covering each sale. The leading art galleries of London—Leger, Agnew, Colnaghi, and the Fine Art Society—have extremely extensive inventories of watercolors, and some of these galleries put on an annual display of these pictures.

Wide price range

The price range of English watercolors is very wide, and it would seem the price difference between the most expensive and the least expensive watercolors does not always reflect differences in quality or in the abilities of the artists. The less expensive watercolors are not by any means poor in quality.

A good English watercolor can still be found for under $100. In the United States, few such watercolors are bought and sold; they are not as a rule in demand either in this country or on the continent of Europe. English watercolors come mainly from English homes and they are sold via auctions and dealers to English homes.

In the larger American cities, English watercolors occasionally turn up in the shops of dealers or at auction, and the smaller auctions from time to time offer a few such pictures for sale—competent, attractive, signed paintings.

The chance of purchasing a fake English watercolor is far less than in the case of a painting by a known master. Where there is a limited market, there is little inducement for fakers to ply their trade.

With the exception of J.M.W. Turner and a very few other watercolorists, the "name" artists in this field are not well known in the United States, and when dealers or auction houses offer such works for sale they simply describe them as, for example, "Watercolor, 8 by 10 inches." Sometimes the fact that the painting is English is not even noted, if that fact is known.

On the present market, a fine Turner watercolor will sell for $100,000 on occasion. Yet a fine landscape by the "Father of English Watercolors," John Varley, may still be purchased for a few thousand dollars.

Historical background

A watercolor has water instead of oil mixed with the pigment. The color and water are applied to paper with a fixing medium. Watercolors are in no way inferior to oil paintings, except sometimes in price. In fact, the watercolor artist may well need to possess talent that is superior to that of the oil painter, for if he does not apply the watercolor to the picture properly the first time he cannot correct his error, unless he uses opaque watercolor. In an oil painting, the artist can rectify his error by painting over in various ways. An oil can be painted, painted again, cleaned, and again painted.

Watercolors did not originate in England. The great German artist, Albrecht Dürer (1471-1528) was an excellent watercolor artist, and did watercolors of the Alps and of his native city, Nuremberg. These watercolors still have an amazing freshness and modernity about them.

In seventeenth-century Holland, the leading landscapists used watercolors, but mainly to add warmth and liveliness to their drawings. By the time Rubens came to England to work for Charles I in 1629, he had already been a watercolorist for twenty years. Three years later Van Dyck arrived in England, and he too was at that time a mature watercolorist.

It was in the eighteenth century that English watercolors proliferated. Three artists form the transition to that century's watercolor art: Wenceslaus Hollar (1607-1677), his follower, Francis Place (1647-1728), and Francis Barlow (c.1626-1702).

English watercolorists excelled

No other country produced so large and significant a school of watercolor artists as England. The art of painting with watercolors reached a degree of excellence in eighteenth-century England never achieved before or since. This fact is of great importance to the collector because he has an enormous selection of watercolor art to choose from and can find virtually any picture he wants from the point of view of subject matter, quality, and price.

The work of four pioneers of English watercolors can be found regularly on the market: John Varley, Paul Sandby, Thomas Girtin, and J.M.W. Turner. They painted in the late eighteenth and early nineteenth centuries.

One fact of importance to collectors is that the works of the very finest and best-known watercolorists appear on the market fairly regularly. It is not necessary to wait three decades for the privilege of bidding on a Turner.

Another important fact is that the price range of English watercolors is so wide. One collector may put $1 million into a collection while another may put just $10,000 into a collection of the same size, and the less expensive collection will still contain quality pictures. It is a matter for wonder, when looking at the price tags on watercolors, that it is possible to acquire such competent pictures for so little money.

High-priced group

The English watercolorists can be divided into two groups from
the point of view of price. The first is the high-priced group, the
greats of English watercolors.

At the very top of the list, in price and in artistic recognition,
stands J.M.W. Turner. His is the most prestigious name in watercolors at the present time. A short time ago Turner's *Sallenches
Savoy: Saint Martin* was on the market. A landscape with a stream,
mountains, a village, and figures, it is not large, measuring 11⅛
by 15¾ inches. It is, however, an important Turner. It had been
exhibited at Grosvenor Place in 1819, and was once in the collection of Agnew, the London dealer. The picture was in the Farnley
Hall collection—Walter Fawkes of Farnley Hall had been a good
friend of Turner.

The price history of this picture is worth noting. In 1862, Christie's of London sold it for 111 guineas—not much over $500. They
sold it again in 1876, but this time it reached only 103 guineas. To
bring the price level of such a work more up to date, fifteen to
eighteen years ago it would have sold for about $6,000. Its recent
price was about $72,000.

The next great watercolorist to be considered received the highest praise for his work—Turner himself said about Thomas Girtin,
"If Girtin had lived, I would have starved." Fortunately for Turner,
but unfortunately for art, Girtin died at the age of twenty-seven.

One of Girtin's greatest works was on the market a short time
ago—*Jedburgh*, a Scottish village, signed, and dated 1800. The
dealer who had this painting in stock paid its owner about $48,000
for it. In 1932, it was possible to buy this Girtin for a little over
$500.

Turner and Girtin stand almost by themselves in the top rank
of watercolorists. The really great paintings by these two artists
bring disproportionately high prices, but some of their pictures
are within the price range of a good many collectors.

In November of 1973, at an auction in London, a fine, but small
Turner watercolor of *Pendennis Castle and Entrance of Falmouth
Harbour, Cornwall,* only 6⅛ by 9¼ inches, sold for $39,375 to the
Leger Galleries of London. It is important to know who buys water-
colors because, if a top dealer buys such a work, he puts his stamp
of approval on it and in a real sense "attributes" it.

The previous lot, however, also cataloged as by Turner, entitled
An Archway in Kenilworth Castle, 7⅞ by 11¾, brought only
$2,100.

Earlier in 1973, another fine Turner was sold at auction—to
Leger—for $36,440. This watercolor was only 6⅛ by 9½, but was
a fine and typical Turner landscape. It, like the previously men-

A View of the Tchin-Shan, or Golden Island, in the Yang-Tse-Kiang, or Great River, of China by William Alexander sold in 1973 for $32,500.

tioned Turners, was fully recorded and had an illustrious history.

Still, the very next lot in the same sale went for far less. It was tiny—3 by 4⅝ inches—and was a scene containing ruins, not a landscape. It achieved $3,024. In the same sale, less illustrious works by Turner sold for even smaller sums.

To turn now to Girtin's lesser-priced works, in November, 1973, two Girtins went for $4,463 and $2,625, respectively. The first was a scene of a bridge, 13¾ by 20½, a picture of very good size and well documented. The second was a Paris scene of the Seine and the Louvre, 7¼ by 11¾.

Another high-priced English watercolorist is John Sell Cotman. A short time ago, Cotman's *Mount Saint Catherine, Rouen* was on the market for about $24,000. While this watercolor was being examined, an old letter fell from the back of the frame to the floor. The letter was dated 1897 and it stated that at an auction, presumably held in 1897, two Cotmans had been offered for sale, each with a reserve of 100 guineas (about $500). The letter also stated that Cotman's *Cathedral* had been sold unframed in 1843 for two pounds, ten shillings (a little over $10). The purpose of the letter was apparently to show that watercolors by Cotman were rising in price and that the *Rouen* watercolor was worth at least $500.

In the early part of 1973, a Cotman sold at auction for about $10,000. This was a 10¼-by-7¼-inch watercolor of *A Spanish Chestnut Tree Blasted by Lightning*—not the most attractive subject. Later in the same year another Cotman sold for about $4,725. Agnew's of London bought this picture, measuring 13 by 9 inches, of *Abraham and Isaac*.

The next of the high-priced watercolorists is Samuel Palmer. In the case of many artists, certain periods in their artistic life are worth more than others. For Palmer it is his "Shoreham period"— 1824 to 1835—that is the most wanted, and this period in the artist's life is almost instantly recognizable by watercolor collectors.

A short time ago a very small (6-13/16 by 10¼) Shoreham period Palmer was on the market. It consisted mainly of golds and darks, and depicted a barn with sheep, some trees, and a rising moon. The price was about $45,000. The non-Shoreham period Palmers sell for a good deal less money. In mid-1973 two Palmers were sold to the London dealer Agnew—one for about $7,500 and the other for about $9,500. The first was an evening landscape, 10½ by 20¼; the second was a study for Palmer's *The Shearers*, 10¼ by 14.

Samuel Palmer's mentor was William Blake. In a decade Blake rose about ten times in price. A while ago Blake's *Saint Paul and the Viper* was for sale. It is a fairly large painting as watercolors go, 19 by 15¾ inches. The fact that the subject is religious may have cut down on its price, as religious paintings are not usually as much in demand as landscapes. The price, however, was not low— almost $25,000. If we go back to 1949, this same watercolor sold for under $2,500 in London.

Lower-priced group

At the very top of the list of lesser-priced English watercolorists must be placed Thomas Gainsborough. This placement may make him the biggest bargain in the entire watercolor market. Gainsborough was the greatest eighteenth-century English portraitist, and a good, large Gainsborough portrait or group portrait will sell easily for $250,000. So will his smaller landscapes in oils, particularly those that contain figures.

Gainsborough also painted watercolors, and these appear on the market from time to time—highly competent, colorful works. His watercolors are in a completely different price category from his oils, and seem to be a remarkable bargain.

A few years ago a fine Gainsborough charcoal and watercolor landscape was offered for sale in New York. It measured about 15 by 18 inches. The asking price was $3,500. Today, $10,000 should buy one of Gainsborough's beautiful watercolor sketches. Such a price would represent not only one of the great buys in watercolors but one of the better buys in the entire field of art.

Crossing the Ford, signed and dated 1846, is by Samuel Palmer, whose water-colors bring high prices.

Another of the medium-priced artists is one of the pioneers of English watercolors, Paul Sandby. At the end of 1973 one of his finer works brought $14,438 at auction in London. It is entitled *Dartmouth Castle and the Mouth of the Dart* and measures 19¾ by 28. In the same sale, however, lesser works by Sandby brought less than $1,000. One was sold for $656, two for $840 each, and one for $368. All were in pen and ink and watercolor; not great works but authentic works by this artist.

John Varley had many pupils who turned out to be leading British masters, including William Henry Hunt and John Linnell. In late 1973, a typical Varley, *Fisherfolk on the Shore Facing Conway Castle,* signed, and dated 1803, measuring 15⅛ by 22⅛, was sold in London. It brought about $2,500. Varley's relatively low prices can be explained in part by the very large volume of his watercolors on the market. On November 6, 1973, no fewer than ten Varleys were offered for sale by Christie's in London. Actually, $2,500 is a high price for a Varley, and they range down in price to below $250. Still, ten years ago they were one-tenth of the price they reach today.

Thomas Rowlandson is a favorite of American buyers because of his literary associations, as is William Blake. Rowlandson is essentially a caricaturist and very much on the inexpensive level, considering the artistic merits of his work. In late 1973, *The Royal*

Oak, With Revellers, and Shipping on the River Beyond, 10⅝ by 16⅜, brought $14,438 at auction in London and was purchased by Leger, a very high price in light of Rowlandson's prices about two years previously.

In a two-year period Rowlandson's prices about tripled, at least for his best watercolors. Still, his lesser paintings could be purchased for relatively little in early 1974. In the sale in which the Rowlandson was bought by Leger, nine other Rowlandsons sold for a maximum of $1,500. His works are not rare on the watercolor market by any means.

William Callow is another excellent nineteenth-century watercolor artist in the medium price range. Late in 1973, two Callows went for $1,103 and $1,260. The first is *Sidmouth From the Shore,* measuring 10¼ by 14⅛. The second, *East Lynn Valley, Devon,* measures 9½ by 14⅜.

Francis Wheatley, who was an excellent painter in oils, produced some fine watercolors which are not high in price as compared with other watercolor artists. In late 1973, *The Faggot Gatherers,* 14 by 10, signed with initials, and dated 1797, brought $1,000 at auction in London. At times, Wheatleys sell for much less.

Tips on collecting watercolors

One of the first things that a would-be collector of English watercolors might do is to buy *English Water-Colours* by Stanley W. Fisher, Ward Lock Limited, London. It sells for about $4.60, and while there are many books on English watercolors, this is a relatively small, easy-to-read text which includes plates of the works of many of the watercolorists of the eighteenth and nineteenth centuries. In addition to this book, several of the recent catalogs of watercolor sales held at Sotheby's and Christie's in London should be purchased by mail. These materials should give the collector a good idea of just what these watercolors are, the prices being asked for them, and the trend of the market.

In 1973-74 the market for English watercolors rose materially. The "greats" rose in value. So did the least important and least expensive watercolors—those selling for $100 and less. It was the middle group that did not rise much in price.

At the very bottom of the price range, the average $25 watercolor about tripled in a period of less than two years. It now sells for $75. These watercolors are available in quantity all over England at small auctions and in small shops. Some are signed and some are not. Since they are so inexpensive, they should be bought strictly on the basis of quality, rather than on name. In England the artists' names, if they are important, tend to assure high prices. The unattributed watercolors and those painted by the lesser-known artists still sell for very little, but they are rising in price at an amazing rate.

In the United States, English watercolors are still not in demand and are still largely unknown. In the course of a season in New York, a collector might accumulate 100 good watercolors by lesser-known artists at a maximum price of $100 each, and more likely a maximum of $50 each.

The cash risk is so low in relation to the artistic merit of the pictures and in relation to the rising price trend of the less expensive watercolors that it might pay to invest in a group of these works of art which could hardly discredit any office or residence.

Riding School, a drawing by the seventeenth-century Dutch artist John Vanderbank, was auctioned in 1973 for $3,900. Many drawings by Dutch artists of the seventeenth century are on the market today at reasonable prices—often one-tenth the price of comparable paintings by these artists.

CHAPTER 6

Drawings

There is a fairly definite relationship between the prices of paintings and drawings by the same master. Mary-Anne Berman, who is head of modern paintings at Sotheby Parke Bernet in New York, has referred to the "one-to-ten ratio" which is the relationship of the value of a drawing to the value of a painting by the same artist. Thus, according to this rough rule of thumb, if a painting by a particular master is worth $100,000, his drawing might sell for $10,000.

It is possible to buy at a moderate price a very fine drawing by a particular artist whereas a painting of similar quality by him may well be beyond the reach of most collectors or else totally unavailable.

Drawings are usually done in pencil, or pen and ink. Some are done with crayon or charcoal. Sometimes a watercolor wash is used and there are highlights made with Chinese white, chalk, or white tempera. Most drawings are linear rather than three-dimensional. There are often free curves and open lines rather than carefully worked out details. Usually they are done quickly and thus contain a degree of freshness and spontaneity which capture the mood and inspiration of the artist. In a sense, drawings are more personal and intimate than paintings. For this reason, collectors sometimes prefer drawings and oil sketches to finished paintings.

Modern drawings soar in price

Modern drawings have risen in price fairly steadily along with modern paintings. A Chagall gouache was sold in the Helena Rubinstein sale held in 1966 for $23,000. In 1973 this gouache brought $57,500.

Under the impact of Japanese buying, impressionist and French modern drawings rose tremendously in value through the end of the 1973 season. Then, as demand from this source tapered off, the surrealists and the cubists—Tanguy, Magritte, Delvaux, Picasso, Victor Brauner, Dali, and Max Ernst—tended to take the spotlight and rise in buyer interest. The postimpressionists—Signac, van Gogh, and Cézanne—were in demand, as were the abstracts— deStaël and Dubuffet.

In general, modern drawings are very high in price and beyond the reach of the collector with a modest budget. Many of the modern artists have been subject to speculative demand and there has consequently been a steep rise in prices that tends to make other schools of drawing seem to be a better investment.

In the very important New York auction of modern drawings held October 18, 1973, a few drawings did sell at fairly reasonable prices. A Lyonel Feininger, 4½ by 9½ inches, a very small drawing in pencil of a locomotive, brought $800, and a Feininger painting of this subject and size would have brought at least ten times this sum. A Feininger pen and ink with pastel, 7⅜ by 10⅝, entitled *Ship, Sea and Mountains,* sold for $3,500.

At that time the artist Foujita was extremely popular with Japanese buyers and a pen and india ink drawing of a cat, with wash on paper laid down on board, 8¾ by 7¼, brought $5,000.

Jules Pascin, a French modern, was represented by a charcoal drawing, 23¼ by 18¼, of a young girl seated. It realized $5,250. A drawing by another French modern, Modigliani, *Head of a Woman,* 13 by 9¼, in pencil, brought $6,000. Matisse, one of the four leaders of the French modern school, was represented by a nude, 10⅞ by 14½, in pen and india ink, which was sold for $16,000.

Two surrealists represented were Yves Tanguy and Victor Brauner. A simple double-sided drawing by Tanguy in pen and india ink, 7¾ by 5½, realized $3,750, and the Brauner *Pictogram,* in the same medium, of several little figures and faces, 7½ by 13½, brought $3,400.

In that sale and at that time in the art market, anything by Picasso was eagerly sought after and at very high prices. Two female figures bathing, a simple line drawing in pencil, 19¾ by 12¾, reached $15,000. A Chagall pen-and-ink drawing entitled *L'Ane Jouant du Violon*, a jackass playing a violin, 16⅜ by 10½, brought $7,500.

On November 28, 1973, a good Modigliani self-portrait in pencil —a rather simple sketch—15 by 10¼, brought $14,000. In the same sale two half-length nudes by Foujita each sold for $3,500. Both were pencil and chalk on paper laid down on canvas. The first measured 17⅝ by 13¾ and the second was slightly larger.

A collector's discovery

In 1956, New York's Metropolitan Museum of Art sold some works of art it no longer required. Among the items was a drawing, or sketch, in brown and black heightened with white, by the Italian baroque artist Castiglione, one of the top artists of the Genoese school.

In late 1960 the drawing appeared in the shop of Herman Galka, the New York art dealer and appraiser. Mr. Galka was not certain of the artist and so offered the drawing of *The Prodigal Son Among the Swine* for $70. A potential buyer stated that he might be interested in purchasing the drawing provided he could take it on approval for study. The dealer agreed and the collector proceeded to prove it out as the Castiglione once owned by the Metropolitan.

At this point the collector decided to make an offer on the drawing—$60—which the dealer readily accepted. Later the drawing was shown to Robert L. Manning, director of the Finch College Museum of Art, who placed the drawing on display some time later. While it was being exhibited another collector saw the drawing and made an offer to the owner for it. After some negotiating, the drawing changed hands at $2,250.

Shortly thereafter the drawing appeared in the sales catalog of the Hazlitt Gallery in London, where it was believed to be priced at a little over $10,000. It was sold a short time later to David Rust, of the National Gallery in Washington, D.C., who displays it fairly often as one of the finest Castiglione sketches in America.

In a way the value rise of this drawing is not atypical of the price rise in old master drawings generally. It was possible to buy a good drawing by a Dutch artist or by an Italian artist of the seventeenth or eighteenth century for $50 in 1959, and a group of Italian baroque drawings was sold at the Plaza Art Galleries in New York for sums under $30 each in 1964.

Prices of drawings began a gradual rise in 1964. Dutch and Italian drawings could still be purchased in 1969 for fairly small

The Prodigal Son Among the Swine by Castiglione was purchased for $60 in the late 1960s and resold a few years later for $2,250.

sums—a few hundred dollars—and a fine Gainsborough charcoal, chalk, and wash landscape sketch was for sale in New York for $3,500.

Between 1969 and 1974 drawings of the old master school increased about ten times in value—from a price in the hundreds to a price in the thousands. Still, prices of these drawings are low by two comparisons: the relationship of the price of a drawing to the price of a painting by the same master, and the relationship of the price of an old master drawing to that of a modern drawing. Modern drawings are, in general, extremely high in price as compared with those by old masters.

Italian drawings

Few good Italian Renaissance drawings are available at reasonable prices. In 1973 a pen and brown ink drawing by Beccafumi was sold for $5,500 in London. A Parmigianino of *Daniel in the Lions' Den* brought $5,775 and a Zuccaro realized $6,300. These last two drawings were half the size of a sheet of typing paper.

In the baroque and eighteenth-century Italian schools of art, considerably more distinguished drawings can be purchased for relatively little money. A Castiglione of *Jacob Leading the Flocks of Laban*, 7⅝ by 11½, sold for $3,276 in London in 1973, but a really important Castiglione of larger size might well bring three times this sum.

Christie's in London in late 1973 sold a splendid landscape by the eminent Venetian artist, Marco Ricci, 12 by 17½, for $10,500. A fine Gian Domenico Tiepolo of *Three Dromedaries Passing a Pyramid*, 7½ by 11¼, brought $12,600. On occasion it is possible to buy a fine Guardi for about $12,000, but a Venetian scene by Guardi in black chalk, pen and brown ink, 8¾ by 10, achieved a price of $18,900 at auction in London in the 1973 season.

In that same season, Sotheby's of London sold a Guercino drawing of a young girl looking at a drawing, in pen and brown ink, for $5,500. A Gian Domenico Tiepolo of the *Adoration of the Magi* brought $5,000, and a good Salvator Rosa landscape with peasants and a hill sold for $1,500.

Dutch drawings

Dutch drawings, principally those of the seventeenth century, are on the market for roughly the same price as Italian baroque drawings. Rembrandt is so high in price as to be very nearly at painting price levels, but a Jacob van Ruisdael drawing can at times be secured for less than one-tenth of the price of a comparable Ruisdael painting. In the 1973 Antiques Fair in Delft, an excellent Ruisdael landscape drawing was offered for sale for about $10,000.

During the 1973 season, a *View of Tivoli* by Willem van Nieu-landt the Younger brought $3,250 in London, and a small drawing by Willem van de Velde the Younger of *Dutch Flagships Under Sail,* 5¼ by 8⅛, brought $2,772. In contrast, a painting by the latter artist would probably bring upwards of $50,000.

A Pieter de Molyn landscape with travelers, also a small draw-ing, 5⅞ by 7⅞, went for $2,530, and an Abraham Bloemaert *Win-ter Scene With Travelers Approaching a Tree,* 6¼ by 8¼, brought $7,056.

French drawings

If one considers the international prominence of the artists, it appears that French drawings offer something of a buying oppor-tunity on the present market. At Christie's in December, 1972, a fine black chalk drawing heightened with white, *Head of a Youth,* 6⅛ by 5⅝, by Boucher, certainly one of the two or three greatest French artists of the eighteenth century, sold for $2,268. A larger Louis Moreau, 9⅛ by 13¼, *Extensive Landscape With Sportsmen,* brought $3,276 at Christie's in March, 1973, and a superb drawing by Jean Louis Desprez, 8⅜ by 13½, of the Piazza del Duomo in Palermo, in pen, black ink, and watercolor, sold for a little over $4,000.

A Hubert Robert architectural drawing brought about $5,000 at Christie's in the same March, 1973, sale. It was circular and a little under eight inches in diameter. A splendid Lepicié of three male figures, in pen, gray ink, and watercolor, 8⅝ by 7¼, went for $3,276 in that sale. Also during the 1972-73 season, Sotheby's in London sold a sheet of figure studies in red chalk heightened with white, by Watteau, for $10,000.

At present there seems to be no shortage of French old master drawings for sale. Good-quality drawings at relatively reasonable prices are available in fairly large numbers in Paris.

Guidelines for buying drawings

If you decide to collect drawings, keep these points in mind:

1. The "big name" impressionists, Central European expression-ists, and French moderns have taken a large jump in price in recent years and are so high in present value as to diminish future possi-bilities of rises. The lesser-known artists may now show more po-tential for price increase.

2. Modern schools are subject to faking and should be purchased from well-established, reputable dealers and from auction houses which offer a guarantee as to authenticity.

3. It is better to purchase modern drawings of substance—

Les Sept Ages de la Vie, by Fragonard sold for $39,000 in 1973. Other Fragonard drawings sell for less than $10,000.

beautiful, well-executed pictures—than scribbles whose value depends on the name of the artist who did them.

4. Old master drawings have not risen on the average as much in recent years as modern drawings have, and for a low four-figure investment very important artists can sometimes be secured.

5. The ratio that an old master drawing's price bears to the price of a painting by the same artist may well be less than that for modern drawings versus paintings. For a few thousand dollars, a drawing might be secured which was done by an artist whose paintings sell in the high five-figure and six-figure range.

6. The important names should be concentrated on in old master drawings as certain of these can still be purchased for sums under five figures.

7. Seventeenth-century Dutch artists and Italian baroque artists offer good purchasing opportunities as there are many drawings in these schools on the market. Earlier drawings in the Flemish, Italian, German, and even French schools are very rare and very high in price.

8. French drawings of the eighteenth century by the most eminent artists, such as Boucher and Fragonard, are still available in the four-figure range at times. They can be bought in some volume in Paris, and on the present market they may be underpriced when compared with Dutch and Italian drawings.

9. English drawings of the nineteenth century and even eighteenth century can still be purchased for reasonable sums, particularly in London. They have not been described here as they tend to have about the same value as the English watercolors already described, and the watercolor artists of the period did drawings as well. Drawings by famous portraitists such as Gainsborough and Romney can be secured for lower four-figure investments.

10. Lesser names in all schools bring very much lower prices— those names on a level lower than van Goyen, Ruisdael, and Hobbema in the Dutch school and Guercino (real name Giovanni Francesco Barbieri), Il Domenichino (Domenico Zampieri), and the Carracci family in the Italian school. There are at least two dozen major names in each of these two schools—Italian and Dutch—and hundreds of lesser names, and the same situation prevails in the French school except that there are fewer top-grade eighteenth-century French artists in relation to the lesser names.

11. In general, concentrate on drawings which are in good condition, preferably those that can pass this test:

   • No fading, wear, or damage to the image itself—defects in other parts are less important;
   • No tears or creases;

- No trimming of the paper by the framer or someone else;
- No broken off, worn, or torn corners—a very common place for wear;
- No fading or water stains;
- No holes or thin places in the paper;
- Little or no foxing (a brownish discoloration of the paper) ; and
- Rag fiber for framing, not wood fiber, as wood fiber causes foxing.

12. In drawings, unlike many other collectibles, damage is not usually difficult to repair and does not greatly affect value. Stains can be bleached out and repairs made; foxing can be arrested.

13. Tiny drawings do not have the value of larger drawings, all other things being equal.

14. Pleasant works, including landscapes, should be purchased. There are many drawings which have subject matter that greatly diminishes their value no matter who the artist was, such as *The Massacre of the Innocents* and *Judith and the Head of Holofernes.*

15. Works typical of the artist should be collected, not atypical works that depend on someone's attribution to determine who created them.

16. Drawings from the artist's best and most wanted periods should be purchased.

17. If possible, signed works should be purchased.

18. Drawings should be framed, preferably by an expert framer or by a restorer to avoid damages which can occur in framing.

19. Above all, good works of art should be collected rather than simply the names of important artists.

Toulouse-Lautrec's excellent color lithographs can command high prices. This print of *La Clownesse Assise: Mlle. Cha-U-Ka-O* brought $42,500 at auction in New York in early 1974. Lautrec prints of lesser quality sell for one-tenth this price.

CHAPTER 7

Prints

If collecting is looked at from a broad angle to include the whole range of collectibles, we might place coins at one end and prints at the other.

A coin bears a fairly standard classification and it can be bought from a description in a sales catalog without examining the coin itself. A coin can, of course, be represented as "very fine" when, in reality, it is only "fine," but any difference of opinion between seller and buyer can usually be straightened out and agreement reached as to its quality.

In prints there is no standard classification. The collector must know what he is buying, and he must examine it in some detail. When considering a particular item, the collector might begin by asking: Is it a print?

Several years ago a "drawing" was offered for sale at one of the smaller auction galleries in New York. It was framed and under glass. A collector of old masters and a dealer were examining the item at the same time. Both decided to take it out of the frame, and received permission to do so. Both prospective buyers examined the item closely, and both come to the conclusion that it was a print rather than a drawing.

If a prospective buyer is certain that what he is considering is indeed a print, that is only the beginning of assessing its artistic importance and value. Did the master do it himself or was it done by a copyist? Is the print an early-off copy or is it a later and less desirable "pull"?

Was the original plate altered by the master before he did a second run of prints? Were the plates discovered much later, then sharpened up by someone and a new set of prints run off? Finally, is the print an outright fake?

Difficult to detect fakes

Few knowledgeable buyers get stuck with modern fakes of old master paintings. It is not so easy, on the other hand, for knowledgeable buyers to avoid acquiring modern fake prints of old masters or even of modern art. Marc Rosen, head of the print department of Sotheby Parke Bernet in New York, had some interesting comments to make in 1974 about recent fake prints on the market:

"There have been a couple of major clusters of fakes that have come up in the past few years. I am pleased that two of the 'fake rings' involved were actually stopped by us here in Sotheby Parke Bernet. Groups of prints by Giorgio Morandi have always been very rare. In the course of one year, however, quite a few Morandi prints were coming onto the market, and it became sort of conspicuous. . . . At one point our gallery was sent a large group of them. It was, however, difficult to secure any genuine Morandi prints for comparison purposes.

"Once the possibility of a fake ring came to mind, however, we began to look very critically at every Morandi offering. Then, with that frame of mind, it became quite easy to see that these offerings were not genuine.

"I think the problem of fakes throughout history is that people have a dominant wish to accept rather than reject things, and it is really a question of the point of view with which one looks at things. Most people are not looking for fakes—in spite of all the sensationalism about fakes. People are generally inclined to take things at face value.

"So this was really an instance of having to look at the prints with the possibility in mind that they were not genuine. Once I had done that, it was transparently clear that they were not genuine. Yet when I placed calls to several people who I knew had recently acquired Morandi prints elsewhere and asked them to bring their prints in for comparison because I had a group of prints that were suspect, do you know they had simply never asked themselves the question, 'Is it a fake?'; and I called many very fine collectors and dealers, all people with generally high standards and good judgment.

"Once it was clear to these people that they had bought fakes, they tried to scurry and return things they had bought. Although I think Interpol knew of the fake ring, I'm afraid they never really pinned it down completely. There is a strong bias in the public mind of not wanting to prosecute the faker. Everyone sort of has sympathy with the clever con man in a way. The only thing that happened was that the fake prints were confiscated. . . .

"A couple of years ago there was another group of fakes in California, involving a former policeman—somewhat the same situation and again a matter of focusing a critical look at the prints. You just can't let down your guard."

What are prints?

Prints are reproductions. They are thus, in a sense, not original art since the hand of the master technically did not create the print, and in some cases did not even create the plate from which the print was made.

At most, prints are a kind of extension of original art, at least in those cases in which the artist himself worked on the plate from which the prints were made. If they could be turned out like books or newspapers, prints would be in quite a different category from what they are now in the esteem of collectors and museums as well as in price. Prints, can, however, be turned out only in very limited quantities, as the quality of the plate deteriorates rapidly and the last "pulls" are of far inferior quality to the early and vastly sharper pulls.

"Print" is a generic or catchall term for several processes which result in multiple copies. The term includes etchings, engravings, woodcuts, and lithographs.

Etchings are impressions produced on paper by a metal plate. The usual metal is copper but iron has also been used on occasion, notably by Albrecht Dürer. The design in the metal is achieved by acid.

Sometimes a cutting tool is applied directly to the metal by the artist. If incisions are made directly on metal, wood, or stone, the resulting prints made from the "master" are called engravings.

A woodcut is an engraving on wood or the prints produced by a wood block.

In lithography, lines are put on a stone (and sometimes on other materials) using a greasy substance, and when the stone is applied to paper a lithograph results.

Determining a print's value

A print's value depends on:

1. Prominence of the artist. Probably in the old master group Rembrandt is the greatest and most valuable. In this same category is the German, Albrecht Dürer, followed by the Italians Canaletto, Giovanni Battista Tiepolo, and Piranesi. In the modern field the most prominent names are Picasso and Toulouse-Lautrec.

2. The greatness of the print as a work of art. Is the print in its own right a work of art, one of the best things done by the master?

3. How fine is the particular impression, how near to being the first off the plate?

4. How rare is the print? Are there only a few from the same plate in existence or are there, say, eighty of them extant?

5. Is the print one of the originals printed rather than one from a plate made after the death of the artist or from a resurrected plate that has been reworked?

6. Is the plate the work of the artist himself, although there are many fairly valuable prints that were done by other artists from an original work by the master?

7. What is the condition of the print? How well has the image been preserved—not the background, but the actual printed image? If anything defaces the image, such as a rip or fading, the value drops. Next in importance is damage within the margins. Is there a crease or a tear? Some damages can be repaired with hardly a trace, and excellent repairs largely restore the original value of a print.

How to buy prints

A novice collector should spend considerable time getting acquainted with the field of print collecting before actually laying out his cash. The field is extremely complicated and the quality and value of a particular print are difficult to judge.

The beginner might well concentrate not on the lesser, relatively inexpensive artists but on those whose place in art history has been established, buying fewer but more costly works. Dealer and auction house catalogs with prices should be secured to get an idea of what is offered in the market and at what price. Exhibitions of prints should be visited.

Articles and books on the subject of print making and collecting might well be read, possibly including Geraldine Keen's book, *The Sale of Works of Art,* published in England by Thomas Nelson and Sons, 36 Park Street, London, W1, and Paul J. Sachs's book, *Modern Prints and Drawings,* Alfred A. Knopf, New York.

The Virgin and Child With the Pear by Albrecht Dürer, one of the greatest print makers, was sold at the end of 1973 for $6,000.

This preliminary investigation should accomplish three purposes: acquaint the would-be collector with what is fine in the market; inform him regarding present values; and enable him to decide what he personally likes, since the prints will be likely to serve a decorative as well as a speculative purpose.

A worthwhile objective might be to acquire a substantial collection in one important area, not necessarily works by one artist, but a collection of the same school of prints. In addition to the satisfaction of possessing a well-rounded collection, this approach provides the important advantage of having a collection that an auction house or a dealer would be willing to take in its entirety. Single works of art or a few pieces do not attract a great deal of auction house or dealer interest, whereas a collection put together with taste and knowledge does. An auction containing such a collection focuses buyer attention on what is for sale and is also likely to draw more buyers because there is more for sale. The more potential buyers there are, the higher the prices generally. Putting together a collection and selling it all at once is becoming a more or less recognized procedure in the marketing of prints as well as in many other areas of art.

Prices of prints

The new collector is at somewhat of an advantage from a price point of view. True, today prices are high, very high, in relation to the past, but the new collector cannot remember nostalgically "when this Toulouse-Lautrec would have sold for a tenth of this price."

In buying prints today, or possibly in any other day, you cannot look for immediate profits. In the present, generally rising, print market it is not at all unusual for a collector who bought a print six months ago to telephone the dealer or auction house to ask what his purchase would bring today. Actually, a longer period of time than six months is required for substantial price appreciation.

Prints are rising in value, and especially recently. Plateaus are reached, and it is sometimes necessary to wait for a fairly long time before the particular artist purchased takes a jump. Upward movements in price by jumps are not at all uncommon in the print market.

In 1972 and 1973 the prices of Chagall prints boomed. In the same period the prices of Rouault prints by no means kept pace with Chagall, but in 1974 a new leap in price for Rouault appeared to be near. Braque is somewhere between Chagall and Rouault in price movement. Braque prices were not booming in 1974 but they were by no means on a flattened curve.

For a time Picasso prints seemed to be outdoing Picasso drawings, although the drawing is the original work of art and the print the reproduction. The reason might be that Picasso's drawings seem somewhat plain and uninteresting in comparison with his prints. Recently his print price increases began to lose ground as compared with prices for his drawings. Also in the modern school, while Paul Klee's paintings and drawings have been soaring in price, his print prices have been lagging. In the old master print field, Dürer has been shooting up in price as rapidly as any of the moderns.

Prices of modern prints

In 1896 and 1897, Toulouse-Lautrec turned out a series of color lithographs of excellent quality into which he put a tremendous amount of hand work. In color lithography the artist must use several stones, one for each color, placing them on the paper one after the other.

One such lithograph of excellent quality made by the artist in 1896 was entitled *La Clownesse Assise* (Seated Female Clown). The subject was not the most beautiful woman by any means. This litho in red and yellow over dark green is from the *Elles* series and depicts a clown with outspread legs. This series did not sell well when it was first produced by the artist, probably because of the subject matter.

In the 1966-67 season, the set of ten sold for $22,400 at Sotheby's in London. In November, 1972, one print—*La Clownesse Assise*—brought $16,000 when it was sold by Sotheby Parke Bernet in New York.

In May, 1973, one print of *La Clownesse Assise* brought $25,500 in New York. In June of the same year, another print of the same subject brought $48,000 when it was sold by Kornfeld and Klipstein, the Swiss auction house. In February, 1974, approximately the same price was achieved for a similar print of the same subject—$42,500—by Sotheby Parke Bernet in New York.

La Grande Loge by Toulouse-Lautrec, a fine color lithograph of two women seated in a box at the theater, shows a similar sharp rise in price. In the 1966-67 season, it brought $15,400. On June 22, 1973, Kornfeld and Klipstein of Switzerland sold one of these same lithos for $160,000. The print was number nine of a limited edition.

Picasso has been an extremely high riser in the field of prints. A few years ago an entire set of Picasso prints known as the *Suite Vollard* sold for about $225,000, certainly a high price at the time. In June, 1973, in Switzerland, just one early Picasso print, *Le Repas Frugal* (The Frugal Meal)—from the first edition

This Renoir color lithograph, *Le Chapeau Epinglé,* brought $14,600 when auctioned in 1973. A good trial proof sold for $13,000 in early 1974.

of only thirty prints made in Paris in 1904—brought about $160,000, not very much less than the entire *Suite Vollard* had brought just a few years earlier.

Fortunately, not all prints are this astronomical in price. In the February, 1974, sale of prints in New York, in which *La Clownesse Assise* brought $42,500, the very next lot was also a Lautrec from the *Elles* series, a litho entitled *Femme au Plateau* (Woman With Tray). It sold for $3,500. The next lot, also from the *Elles* series, entitled *Femme Couchée* (Woman in Bed), brought $6,000. These two lesser-priced lithos were not in perfect condition but they were certainly not in poor condition. Toulouse-Lautrec's famous *Le Jockey,* a fine impression from a series of 100, brought $40,000.

A print by Picasso, in the February, 1974, sale in New York, *Femme au Corsage à Fleurs* (Woman With Flowered Blouse), produced in 1957, number four of fifty, was sold for $19,000. An illustration of it occupied an entire page in the catalog. A somewhat similar bust of a woman, a much later copy and a much simpler picture, produced in 1957, number eighteen of an edition of fifty, brought $4,500. *Le Homard* (The Lobster), also illustrated in the sales catalog, number twenty-nine of fifty, dated 1949, brought $2,600. Many Picasso prints can be purchased under $5,000 and a number of them at the $1,000 level.

In February, 1974, an excellent large Renoir lithograph—a good, fresh trial proof—printed in red, pink, ocher, two greens, gray, and black, 24½ by 19½ inches, dated 1898, sold for $13,000. The very next lot, however, was also an attractive Renoir of a child with a biscuit, 12½ by 10⅜. It is from an edition of 100 and it brought $3,400.

In that sale, a Cézanne color litho, *The Bathers,* a fine, bright impression with no defects listed, sold for $8,750. Essentially the same print, this one a black proof impression with a few defects, brought only $3,700.

Chagall is yet another leader in the field of prints. In February, 1974, the color lithograph by Chagall entitled *The Bird Chase,* 16½ by 25¼, brought $6,000, a very strong price for Chagall. Aside from a slight discoloration, it was in good condition. In the same sale *David Presenting Saul With the Head of Goliath,* a trial proof etching but in good condition, brought $500. This price level for simple prints is not unusual for Chagall.

An excellent Braque entitled *Le Char Verni* (Varnished Chariot), a litho printed in colors, brought $3,250, and his *Athenée,* also a color litho, sold for $2,500 at the 1974 sale.

Leading American artists also produced prints, and in the same sale a Whistler third-state etching, *San Giorgio,* a Venetian scene, 8¼ by 12, brought $2,300. It was significant enough to merit a full page in the sales catalog. The next lot, entitled *Nocturne,* a typical Whistler subject, also an etching, brought $1,800, and other Whistlers sold for $1,000 and less.

In the present market for modern prints, a very good colored litho can usually be secured for a price of from one-tenth to one-twentieth of a painting by the same artist. As examples, an excellent Matisse litho can be purchased for $3,000 to $4,000 and a Miró litho for $1,000 to $3,000.

Prices of old master prints

Up until 1969 the London *Times,* in conjunction with Sotheby's auction house in London, prepared a price index of old master prints. The charts indicate that in the twenty-year period between 1950 and 1969, old master prints rose thirty-eight times in value. The index was made up of prices for a number of prominent old master print makers, and among individual price plottings presented were: Albrecht Dürer, the German Renaissance artist, rose twenty-six times in value; Rembrandt, forty times; Canaletto, thirty times; Piranesi, thirty-three and a half times; and Goya, nineteen and a half times.

Rembrandt is almost certainly the leading old master print maker, both from the point of view of artistic excellence and from the point of view of price rise. In 1950 his *The Woman With the Arrow* sold at auction for $500. On May 10, 1973, this print was sold at Sotheby Parke Bernet in New York for $58,000—over 100 times the 1950 price. In addition to Rembrandt, the print makers concentrated on today seem to be Dürer, Canaletto, Giovanni Battista Tiepolo, and Piranesi.

Top artists of the Dutch-Flemish school whose work can be secured in the present market include, in addition to Rembrandt, the greatest Dutch landscapist of the period, Jacob van Ruisdael, and Van Dyck.

Some of the artists of the French school who appear fairly regularly in the quality print market are Jacques Callot, Jacques Bellange, Claude Lorrain, Boucher, Moreau, and Watteau. A Callot print can sometimes be purchased at the $1,000 level.

In the Italian school, the eighteenth-century artists, particularly the Venetians, produced quality prints that are offered at substantial prices at the present time, yet prices which are far under those asked for their paintings. Such artists include Canaletto, Bellotto, Marco Ricci, Giovanni Battista Tiepolo and his sons, Gian Domenico and Lorenzo, and Piranesi.

Among the Spanish old masters, the most eminent print artist is Goya.

If we start with the most prominent print maker, Rembrandt,

The Woman With the Arrow by Rembrandt, the leading old master print maker, sold for $500 in 1950. In 1973 it brought $58,000.

we find that *Saint Jerome Beside a Pollard Willow,* an etching and drypoint, sold in New York for $48,000 in the summer of 1973. A little later in the same year Rembrandt's etching of the print seller, Clement de Jonghe, brought $57,500 in London, and in the same sale a portrait of goldsmith Jan Lutma sold for $55,000.

While Rembrandt's paintings and drawings never go at low prices unless the attribution is questioned, once in a while a large number of Rembrandt etchings appear on the market and prices have run as low as $1,000 for the less important examples. *The Bust of an Old Man With a Fur Cap and Flowing Beard* went for $6,750 in the 1972-73 season.

At the end of 1972 a fine Jacob van Ruisdael, *Three Oaks on a Mound,* a drypoint etching, sold at auction in London for $7,750.

A Jan van de Capelle landscape can easily bring $100,000, but a print by this prime seventeenth-century Dutch landscapist and seascapist might sell at times below $1,000. A very good Van Dyck etching can also sometimes be purchased for as little as $1,000.

In early 1973, a very important woodcut by Albrecht Dürer, *The Four Horsemen of the Apocalypse,* sold for $17,500, but a woodcut from a very large edition may be purchased for a few thousand dollars. Later in 1973, a Dürer woodcut entitled *The Martyrdom of Saint John the Baptist* sold in Christie's in London for $5,775.

The most available of all prints from the Italian school are those by Piranesi, and these appear regularly on the market in great numbers. Recently a *View of the Interior of the Temple of Neptune,* an etching, brought $4,250 in London. In the March 28, 1974, sale of prints at Sotheby's in London no fewer than ninety-one lots by Piranesi were offered. However, not all of them went at low prices simply because they were numerous, and a price of $5,000 is not unusual for a fine Piranesi etching. On the other hand, for a maximum of $1,000 a good, typical Piranesi architectural etching can be secured. It has a tremendous amount of decorative value in addition to being an excellent work of art.

In late 1972, Canaletto's *Imaginary View of Venice* sold in London for $21,000, but lesser examples of the work of this great eighteenth-century canal painter could be purchased in 1974 for about $1,000. These less expensive works have some defects, but not great defects.

Etchings by G.B. Tiepolo can be purchased for $1,500 to $2,000, as can the work of his sons. For about the same sum a very good etching by Castiglione can be secured.

Something of a unique print maker was Marcantonio Raimondi, who apparently specialized in prints based on the work of Raphael. Although Raimondi is clearly a copyist, his works come onto the market with some regularity and one appeared in the March 28,

1974, sale held by Sotheby's in London. These prints can be purchased for under $1,000.

Cautions for the print buyer

While one can buy a print for a sum of money of from one-fiftieth to one-hundredth of the price of a painting by the same artist, there are two cautions for the print collector:

Prints are not original works of art, for the most part. For a print, the master made the plate, and the plate was pressed on a piece of paper. Sometimes the artist touched up and improved the print. Usually he did not, and one plate may have turned out more than 250 prints, so that a particular print is not unique. Still, it may be the nearest thing to original art that the collector can afford.

A second drawback in print collecting is the rapid rise in the market. The name of the French artist Jacques Bellange is great in print making, although not particularly great in the field of original art. Still, his etchings can reach five figures. When such huge prices will peak is impossible to say. The great prints have risen the most in the past, but the new collector might well concentrate on the perfect, or near perfect, examples of lesser works by the great print makers that can be purchased for sums ranging from under $1,000 to $2,000.

Brancusi polished bronze, *La Negresse Blonde,* was bought for $750,000—an auction record price for a piece of sculpture—in May, 1974. While modern pieces are often priced beyond the reach of most collectors, there are bargains available in the sculpture of earlier times.

CHAPTER 8

Sculpture

Several years ago the Austrian government decided to buy a house in Washington, D.C., to be its new embassy. The bank handling the sale of the estate which included the house indicated to the Austrian ambassador that the house's contents, or any part of them, could be purchased by the government of Austria, and items that the Austrians did not want would be offered to the public.

At a dinner party, the wife of the ambassador told an art collector that she had made her selection of the house's contents which her government would buy and suggested that a number of items remained which might be of interest to the collector. The collector was interested, and the next day he met with a vice president of the bank and the ambassador's wife to look over the things that were for sale.

The collector looked for some time at the paintings and antiques, but could not find anything that interested him. In desperation he asked for a description in the bank's records of a marble head of a man. The vice president looked at his inventory sheets and read, "Statue on Pedestal—$50."

So that the ambassador's wife and the bank official would not think him simply a time waster, the collector quickly said, "I'll take it."

The "taking it" was not as easy as he had imagined, however. The statue was too heavy to lift. So the collector got his convertible and placed it as close as possible to the front door of the new embassy. He slid the statue across the marble floor to the door, and then got the statue into the car end over end, damaging his car somewhat in the process.

When the collector got the statue home, his wife was totally uninterested in his purchase, even as a prop to hold open a door. The collector then thought about donating it to a museum but decided against this course because he knew nothing about the statue and was afraid that it would turn out to be just a copy of a Greek or Roman head done some time in the late nineteenth century.

He thus decided to drive it to New York to a small dealer in art, antiques, and sculpture. He parked the car with the statue in the trunk in a dark corner of a garage so the dealer would not get too close a look at the statue and pronounce it a fake of no value. However, the dealer did look at the statue in the car and purchased it immediately for $250, but the biggest service he performed, as far as the collector was concerned, was to have his crew of helpers remove the statue from the collector's convertible.

The dealer offered an attribution of the statue: Roman, first century A.D., and the pedestal, also of marble, of the same period and place of origin.

The collector learned later what happened to the "Statue on Pedestal—$50." The dealer soon sold it, but first he divided the statue from the pedestal. Each part he sold for $800—$1,600 for the two pieces—to a Madison Avenue art and antique shop. There the prices asked of buyers were $1,600 for the head and $1,600 for the pedestal.

Reasonably priced statuary

Although it is not likely that a collector will find an ancient Roman head for $50, there are still major categories of statuary in which one can fine good pieces at reasonable prices:

• First-century A.D. Roman, which is, however, becoming scarce;

• Sixteenth-to-eighteenth-century marble, terra cotta, stone, bronze, and wood; and

• Eighteenth-century French in terra cotta and sometimes marble.

Terra-cotta figure of a lion, French or Italian of the early eighteenth century, sold for $750 in March, 1974.

Roman statues of the first century A.D. are not extremely rare on today's market. Once in a while one appears in a minor auction. Very often the nose or chin, or both, have been broken off and replaced. Such pieces are generally not of museum quality, but they are genuine and do have some value. The auction house of Adam A. Weschler and Son, in Washington, D.C., sold a fair one of these restored statues in 1972 for under $1,000 and they can still sometimes be procured for a sum in the low four figures. They have increased in price in recent years—about 10 percent per year.

A very good, but by no means perfect, Roman head of that era was on offer to billionaire collector J. Paul Getty in 1973. It was not quite of "Getty quality," but was nevertheless a good specimen. The offering price was $7,500, and it might have been bought for a little less.

Roman statues of the first century A.D. are essentially copies of the style of Greek statues of the pre-Christian era—from the fourth century B.C. down. Greek heads are, however, priceless when they are in anywhere near perfect condition, and if they can be identified as to sculptor they are in the super-priceless category. J. Paul Getty purchased six of these heads in 1973 for a sum believed to be well into seven figures.

Later bargains

If we move forward to the seventeenth century we find that a variety of statues appear on the market from time to time and at bargain prices. A few sixteenth-century statues also appear in this category occasionally at auction.

On March 2, 1974, Sotheby Park Bernet in New York offered a fine collection of "Renaissance and Later Works of Art." In the sale was a very attractive marble bust of a nobleman, Scandinavian, seventeenth century. It was large—27¼ inches high—with good carving and an excellent patina, and it was in very good condition. It sold for $300. For $300 it would be hard to buy any more impressive antique piece—a painting, a piece of furniture, or anything else.

If a would-be collector could not afford $300 for a work of art, he might have bought the very next lot, a marble portrait miniature of Sir Joshua Reynolds, the artist. This was an English sculpture done in the late eighteenth century. It realized $50.

In The Hague there is a dealer by the name of Han Jüngeling on Noordeinde. The visitor entering his shop could look to the left and see in a niche a life-size bust of a nobleman in marble from eighteenth-century Holland. It was not greatly inferior in quality to similar marble busts in the Rijksmuseum in Amsterdam. The price was $200 and the price had been $200 for at least the ten years that the dealer had owned the statue. Finally, in 1973 it was bought.

Antique statuary—attractive, absolutely genuine—provides a considerable amount of art for very little money. Statuary is by no means plentiful but it does appear from time to time in estates which are sold in many parts of the country. Such statuary is not important enough from a price viewpoint for it to be shipped to the major auction houses or dealers of New York, London, or other large cities.

There is much more terra-cotta than marble statuary for sale, and in this general area the first major division might be Italian terra cotta. This type of statuary is available in Italy in fairly large volume and at prices of $2,000 and under, but usually the sculptor is not known. A few years ago, Leone Cei, a dealer in Florence, had a fine terra-cotta bust of a man, Italian, seventeenth century, almost perfect in every detail, for about $1,200.

The March 2, 1974, Sotheby Parke Bernet sale in New York offered a fine terra-cotta figure of an apostle, Italian, early eighteenth century, 17¾ inches high. It brought $750. Just a few lots earlier in the sale, an Italian seventeenth-century terra-cotta head of a man, 10¼ inches high, brought $700, and an Italian eighteenth-century figure of the Virgin, 18½ inches high, brought $700. None of these three figures brought above the low estimate of the gallery. Such pieces usually do not catch collector or dealer interest, and Italian dealers who were present at the sale did not bid much for them.

A polychromed terra-cotta group of Saint Joseph and the Christ Child, Spanish, eighteenth century, 19¾ inches high, did even less well pricewise. It brought $450. A terra-cotta group of the Virgin

Early eighteenth-century Italian terra-cotta figure of an apostle, 17¾ inches high, brought $750 when auctioned in March, 1974.

and Child with a female saint, Italian of the late seventeenth-early eighteenth centuries, 9½ inches high, went for $550, whereas the low estimate of the gallery was $1,000 and the high estimate $1,500. This is not only a piece of later Italian sculpture, which is in general out of favor with collectors, but it is religious in subject, and religious subjects are not usually in demand by collectors of works of art.

Finally, two terra cottas went for very reasonable prices in the March, 1974, sale. The first was *Neptune,* European, of the late seventeenth-early eighteenth centuries, 13 inches high, which realized $275. The last "bargain" was a figure of Apollo, Italian, late eighteenth century, 10¾ inches high, which brought $400.

Stone statuary provides the opportunity for even better "buys" than do pieces made of terra cotta or marble. In 1973 a fine stone figure of Saint Ursula, Italian, seventeenth century, perhaps a shade under life size, was purchased in Florence for $170. It was trucked to the vicinity of Venice and installed in a niche in a famous villa, where it will probably remain as long as the villa stands. The trucking was included in the price of the statue, incidentally. Such pieces of stone statuary generally have been available at reasonable prices in Italy and sometimes appear at auction in the United States, where they rarely bring large sums of money.

There are in Italy some magnificent wood statues, some by famous sculptors. For several years now, Venetian art and antique dealer Pietro Scarpa has had for sale a life-size figure in beautifully polished wood. The statue was finely carved in the eighteenth century by wood sculptor Giacomo Piazzetta, a member of the famous family which produced the artist of the same century, Giovanni Battista Piazzetta. The statue was on display in the Art and Antique Fair held in Florence in the autumn of 1973. Its price was $1,600.

Also in Florence in 1973 there was a set of four life-size terra-cotta figures representing the four seasons. The price of the four was $12,000—$3,000 apiece, certainly a good deal of art for the money. Such statues are still available in Italy. They also sometimes appear at auction in the United States, as do statues from Germany and other countries from as early as the sixteenth century. Unless they are truly great works of art, they achieve prices not over a few thousand dollars, and in the slack year of 1970 a fine sixteenth-century statue of a saint brought only a few hundred dollars at P.B. 84, the New York auction house.

It is still possible to secure excellent French statuary of the eighteenth and early nineteenth century for not very large sums. However, the great and popular names of this era, Clodion, Falconet, and Houdon, are not by any means low in price. Groups and busts by these sculptors which appear on the market from time to time are generally in the five-figure range, and a very good Clodion terra-cotta group can easily bring $30,000.

One of the great names in sculpture of the eighteenth century is Pajou, and for the work of this artist the market price would seem to be low at present. A signed Pajou statue of a pretty woman can be purchased for about $3,000. This is also the approximate price of certain lesser works by Jean Baptiste Carpeaux and by Jean Baptiste Lemoyne. On the present market, eighteenth-century French statues whose sculptors are unknown can be bought even in Paris for about $1,000.

Fakes turn up

In the March 2, 1974, auction sale at Sotheby Parke Bernet in New York, one lot was a marble bust of Henry IV, 25 inches high. It was inscribed on the back "Lemoyne" and dated. It realized only $950 because this statue was almost certainly not by Lemoyne, and it may well have been nineteenth century instead of eighteenth century.

Faking has caused a setback in sculpture collecting. The faking of sculpture is by no means a new thing. The great Michelangelo tried his hand at it, not so much to make money but to prove himself a great artist.

Faking was done in the seventeenth century in France when sixteenth-century bronzes were "repatinated." In the nineteenth century there were two sculpture fakers whose work surpassed even that of Han van Meegeren in art. Their names were Bastianini and Dossena, and the name Dossena is even now spoken in respectful tones by those familiar with the quality of his work. The works of Bastianini and Dossena are on display in various European museums. One major American museum once purchased a Dossena fake, thinking it was real, for a price reputed to be $100,000.

Not all fakes are so outright as these. About a decade ago a collector found a terra-cotta bust of a woman in a small shop on New York's Third Avenue. The statue appeared to be eighteenth-century French, but something about the patina did not seem quite right. The collector received the dealer's permission to take the statue on approval. He then placed it in the trunk of his car and took it to a painting and sculpture dealer and export, Spencer Samuels, formerly president of French and Company. Mr. Samuels examined the statue carefully and came up with a somewhat unexpected pronouncement: "This probably started out as an eighteenth-century French terra-cotta statue, but in the nineteenth century it was refinished and in certain ways resculpted, so now it is neither fish nor fowl."

The collector promptly returned the statue to the dealer and saved himself $550 for a piece of sculpture that was worse than a damaged period piece. In the March, 1974, Sotheby Parke Bernet auction a genuine eighteenth-century French terra-cotta bust, 11½ inches high, of Count Mirabeau, sold for only $1,000. It was a far better piece than the altered statue, and a decade later on the market.

Museums not competing

There are essentially two general categories of antique sculpture: the fine pieces which are extremely rare and extremely high in price, and the lesser pieces which are anything but popular with collectors at the present time and not sought by museums. In fact, museums are not a significant factor in this market at all, a fact which contributes to the reasonable prices of much antique sculpture—from the first century A.D. to the late eighteenth and early nineteenth centuries.

Museums are usually not active buyers in the present market for three reasons: Their collections are often well rounded; pieces of a quality equal to what they already possess rarely come onto the market and, when they do, only at very high prices; and boards of trustees and patrons are not particularly interested in sculpture collecting today.

The March, 1974, auction held in New York was by no means a sale of inexpensive sculpture that nobody wanted. There were some very fine pieces. In this category was a pair of bronze tritons made in the workshops of Nicolo Roccatagliata, late sixteenth-early seventeenth century. They are small—only 6½ inches high—but they brought $14,500 as against a sale estimate of $6,000 to $9,000. They were purchased by a private collector who had been collecting for about ten years. In fact, most buying of such works is done privately at the present time.

The finest antique sculpture cannot be collected in volume or for reasonable sums of money. From this great sculpture there is a steep drop in artistic merit and in collector interest to all the other sculpture described in this chapter. In general, these latter pieces of sculpture are not in great demand at the present time. Still, although they are not the greatest works of art, they should not be dismissed by would-be collectors, particularly by those who are looking for a collecting area which has not risen to sky-high levels.

Most sculpture of the sixteenth through eighteenth centuries, both great and lesser pieces, has risen gradually. Joseph Kuntz, head of European works of art at Sotheby Parke Bernet, estimates that prices of such sculpture have risen at a fairly steady rate of about 10 percent a year since 1960.

A record price for Art Nouveau was achieved when this gilt-bronze bust, 27½ inches high, by Alphonse Mucha, sold in 1971 for $27,500.

Value factors

The value of a piece of sculpture is determined by these factors:

1. *Quality* is most important, and this holds true for sixteenth-century bronzes as well as for eighteenth-century terra cottas or eighteenth-century wood carvings. A knowledgeable collector instantly recognizes quality in his field of connoisseurship and will not pay a high price unless the quality is evident to him.

2. *An attractive subject* arouses the interest of collectors and dealers alike. Profane subjects as opposed to religious ones are usually preferred, with the exception of highly important works by rare and well-known sculptors.

3. *Size* can also be a factor determining value. A collector may not want something that is too large to live with.

4. *Patina* in a bronze is important. It must be true to the period and area of origin of the piece. The work of each country and period has characteristics which must be learned by the collector. The color of the bronze varies. The patina and detail vary. A bronze from the workshop or by the hand of Giovanni da Bologna would have a smooth and beautiful finish. An early Florentine bronze would have a rough and crude finish—no less appealing to a collector. There is no lab test for bronzes. The collector must know how these pieces were cast and finished in each period, and the characteristic styles of dress, pose, and artistic concept. The would-be collector should be aware of such facts as that early sixteenth-century casts had armatures in them for support, and that if the piece is just a copy made in the nineteenth century, there will be no armature.

5. *Original paint* on a wood sculpture is more important than the original patina on a bronze. Usually little happens to bronzes over the centuries, but wood carvings are seldom intact as far as the original paint surface is concerned. They are usually stripped or repainted. If one is valued at $5,000 or $6,000 in the "stripped" condition, it would probably sell for $25,000 with the original paint intact.

6. *Completeness* of a "modeled" piece is of importance. Terracotta pieces may be repaired without much diminution of value. This is true of any modeled material. It is not so important that a piece be perfect as that it be complete. Of course, if a piece has not been damaged, it is more valuable, all other things being equal.

Opportunities for collecting

The sculptors of the twentieth century, such as Arp, Brancusi, Giacometti, and Moore, are all but priceless, and sculpture of the periods up through the eighteenth century has been avidly collected for so many years that few really fine early pieces are available for the new collector in this field. However, prices for lesser works and casts from important early workshops and for later works are in many cases still so low as to represent that phenomenon of the mid-1970s—a bargain!

A very interesting collection of bronzes, wood carvings, marble busts, and terra cottas could be put together now, and the worth of such a collection might increase materially if it were collected with an eye for quality, condition, and subject matter. The field is certainly not a fashionable one at the moment, and there is little competition for the good, but lesser, pieces. If you are willing to devote a great deal of time to studying, looking, searching, and learning, it is quite likely that you will find some very good pieces and put together a collection of sculpture which will be a pleasure to live with as well as an investment.

PART THREE

Investing in Antique Furniture

This Chippendale carved mahogany corner chair, attributed to John Goddard of Newport, Rhode Island, circa 1760, was bought in 1964 for $24,000. Eight years later it sold at auction in New York for $85,000. Although prices are rising, many American antiques are priced under $1,000.

CHAPTER 9

American Antiques

American antiques probably represent the most desirable purchases for the average collector of antique furniture for several reasons:

- They are beautiful additions to the decor of almost any house.
- They are available in almost all major cities of the United States—in shops and at auctions—so that there is a relatively wide selection.
- They are solidly made so that they will last indefinitely with a minimum of repair and restoration cost.
- They are not yet expensive, except for certain top pieces.

The following list of some American antiques that were sold at an auction house in Washington, D.C., provides a good indication of price levels in 1974:

1. Walnut Chippendale slant-top desk with serpentine-shaped front, bracket feet, and an excellent interior, circa 1765—$900.

2. American cherry Chippendale Governor Winthrop desk made in New England, slant-top design, circa 1790—$625.

3. American walnut tilt-top tea table with birdcage, circa 1780, diameter 30 inches—$500. This type of table can be folded and placed in a corner when not in use. The box-like birdcage design indicates that there is a mechanism for allowing the top to turn easily. This device is not only useful in a tea table, but it adds enormously to the value of any tilt top. A table of this type is in tremendous demand and is—along with the slant-top desk—a measure of the market for American antiques.

4. Baltimore mahogany sewing table with one drawer and two wells, circa 1815, 26 by 15 inches—$375.

5. Mahogany Hepplewhite bow-front chest with four drawers and high French feet, circa 1800—$550.

6. American cherry and bird's-eye maple Sheraton secretary, probably made in Massachusetts, height 57 inches, circa 1800—$1,900. This is a large and decorative piece of furniture combining a slant-top desk with drawers under the slant top and doors above the slant top enclosing a cabinet with shelves.

7. Walnut chest on stand, made in Pennsylvania, Queen Anne period, height 78½ inches—$2,450. This is a very large combination bureau and high chest with several drawers.

8. Walnut drop-leaf dining table, from Pennsylvania, Queen Anne period, with high stocking web feet, scalloped skirt, white oak and pine secondary wood, length 51 inches when open, circa 1760—$1,150.

9. Mahogany Governor Winthrop desk from Massachusetts, original gilded cast brasses, concave shell interior, block front, circa 1780—$3,100. The block front design is rare and adds tremendously to the value of the piece.

American furniture has not been a recent "high riser" in the antique market except, perhaps, for the great museum pieces that very occasionally come onto the market. The vast majority of American antiques are still reasonably priced.

The plainer, less-expensive, American furniture of the eighteenth century rose very little between 1972 and 1973 while the corresponding English furniture about doubled in price. However, since American furniture is bought and sold mainly in the United States, and English furniture is traded mainly in England, the markets and demands for the two types of furniture are different.

American furniture of the seventeenth century is a rarity. If a piece of that period is of any quality at all, the price is very high. American seventeenth-century furniture is to a considerable extent rustic, dark in color, and is sought by collectors who often run

The Increase in
American Antique Furniture Prices

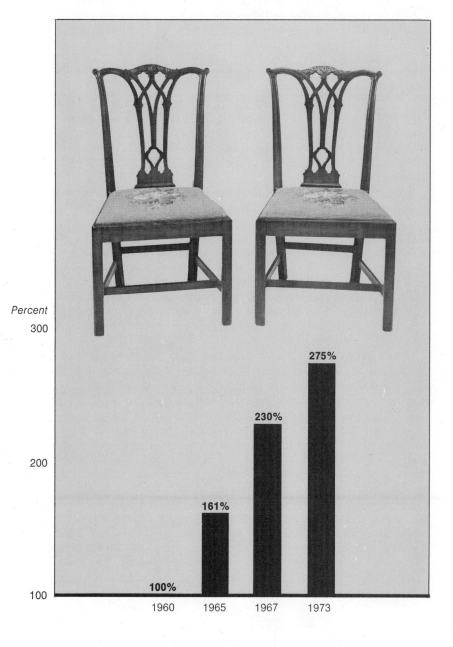

Percent

300

275%

230%

200

161%

100%

100

1960   1965   1967   1973

up prices to four-figure levels, even for simple pieces. This type of furniture is generally not comfortable nor especially useful.

The finest and most sought after American furniture is from the Golden Century—the eighteenth. This furniture is for the most part based on English furniture of the same period. American furniture makers tended to follow the English styles seen in pattern books and in actual pieces of furniture shipped from England to America. The names of the American styles are the same as the English styles.

William and Mary furniture

This furniture was made in America slightly later than the reign of the British monarchs William and Mary. Its dates in America are 1700 to 1725.

William and Mary furniture is not plentiful, partly because it was made for a relatively few years and partly because much of it has been destroyed.

Of all of the antique furniture of the eighteenth century, William and Mary pieces are probably the least attractive and poorest in design. They are generally large, made of dark wood, and bulky looking.

One of the characteristics of this furniture is that it makes use of lathe turnings. The legs on tables and on highboys and other case pieces are often elaborately turned into trumpet and other bulbous forms, giving the furniture a somewhat heavy appearance.

As recently as 1969, William and Mary furniture was not in much demand at high prices, but in 1973 particularly good pieces brought very much higher prices.

In early 1973 a very fine William and Mary highboy from Connecticut or Massachusetts, made circa 1700-1720, sold at auction for $9,500. The highboy was in two parts. The top half had three long drawers and two small parallel drawers above these. The top above these two drawers was flat. The bottom half had three parallel drawers, which were placed above six well-turned legs. The piece was 62½ inches high and 40¾ inches wide. It was made of walnut. This is one of the most expensive, but more beautiful, William and Mary pieces. A good highboy, but not a top-grade one such as this, could be purchased for $5,000 or less.

In the same sale in New York City, there was a New England William and Mary butterfly table with turned legs. The legs were rather small and well proportioned. However, the piece had been restored, and was not in the finest condition. It was 27 inches high and 40 inches wide. The top was oval with drop leaves. The price realized was $550. Had this table been in good, unrestored condition, it might have brought $1,500.

William and Mary flat-top, trumpet-leg highboy, made in New England, circa 1700-20, was to be auctioned in 1974.

The Queen Anne period

William and Mary furniture was a transition style from the large and heavy seventeenth-century furniture made in England and America to the beautiful, smaller Queen Anne furniture which, in the United States, was made between the years 1725 and 1750. These are some of the major characteristics of this furniture:

- Emphasis on curves, especially for chair backs, legs, and seats.
- Cabriole, or double-curved, legs.
- Elimination of stretchers (braces to hold the legs together) on chairs.
- Rectangular shape.
- Bonnet tops and broken-arch pediments on tall case pieces.
- Spoon backs for chairs.
- Curved or horseshoe shapes for seats.
- Shaped aprons.
- Great use of the shell design for ornament.
- Vase-shaped chair splats.
- Extensive use of walnut and walnut veneer.
- Club feet, pad feet, and ball-and-claw feet, although the last has developed into something of a trademark of Chippendale furniture.

In early 1972 a beautiful and typical Queen Anne walnut and maple bonnet-top highboy from New England, circa 1750, was sold at auction in New York. It had restorations which decreased its value, but it had many fine characteristics, including cabriole legs, small pad feet, two carved shells on the front, and three flame finials on the top. It brought only $1,500.

In the same sale, a much simpler flat-top highboy from Pennsylvania, but in better condition, brought $4,100. It was 70½ inches high and 42 inches wide. It had cabriole legs and more elaborate trifid feet.

A piece of furniture that almost never goes for little money, particularly in relation to its size, is the Queen Anne lowboy, which in many ways resembles the bottom half of a chest-on-chest. In that same sale, a lowboy with one long drawer over three parallel drawers, cabriole legs, and trifid feet was sold for $7,000.

A typical, plentiful Queen Anne piece is the drop-leaf table. In the New York sale, such a table, 27½ inches high and 43½ inches long, made in New Hampshire circa 1740-1760, and restored, brought $800. This is about the usual price for this type of table.

Queen Anne chairs are quite expensive, and sets of American Queen Anne chairs are difficult to find. In sets of four, they might bring $1,000 each and up, even if of a less elaborate design.

Queen Anne furniture is showing the greatest rise in price of all American furniture at the present time. To many Americans it is synonymous with "antiques."

The Chippendale style

The Chippendale style is even more refined than the Queen Anne. It makes extensive use of the cabriole leg, although on some later pieces the straight leg is used. The ball-and-claw foot is also widely used. In the Queen Anne period, large splats were used on the chair backs. In Chippendale chairs the splat is elaborately pierced and carved. Carving is also more often used on other parts of the furniture than in Queen Anne pieces. The broken-arch pediment on tall pieces, while used in the Queen Anne period, is even more common in Chippendale furniture. Carved aprons and skirts are used on chairs, cabinets, and tables. The serpentine front—an attractive design—was developed in this period. Besides the normal Chippendale style, a Chinese style and a Gothic style were developed.

Fine Chippendale chairs and high chests are some of the most expensive pieces of furniture in the world. In the 1973 sale in New York mentioned earlier, a fine Chippendale carved mahogany armchair made in Philadelphia, circa 1760-1770, was offered. This chair has an elaborately carved splat and top rail, cabriole legs, and ball-and-claw feet. The arms and the knees on the legs are fairly elaborately carved. It brought $15,000, not by any means a high price for a chair of this quality.

Also auctioned at that sale, a block-front, shell-carved chest-on-chest, which may have been made by a member of the important family of furniture makers, the Townsend-Goddards of Newport, Rhode Island, brought $65,000.

A very good cherrywood bonnet-type highboy without a block front, from Connecticut, brought $10,500 at that auction, and an example of even simpler tall case furniture, a Chippendale high chest of drawers made in Pennsylvania, circa 1760-1780, with flat top, but with fine curved (ogee-bracket) feet, went for $2,000—a standard market price for such a piece of simpler Chippendale furniture.

At the present time one of the best buys in antique furniture is the American Chippendale chest of drawers. In 1973, a particularly attractive Chippendale cherrywood and birch chest of drawers of serpentine shape, made in New England circa 1760-1780, with double curved feet which had been slightly restored, sold for $1,100 at auction. The piece had four drawers and was 35 inches high and 39⅝ inches wide. In the same sale, a better serpentine chest of drawers with the same type of ogee-bracket feet brought $2,300. If the front is straight instead of serpentine in shape, the price is even lower, and if the feet are straight instead of ogee or ogee-bracket, the price is less still.

The slant-top Chippendale desk of serpentine shape is a decorative and useful piece of furniture for office or home. One such desk with ball-and-claw feet, but restored, brought $1,500 in 1973. A straight-front, slant-top desk with ogee-bracket feet and three drawers realized $750 in the same sale. If the desk had had straight feet, it would not have reached this figure.

If the slant-top desk has a cupboard above and the cupboard is enclosed by wooden or glass doors, the large and impressive piece of furniture is called a secretary or a secretary-bookcase. In the 1973 sale, a very good secretary-bookcase with glass doors, straight front, and ogee-bracket feet, 84 inches high and 48 inches wide, made in Pennsylvania, circa 1769-1780, brought $3,000.

The Chippendale tilt-top table is a very common, useful, and inexpensive antique of this period. In 1973, a very good tilt-top table, with ball-and-claw feet, probably made in Massachusetts, brought $2,000 at auction. It was 30 inches high and 32 inches in diameter, fairly large for this type of table. Its selling price was so high because the top was carved out (dished) and of piecrust design on the edge. If its top had been entirely plain, the table might have sold for only $1,000, or even $750.

Chippendale chairs are rare and high in price. Usually only straight-leg chairs without ball-and-claw feet and with a simple splat can be secured in sets for under $1,000 a chair.

The Chippendale period in America ran from about 1755 to about 1790. Many pieces of furniture were produced during this period, and many of them of the less elaborate variety are on the market at the present time.

The Federal period

The term Colonial furniture covers the furniture made in America before and during the American Revolution. It includes William and Mary, Queen Anne, Chippendale (although the Chippendale period extended to later years), and a style of furniture sometimes classified in the United States as Georgian, although Georgian is a term usually applied to English furniture produced in a large part of the eighteenth century and closely related to Chippendale.

Federal period furniture covers furniture made in the years between the establishment of the federal government in 1789 and 1830, or even as late as 1840. It includes the Hepplewhite and Sheraton styles as well as American Empire and late Empire (1830 to 1840).

Most Federal period furniture is classified either as Hepplewhite (1785-1800) or Sheraton (1795-1815). This furniture is lighter and smaller than the earlier Chippendale furniture and is perhaps better suited to modern apartments and compact houses. Although it is later furniture, it is hardly more plentiful than the earlier furniture. It is also by no means lower in price if Hepplewhite and Sheraton furniture is compared with the simpler Chippendale pieces.

These are some of the characteristics of the Hepplewhite style:

- Small size with graceful design.
- Straight lines, sometimes combined with curves.
- Dependence on classical Greek design.
- Fine carving and fine upholstery.
- Mahogany as the dominant wood.
- General absence of stretchers on chairs.
- Small scale but finely executed moldings and fine flat surface decoration.

Sheraton furniture has even smaller structural members than the Hepplewhite style, and even greater use is made of the straight line. The proportions are prime, and there is the impression of angularity. Veneers and inlays are used for ornamentation, and again mahogany is the dominant wood. Classical ornamentation is used, and tops are almost always of modified pediment design, rarely plain and straight.

American Hepplewhite shades off into Sheraton in design, and some furniture for sale is classified as Hepplewhite-Sheraton. It all can, of course, be categorized as Federal period furniture, but this is perhaps an oversimplification.

Of all furniture of the entire Federal period, the biggest bargain —from the viewpoint of securing the most furniture per dollar of expenditure—appears to be the sideboard. This is generally a large piece of furniture, but it can serve many purposes.

In early 1973, a really fine mahogany sideboard with the label of the maker, Joseph Rawson, Jr., of Providence, was auctioned in New York. The piece was bowed at the center and had a band of light wood above the mahogany. It had reeded stiles and reeded shaped legs. It was 43 inches high and 72 inches long. Its selling price was $2,100. In the same sale, a similar but more classical piece, circa 1815—with leg tops elaborately carved in the form of turbaned sultans—sold for $1,400. It was attributed to Charles-Honoré Lannuier of New York.

One of the most beautiful pieces of American furniture is the satinwood commode made in Massachusetts around 1800. One such commode, of mahogany and satinwood, of serpentine design and with French (splayed) feet, brought $1,400 in early 1973.

Similar to the commode in wood and design is the card table from Salem or Boston. Two such tables sold in that same sale were each 29½ inches high and 33½ inches wide, with fine, slender, reeded legs. Each table brought $850.

The Federal period mirror, gilded, with a large molded cornice, and with a glass upper portion on which a scene is painted, is easily found, very ornamental, and not expensive. One such mirror, 22¼ inches high and 12¾ inches wide, sold in 1973 for $350. A superior version—the Fisler family mirror—36¾ inches high and 21 inches wide, brought only $1,000. The buyer acquired a top-quality antique at a not unreasonable price.

From this era of refined, artistic design, Federal period furniture developed into a much coarser design in the first half of the nineteenth century, when machine methods were introduced into the furniture industry. This type of furniture is usually called Empire, or American Empire. Actually, the typically American style known by the name of its creator and manufacturer, Duncan Phyfe, began as Sheraton in style and gradually became the heavier Empire.

Sheraton and Hepplewhite chairs are extremely difficult to purchase, particularly in sets of four or more. They rarely appear on the market, and in sets they almost always sell for over $1,000 a chair. Empire chairs are easier to find. They are rather heavy, and are made of dark wood, with classic lines, and are often decorated with classical carvings. They can be bought for under $500 a chair in sets and sometimes at prices below $200 a chair. In contrast, at a recent sale, a Sheraton side chair of fair design went for $350, and a good shield-back Hepplewhite side chair with floral decoration brought $900.

In early 1973, a flared-side sofa made in New York, circa 1820-1835, was sold at auction in New York. All the wood on the front of the piece was horizontally reeded. The top of the frame terminated in eagles' heads and the feet were carved in the form of eagles' claws. The piece brought $900. An even more elaborate sofa, with carvings on the front of large eagles with outspread wings, sold for $1,000. A 36-inch-long card table with an elaborately carved center post and elaborately shaped and carved legs brought $550, and a slightly less elaborate one brought $375.

Simpler Empire pieces sell for much less. A very good commode of simple design, but with lions'-head pulls on the drawers, might be purchased for $250. Such a piece has increased only slightly in price during the past five years or so.

How prices have risen

Several years ago, a collector in Westport, Connecticut, began filling his eighteen-room house with American antiques, most of

How Antique Furniture Styles
Compare in Price Increases
(In Percent)

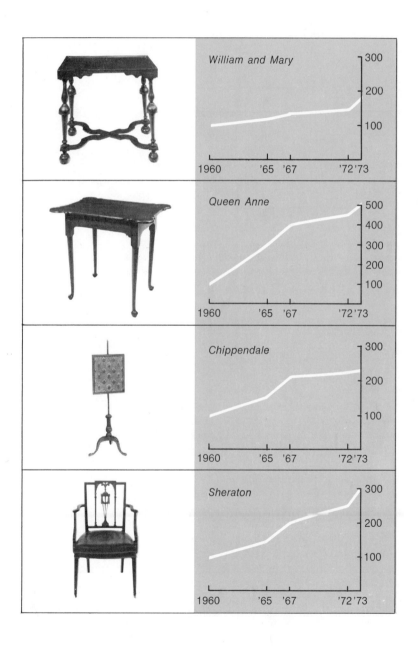

which he bought at auction, particularly at O'Reilly's Plaza Art Auction Galleries in New York. Then he sold his house. The buyer had an apartment in New York that contained enough furniture to fill only five or six rooms of the eighteen-room house. The purchaser's wife consequently began buying at auction in New York when she could, and also visited antique and secondhand shops, seeking suitable American pieces. She bought what she could find, but when the closing date on the house came around she was still very short of furniture. She made an offer on some of the seller's antiques and the offer was accepted. These antiques had been owned about a year by the seller. The price to the new owner was exactly 248 percent of what he had paid for the furniture a year earlier.

One of the pieces was a chest-on-chest from Pennsylvania, made in about 1780. It had the very much wanted double-curved ogee-bracket feet. The chest-on-chest had cost $625 when bought the previous year from dealer Michael Arpad in Washington, D.C. The house seller let the new owner have it for the same figure—$625.

About three years later, a knowledgeable dealer in American antiques came to visit the new house owners. He was a friend, but he was also a businessman. He carried with him a check with which he hoped to purchase the chest-on-chest. The owners of the chest did not want to sell—despite the fact that the check was for $5,000.

Future price trends

If any kind of furniture will rise in the immediate future, American furniture should. The best prospect for a rise is Chippendale furniture, which has risen little in the immediate past. It is fairly scarce. It is of excellent design. It is highly useful and sturdy, and it fits well into the modern smaller home.

Sheraton furniture, if it can be located, is possibly the next candidate for a price rise. It is even smaller and more refined in design than Chippendale.

Next in line to rise would probably be Hepplewhite furniture, which is very close to Sheraton in design.

Queen Anne furniture has had a good rise in price, and it is by no means in the bargain category. Still, this furniture is in demand, and the price should increase in the future.

William and Mary furniture has taken a big jump in price since 1972, even though it is far from being the most artistically excellent furniture ever made. Still, it is something of an "art object" and a rarity, and should continue to rise.

Empire furniture also is not the best from an artistic point of view, but it is fairly plentiful and appears at many large and small auctions throughout the country. It is still so low in price, and so useful, that it no doubt will rise in price. Even if the price should not rise, this furniture is not a bad buy as it is still in the price range of good new reproduction furniture, to which it is very superior as an investment.

The finest quality reproduction furniture also, no doubt, will rise in price on the secondhand market (when first sold it loses value but then gradually rises), as it has been doing, but any anticipated price rise for reproductions must be less than for antiques in the immediate future.

A George II walnut and parcel-gilt mirror, sold for $3,000 in 1973, is shown over an early George III serpentine-fronted walnut chest of drawers, which sold at the same time for $1,600. English antique furniture is generally not as expensive as the much-sought-after French antiques.

CHAPTER 10

European
Antiques

In the United States today, antiques from Spain, Holland, Germany, and sometimes the Soviet Union (originally Russia, of course), can at times be purchased from dealers and at auctions. All of these antiques are relatively unknown in this country, and up until the past few years they brought very low prices here.

The European antiques that have been known here for many years and that have brought and do bring good market prices are from France and England. They are available in the shops of dealers and they appear regularly at auction. The collector might well concentrate on these antiques. If we add to French and English antiques those of American origin we probably have 90 percent of the antiques offered for sale in this country.

French antiques are the most prestigious in the world. They are the most sought after by the greatest and wealthiest collectors. They achieve the highest prices. And they are considered to be the finest quality furniture ever made. In the past few years at least three pieces of eighteenth-century French furniture have reached the $400,000 mark at auction, and these were not very large pieces.

Probably the most active collector of this furniture today is J. Paul Getty, who in the last two years has been quietly buying to furnish his palatial new museum in California. Mr. Getty's French furniture collection is the greatest in America and is probably one of the three or four greatest collections of French furniture in the world—the other collections being in the Louvre in Paris, in the Wallace Collection in London, and in Waddesdon Manor, the former home of the Rothschilds in Buckinghamshire, England.

Mr. Getty did not hesitate to buy a pair of commodes for $250,000 at auction recently. Still it was not always thus with him. Nor was it always thus with French antiques. On July 24, 1939, just before the beginning of World War II, Sotheby's in London sold two carved gilt *fauteuils* (open-arm chairs) covered in Italian needlepoint for $233 the pair. The significant thing about this sale, apart from the excellent quality of the chairs, was the fact that they were sold to J. Paul Getty.

On the same day a pair of *bergères* (chairs with closed arms) covered with contemporary needlework sold for a little less to the same buyer. A beautiful small kingwood *bureau* (commode), 42 inches long and with a marble top, stamped with the initials of the maker, D.F., was sold for $433—to Getty. Finally, a suite consisting of a tapestry-covered *canapé* (sofa) and four *fauteuils* was sold to the same buyer for $580.

The year 1939 probably represents the bottom of the market for Louis XV furniture, which, of all of the furniture ever made anywhere, now represents the ultimate in quality. In the 1932 economic low point of the United States and Europe, this furniture was certainly inexpensive, but by 1939 the 1932 price level had been cut in half.

One of the greatest talents of multibillionaire Getty is his ability to foresee economic conditions and prices. He was certainly right in buying Louis XV furniture in 1939. Still, it is possible today to collect this furniture, as well as Louis XVI furniture, for relatively modest sums of money, including a few pieces that might be acceptable even to J. Paul Getty.

Production system assured excellence

There are several reasons for the preeminence of Louis XV and Louis XVI furniture. The first factor was the tremendous demand by the king and the nobles for pieces to furnish the finest estates in Europe, built and furnished almost without regard to cost. To meet this demand, the furniture makers established a production system that assured excellence of design, materials, and workmanship.

The essence of the production system was the guild, and the chief guild was the Corporation des Menuisiers-Ebénistes. The *menuisier*

Louis XV mahogany and kingwood marquetry table once owned by the Marquise de Pompadour sold in 1928 for $71,000. It sold again in 1971 for $410,000.

worked in solid wood, including decorative elements, and is usually considered a chair maker. The *ébéniste* was a cabinet maker, skilled in the use of veneer on commodes, desks, and such.

Maîtres (masters) were the senior members of the organization. In 1723, when Louis XV came to power, there were 985 *maîtres*. When the guild system was dissolved in 1790, there were still only 985 *maîtres*. The members were limited because a restricted number meant restricted production and consequently high prices, but small numbers also made it easy for the government to control the furniture industry so that the best workmanship would prevail.

An apprentice was taken on by a master at age twelve to fourteen. He served the master six years without pay. If, at the end of that time, his work was satisfactory, he was made a *compagnon*, or assistant, with pay. If the apprentice who graduated to *compagnon* came from Paris, he served three years as an assistant. If he came from outside Paris, he served for six years. Thus there was an obvious Parisian monopoly of the furniture-making industry.

At the end of the *compagnon*'s term he was required to construct a piece of furniture entirely on his own and submit it for inspection to the control committee of the guild. This piece of furniture was known as the *chef d'oeuvre*.

The control committee was called the *juré*. Masters in this group had to have at least ten years of experience. If the piece passed the control committee, the *compagnon* then presented silver pieces to the *juré* and more silver pieces to the *syndic*, the president of the guild.

The *compagnon* then became a master. Four times a year the *juré* visited the shop of every master and inspected every piece of furniture in the shop. Those pieces that did not pass their inspection were confiscated and then either sold for the benefit of the guild or destroyed. The pieces that passed inspection were stamped by the *juré* "JME" or "ME," and this stamp appears on such furniture today. The master was also required by the guild to place his own stamp—such as "B.V.R.B." (Bernard van Risen Burgh) or "I. Dubois"—on the furniture to identify it. Such a signature on a piece of French furniture probably doubles its present value.

The Louis XIV furniture that was made in the seventeenth and early eighteenth centuries is not on the market today in any substantial volume. The finer boulle pieces—inlaid with brass and tortoiseshell—are almost nonexistent, and only later pieces in the boulle style are usually for sale.

The Louis XV style

Régence and Louis XV furniture is plentiful in both elaborate and simple pieces. This furniture was made from about 1715 to

How Louis XV and XVI Furniture Has Increased in Value

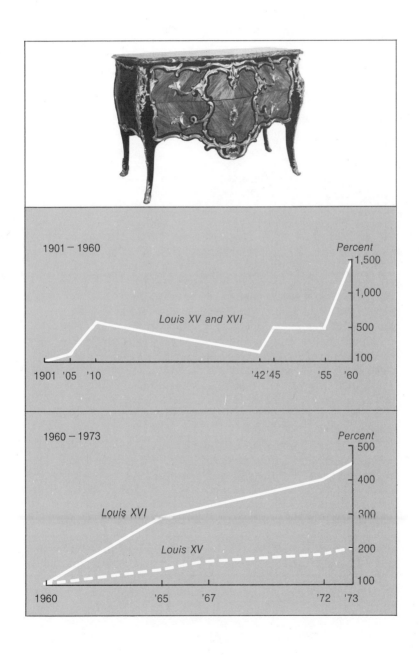

1901 – 1960

Percent

1,500
1,000
Louis XV and XVI
500
100

1901 '05 '10   '42 '45   '55 '60

1960 – 1973

Percent

500
400
Louis XVI
300
Louis XV
200
100

1960   '65   '67   '72 '73

the era of Louis XVI, which began in 1774. The characteristics of this furniture are:

- Cabriole, or double curved, leg.
- Less emphasis on the rectangle and more on the curve for chair back top rails, for all sides of the chair back, and for the overall shape of commodes.
- Smaller sized, less bulky pieces.
- More use of surface decoration, including ornamental metal.
- Elimination of stretchers and underbracing on the chairs, giving them a lighter, more finished appearance.
- Mahogany and walnut as the chief woods.
- Light color through the use of inlays, gilding, polychroming, and painting.

An eminent New York collector of paintings and antique furniture purchased a Louis XV *bureau plat* (desk) for $150,000 a few years ago. On the underside of the desk was a number, which Sir Francis Watson, director of the Wallace Collection in London and keeper of the queen's art treasures, later identified as an inventory number of a royal piece of furniture.

The number, together with a description of the desk, was sent by Sir Francis to the director of the Louvre in Paris. The quick reply stated that the desk was one of the greatest pieces of royal furniture in the world, that it had disappeared from public view decades ago, that it was made by the king's furniture maker—Joubert—and that the value for immediate sale might well be $300,000—twice what the desk had just been sold for. Today it would be worth more.

The biggest bargain in Louis XV furniture is the settee. Sometimes this piece of furniture sells for less money than a chair of the same quality. In early 1973 a Louis XV beechwood settee, 72 inches long, sold for $2,500, but sometimes this type of settee can be bought for less.

Later in the same year a good pair of Louis XV carved and painted open-arm chairs *(fauteuils)*, signed by the maker, I. Boucault, brought $1,900 the pair. In the same sale, a Louis XV carved beechwood *marquise* (large chair) went for $1,000.

In April, 1973, a rosewood commode with elaborate handles and ormolu trim, 47 inches long—an imposing piece of furniture—sold for $2,200. Also at that time, a most desirable piece—a Louis XV kingwood marquetry desk *(bureau plat)*—sold for a reasonable price. It was 29 inches high and 44½ inches long. It brought $3,200.

Earlier in 1973, a beautiful, small *secrétaire* (slant-top desk) with fine brass mounts (ormolu), in kingwood and walnut, realized $3,700.

J. Paul Getty purchased this rare French Régence *bureau plat* in 1944 for $17,245. By 1974 its value had risen to $250,000.

This pair of Louis XVI painted *fauteuils en cabriolet* upholstered in Aubusson tapestry sold at auction in March, 1974, for $1,800.

The Louis XVI style

The Louis XVI style is characterized by these features:

• Straight lines as compared with the curves of the Louis XV style. This is perhaps the main characteristic of this style.
• Smaller size than Louis XV.
• Less elaborate ornamentation.
• Classical Greek influence on shape and ornamentation.
• Rectangular shape.
• More subdued metal mounts.
• More painting of the furniture than in other periods.
• More delicate and more fragile pieces than in the Louis XV era.

The simpler commodes that can be used as bedroom storage pieces or ornamental living-room pieces often sell at reasonable prices. In April, 1973, a mahogany commode with three drawers, a brass gallery, and ormolu handles, brought $2,100. Louis XVI commodes are usually less costly than Louis XV commodes.

In the same year a pair of painted, closed-arm chairs *(bergères)* sold for $750 the pair. Later in 1973, a very useful piece of furniture, a chiffonier of tulipwood and purplewood, 40¾ inches high and 24½ inches wide, containing five long drawers, was sold for $1,500.

The usual Louis XV flat desk *(bureau plat)* is very expensive, and only the simpler ones sell for lesser sums. The Louis XVI *bureau plat* is very much cheaper than the Louis XV equivalent. In April, 1973, a very good Louis XVI *bureau plat* of mahogany with ormolu mounts, signed by Gosselin, brought $1,900.

One of the least expensive of all Louis XVI pieces is the *secrétaire à abattant* (fall-front desk). One such desk, 55¾ inches high and 37 inches wide, signed by the maker, Vassou, sold in 1973 for $2,000. The *bureau à cylindre* (roll-front desk) is another piece of fine furniture not in great demand that can be purchased at about the same price.

Small tables of the Louis XV and Louis XVI eras, especially those with small, slender legs, usually are expensive, particularly in relation to the size of the pieces. Some of these tables, however, at times sell at reasonable prices. In April, 1973, an ormolu-mounted table, 29½ inches high and 25½ inches wide, with a brass gallery around the top, fairly elaborate brass trim, and fluted legs, brought $1,800. A simpler table, rectangular in shape, 30¼ inches high and 21¾ inches wide, sold for $1,200 in the same sale.

A very fine and useful piece of bedroom furniture, a *duchesse*— similar to a chaise lounge—72 inches long, with fine fluted and ta-

How English Antique Furniture
Has Increased in Value

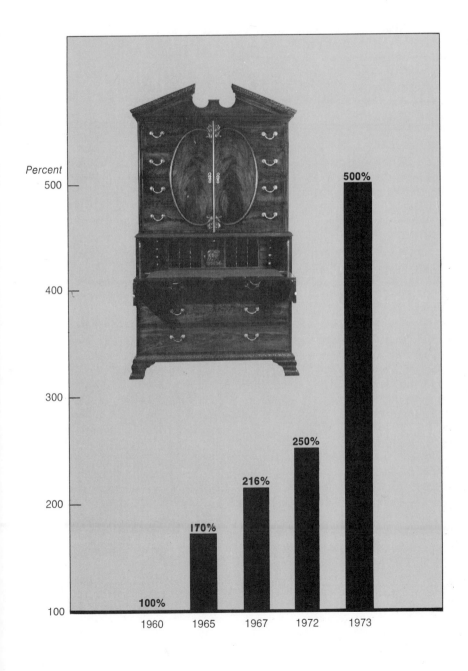

Percent

500%

500

400

300

250%

216%

200

170%

100%

100

1960   1965   1967   1972   1973

pered legs, was purchased for just $1,000 at that auction in 1973.

English antique furniture

The large, dark, rectangular, oak furniture of seventeenth-century England gave way in 1689 to the bulbous and not very plentiful William and Mary furniture. At the end of the reign of William and Mary in 1702, Queen Anne ascended to the throne. A new style of furniture came into being—smaller, less bulbous, more graceful. Queen Anne furniture is on the market from time to time but the better pieces are rather rare and usually high in price.

Chippendale

The Chippendale style was the next to appear. This style was introduced around the year 1749 and lasted to about 1779. Unlike most of the earlier English and French styles that were named after reigning monarchs, the Chippendale style was given the name of the principal furniture designer and maker of that time— Thomas Chippendale.

While this furniture is more plentiful than Queen Anne, it is, in general, high in price. Some collectors have been looking for years for sets of Chippendale chairs with ball-and-claw feet, and with fine pierced and carved splats (seat backs). Such sets are almost always sky-high in price, even the simpler varieties.

In April, 1973, a set of chairs that were certainly of the Chippendale period—but were known as Georgian chairs—was sold at what might be considered a very reasonable price for such pieces. There were twelve chairs, a huge set in relation to what comes onto the market in Chippendale chairs. There were two armchairs and ten side chairs. There were nicely pierced and carved seat splats but no ball-and-claw feet. The twelve chairs brought $6,500—about $550 a chair. Such buys rarely appear on the market, and it is usual to pay about $1,000 a chair for this type, even in smaller sets.

Hepplewhite and Sheraton

Two types of English antique furniture do appear on the market in quantity, both in England and in the United States, and are not out of reach from a price viewpoint. One type is Hepplewhite, made between 1780 and about 1795. The other is Sheraton, made between 1795 and 1810.

Some of the most desirable Hepplewhite and Sheraton pieces are chairs. At times the simpler ones can be purchased in sets for around $100 a chair, and usually not above $200, although finely carved ones bring more. For years, Luigi Cox, a dealer in Canterbury, England, had a good set of eight Hepplewhite chairs of simple design for sale, newly upholstered and in excellent condition. The

The Value of Sheraton Furniture Is Soaring

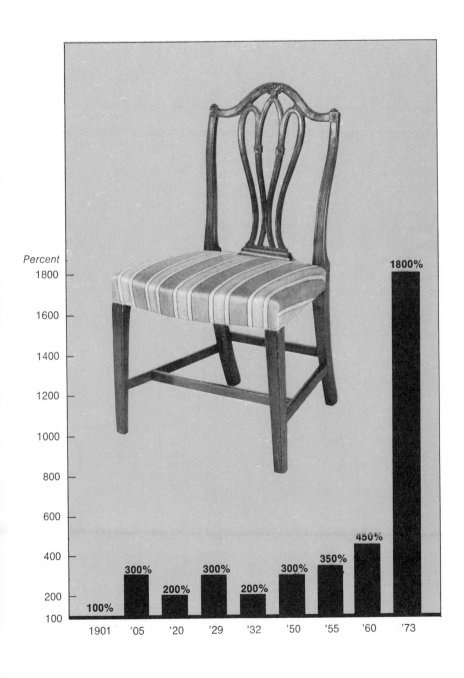

Percent

1800%

450%

350%

300%   300%   300%

200%   200%

100%

1901   '05   '20   '29   '32   '50   '55   '60   '73

price of the set was about $650. Two years ago the price of such chairs began to rise, and the set today might well bring $1,500.

In April, 1973, a magnificent pair of Hepplewhite painted armchairs was sold in New York at auction. The backs were of shield design; the legs were tapered and fluted; and there was a good deal of carving on the front seat rail, on the arms, and on the legs. The pair sold for $1,200.

Another highly desirable and useful piece of furniture is the late-eighteenth-century dining-room table of rectangular design and with two, three, or more supporting columns. One such table, about twelve feet long, sold at Worsfold's auction in Canterbury, England, for the equivalent of $1,700 in 1972. This would have been the market price in New York too. The price of such a table has now risen to about $2,500. An extra-large table—14 feet 6¾ inches long—made about 1800, with fluted and tapered legs, brought $3,200 at auction in New York in April, 1973.

English sideboards, like the American variety, are not in demand, and for a small sum of money a large and decorative item can often be purchased. In the same April, 1973, sale, a small sideboard, 54 inches long, made in the last quarter of the eighteenth century, was sold for $1,400. Generally, the smaller the sideboard the greater its value. This one was made of mahogany, with ornamental lion's-mask drawer pulls, two bowed front sections, and ornamental veneer and inlay stringing.

An especially useful, yet decorative, piece of furniture is the chest-on-chest, which is literally one commode on another. One such piece was offered at the sale in April, 1973. It was 70 inches high. In the bottom section there were three long drawers. In the top section there were two small parallel drawers over three long drawers. The feet were of bracket (straight) design, but there was ornamental inlay stringing. The price realized was $1,300.

Earlier in the year a very good mahogany Pembroke table with curved drop leaves and square, tapered legs ending in brass casters was sold. It contained one drawer and was 28 inches high and 33 inches long. It brought $700. Had it been of simpler design, it might have been sold for as little as $150.

Also sold in the same sale were two highly useful and ornamental pieces—a pair of mahogany settees made about 1800. Each was 66 inches long and beautifully shaped. The frames were molded and inlaid with brass. The price of the pair was $1,600. This, again, is the piece of furniture that rarely seems to bring the price it should, whether the settee is English, French, or American.

In this sale a set of twelve chairs, including a pair of armchairs, made in the early nineteenth century, went for $3,300—less than $300 a chair.

Sideboards can often be purchased at reasonable prices. This George III inlaid mahogany sideboard went at an auction in 1973 for $1,600.

George I upholstered walnut settee was purchased at auction in 1973 for $4,500. Some antique settees sell for under $1,000.

Auctioned in 1973, the George III mahogany tea or games table, below, brought $2,100 and the George II mahogany piecrust tripod table $2,800.

The commode, or bureau, of the late eighteenth and early nineteenth century is widely available, and usually at a reasonable price. It is at the very least useful for storage in the bedroom, and the more elaborate versions can be used as hall or living-room pieces.

Simpler commodes, even those with shaped legs, bow fronts, inlaying, and stringing, can often be purchased for under $1,000. The simplest ones can be purchased for under $500. Fairly good commodes could be purchased in England for $100 in 1971, but all English furniture has risen in price tremendously since that time.

Between 1972 and the end of 1973, Hepplewhite and Sheraton furniture, the most plentiful English antique furniture, approximately doubled in price. The less expensive, simpler Hepplewhite and Sheraton pieces at least doubled. In 1971, demand for antiques was low in England and pieces were plentiful on the market. There was little trouble in finding a commode and a slant-top desk for $100 to $150. Chairs sold for $100 each, and tilt-top tables sold for less. To double these figures was no great achievement. Prices could do little other than rise.

The market today

The finest Louis XV and Louis XVI pieces of furniture by the great makers are in the priceless category, and prices over $100,000 per piece are not unusual. The good furniture (as opposed to the great museum pieces) is high in price as compared with other antique furniture. Demand to a degree has shifted to the finer, later Empire furniture, and this furniture is no longer in the moderately priced category.

In the moderately priced category are the simpler pieces. Compared with other types of antique furniture, these "simpler" pieces are elaborate—with inlays, fine veneers, elaborate brass pulls, carving, and ormolu mounts. Some pieces are gilded and painted. This furniture is generally priced above the less expensive English and American antiques, but dollar for dollar the collector still gets a greater "work of art" for the money in French furniture.

Victorian furniture at times incorporated styles of earlier eras. This porcelain-mounted satinwood and rosewood *bonheur du jour* was made in the mid-nineteenth century in a style reminiscent of French eighteenth-century pieces. It was sold at auction in mid-1973 for $4,000.

CHAPTER 11

Victoriana

Victorian furniture is synonymous with antiques in many parts of the United States. In certain areas it is virtually the only kind of "antique" furniture for sale in dealers' shops or at auctions. Much of this furniture comes from local estates that are liquidated but a great deal of it comes from the large cities, particularly New York.

At the smaller auctions, dealers buy virtually vanloads of Victorian furniture to sell in their shops. Victorian furniture is not always quite plentiful enough to make an entire vanload from one or two big city auctions, but it is mixed with reproduction furniture, secondhand furniture, and perhaps a few earlier pieces, plus rugs, lamps, glassware, and so forth.

Because in many parts of the country Victorian furniture is the only kind of "antique" furniture available for purchase, buyers are conditioned to think that Victorian furniture is antique furniture. The United States Custom Service's determination of nondutiable items uses a 100-year cutoff date, so that anything made over 100 years ago might be called "antique," but the connoisseur will generally not accept anything as antique if it was made after 1830. For him, even this is stretching a point, and he would prefer to use a cutoff date of 1820 or, better still, 1800, the date that divides the Golden Century of furniture making from what came later.

Historical perspective

Queen Victoria reigned from 1837 to 1901, and furniture made in her day is generally known as Victorian. This furniture has a distinct style, although at various periods it incorporated (sometimes slavishly copying) some of the styles of the past. Still, it is instantly recognizable to the trained eye as "Victorian." The furniture was not created by order of the queen—as Napoleonic, or Empire, furniture was created in France when Napoleon decreed the new style.

Victorian furniture was made between the years 1830 and 1900, to use rough dates. It was the product of the industrial revolution, which had its beginnings in the years 1795 to about 1815. The industrial revolution developed the machine, which was applied to the making of furniture in factories. Prior to the advent of the machine and the factory, furniture was made by hand in small shops by craftsmen. The machine and the factory allowed a form of mass production to be applied to the making of furniture, with the result that more pieces could be turned out at lower cost. As the industrial revolution developed, factory methods were applied to carving and other ornamentation that previously had required days and weeks of artistic labor of a fairly high order.

The industrial revolution also created a class of entrepreneurs who had enough money to provide a new market for furniture of good quality. This group purchased the new Victorian furniture. In the United States, in just twenty years—from 1845 to 1865—furniture volume doubled.

It is possible to divide Victorian furniture into three general categories:

1. *Very large and highly decorated with carving.* This is enormous furniture that was made especially for certain baronial homes. Very often it was designed for a particular wall or corner and thus became an integral part of the home. Upon sale or demolition of the house, quite often no one wanted the furniture. It did not fit into more modern, smaller homes; it was too costly to move; and it was considered old-fashioned. Much of it was therefore demolished along with the houses.

2. *Smaller and decorated with carving.* This category contains the most wanted and most valuable of all Victorian furniture. The pieces were well designed and made of attractive woods. The carving was elaborate and often consisted of bunches of grapes and

other natural elements. Laminated and steamed wood was often used, and rosewood gave the furniture an attractive appearance. The most popular maker of this type of furniture in the United States was J.H. Belter and Company. The designs and construction used by this firm resulted in the production of pieces which are very much sought after by collectors and dealers today.

3. *Smaller and almost completely undecorated.* This is the furniture that appears regularly at auction, particularly at the smaller auction houses in New York. It is well designed, sturdy, and useful. Because it appears in such quantities and lacks the approval of antique connoisseurs, it can be purchased at fairly reasonable prices.

What is being offered

In New York City's Plaza Art Galleries, P.B. 84, and Coleman Auction Galleries, as well as in other auctions, Victorian furniture is offered for sale almost every week.

The pieces offered at just one recent New York auction indicate what is on the market and at what price. At the Coleman auction in January, 1974, these were some of the offerings in Victorian furniture:

One lot was a carved walnut and white silk damask settee with a loose pad. It was a fairly large settee, well proportioned and with a three-part ornamental back which was well carved. The upholstery was new and excellent. The cushion on the seat was overstuffed. Possibly the upholstery cost as much as $400. This fairly attractive settee sold for $275.

The next lot was a pair of carved walnut side chairs with upholstered seats which matched the settee. The pair brought $130—$65 a chair—and the upholstery could not have been done for this figure.

In the same sale there was offered a Victorian mahogany center table with a black marble top. It was small and rectangular in shape and had incurvate legs, a somewhat pleasing design. It was not elaborately carved. It sold for $175.

These are typical pieces of the middle category, which in the present market is the preferred category. A Belter settee at auction might well bring $900 to $1,000, and a Belter armchair or fine side chair might bring upwards of $500.

The main offerings at any auction and in the shops of most dealers belong in category 3—the small, relatively undecorated pieces. These were some of the pieces in this category offered at this auction sale:

• A pair of Victorian walnut and gilt upholstered side chairs,

Victorian ormolu and porcelain-mounted *bureau plat* in the French manner was auctioned in January, 1974, for $6,500.

but each chair was upholstered differently. There was no carving. The pair brought $50.

• A Victorian mahogany and plush upholstered slipper chair of simple design and not carved—$40.

• A pair of Victorian walnut footstools with needlework tops. These were very small. The price was $60.

• A pair of Victorian mahogany upholstered open-arm chairs, covered with wine-colored tufted fabric. These chairs were big and of heavy design. The pair brought $80.

• A Victorian walnut and gilt upholstered side chair of plain design and not carved—$30.

• A Victorian carved mahogany side chair with needlepoint seat. There was relatively little carving, but the design of the chair was fairly attractive. It sold for $25.

• A Victorian carved mahogany settee. This was a settee of medium size and medium quality. It brought $80.

• A tall chest with five drawers. This was an early Victorian veneered piece with fine finish, not huge or bulky, and without carving or much decoration of any kind. It went for $60.

• A Victorian carved mahogany upholstered settee. This was an attractive piece of furniture with very good upholstery. It realized $100.

At this one sale, enough furniture of Victorian design could have

Inlaid burr-walnut side cabinet, 70 inches long, made in England about 1860, sold in early 1974 for $1,100.

been assembled to furnish more than one room of a home. When an entire room is furnished with Victoriana, including lamps and other items of the period, the effect is reasonably good. On the other hand, some attractive pieces of Victorian furniture are suitable for homes which are mainly decorated with eighteenth-century antiques. There is also little or no incongruity if Victorian pieces are mixed with modern pieces of furniture, and at the above prices there is some inducement to buy at least a few pieces of Victoriana for almost any home.

Victorian styles

There is a wide variety of Victorian styles. Those of the earlier nineteenth century are:

Classical. From 1800 to about 1840, England produced a classical style of furniture which was essentially based on Greek forms. American Victorian furniture followed a little later, from 1820 to 1850. By 1840, cabinetmakers were turning to the rococo style and by 1850 the transition was fairly complete.

Gothic. The heavy, angular Gothic style did not replace the classical but ran parallel to it. This style was nothing new; Chippendale had developed a Gothic style in the middle of the eighteenth century. It was simply a revival of an already well-developed style. This style was introduced in America around 1830 and was an immediate success. By the mid-1800s the Gothic style had run its course.

Elizabethan. This was another reversion to the past, as is almost all furniture produced in the nineteenth century. This style also paralleled the classical but did not equal its popularity.

Rococo. This was the style of Louis XV which was revived in France with the coming to the throne in 1830 of Louis Philippe. By mid-century the style had spread to America, where its leading exponent was J. H. Belter. It is a matter of some interest that a clearly Victorian settee described earlier was listed in the catalog of the auction house as "Louis XV."

The balloon-back chair was developed in this period. This design vaguely resembles the Louis XVI back. Such chairs are regularly on the market.

By the period 1850-70 machines had been developed that could cut scrolls and frames of irregular design. There were also machines that could carve fairly elaborate ornaments. Mass production was applied to the entire furniture industry with resultant lower furniture prices.

It is worthy of note that even in those times of mass production there were furniture makers who designed pieces and then executed the designs by hand, charging as much as $250 for a handmade sofa—not a low price for the nineteenth century.

Victorian styles of the later nineteenth century are:

Louis XVI. In the 1850s and 1860s, Empress Eugénie of France commissioned the German cabinetmaker Grohé to redecorate the royal residences in the style of Louis XVI. In 1860 the American cabinet shops began to produce furniture of this style, which was a heavier version of Louis XVI but also contained elements of the earlier and heavier Louis XIV style.

Renaissance. In France in about 1855 the Italian Renaissance style was revived. It spread to England and the United States. This furniture was made almost until the close of the nineteenth century. It is heavy, dark, rectangular, and architectural.

Near Eastern. This was a kind of Moorish furniture developed by English and American designers because little actual Eastern furniture was available to copy in Britain and the United States. This is the style of the P. T. Barnum home in Bridgeport, Connecticut, known as Iranistan. Persons of wealth ordered entire rooms of this type of furniture during this era.

New Classical. In the latter part of the nineteenth century Victorian designers turned to a new classical revival, this one based on the designs of Robert Adam, a fine, well-proportioned style. The

Among the Victoriana sold in London in early 1974 was this English mid-nineteenth-century papier-mâché work table inlaid with mother of pearl. It was bought for $200. The walnut dining chair is one of a set of six made in England about 1860 that sold for $700 in early 1974.

new pieces were very close to the original eighteenth-century designs, and some fine furniture was produced at this time.

Pre-Raphaelite. By the mid-nineteenth century furniture design had fallen to a low level. To improve its quality and appearance, William Morris of England, in company with pre-Raphaelite painters Rossetti and Burne-Jones, and others, organized a company to design and make fine furniture based on much earlier designs and to make it by hand. The lines were straight and the carving was simple and sharply cut. There was some painting of figures and decorations.

Eastlake. Designed by Charles Eastlake, this was a very popular and very common type of furniture which can still be purchased in its American versions in Goodwill Industries shops and in Salvation Army and Thrift shops, as well as in dealers' shops and at auction. The pieces are generally small, with straight lines and little ornamentation. There is at present something of an Eastlake revival.

Japanese. This style of furniture appeared in France in the 1860s, and was very popular in England in the 1870s and 1880s. The pieces are decorated with Oriental motifs, generally little figures. Furniture in this style does not appear on the market in any great quantity today.

Price trend of the past

The price trend of Victorian furniture is dissimilar to that of true antique furniture. In 1943, the Parke Bernet Galleries in New York sold a "triple back" settee for $450. This was a settee very similar to the one sold at the Coleman Galleries in January, 1974, for $275, although it is unlikely that the fabric on the settee sold in 1943 compared with the new silk fabric on the 1974 settee.

During World War II old furniture was bought for utility when new items could not be purchased. There was also increased buying of antiques and antiquities with money that could not be spent for such items as automobiles, dishwashers, and clothes dryers. When the war was over, auction sales dropped off while accumulated dollars were spent on postponed purchases of modern products.

Victorian furniture went into a decline, and as late as 1960 there was no demand for this type of furniture, with the exception of the very finest pieces. In fact, even later than 1960, a collector purchased a set of four attractive carved side chairs of small design for $50. These cost $7 each to put into good condition.

Between 1960 and 1965 there was a revival of interest in Victoriana and the prices of Victorian furniture approximately doubled. Still, in 1965 the price level, item for item, may well have approximated the wartime price level. In the last decade the prices of

Victorian furniture have probably doubled. This degree of price rise is not great when compared with the performance of genuine, earlier, antique furniture.

In making overall price estimates of the degree of rise one must exercise caution. The very finest Victorian furniture of the second group, which includes Belter furniture, has at least doubled in price since 1965. The first group—large, highly decorated furniture—rarely reaches the market and its price behavior is hard to measure. The third group—the smaller, plainer pieces—probably did not reach the average of doubling in price.

The degree of price rise for Victorian furniture is difficult to determine because prices vary according to where the items are sold. In the New York City auctions, prices are very low. In a city in the central west, prices may be several times higher due to the fact that only a small volume of furniture can be bought from local estates by dealers and offered for sale. To meet the demand, Victorian pieces may be purchased in Chicago, New York, or in other large cities and trucked more than two thousand miles before being offered for sale. The cost of such haulage is high, and this must be added to the selling price.

The vast majority of Victorian furniture offered is in the simpler third category, and the price rise in this group should be compared with the rise in reproduction furniture or ordinary second-hand furniture, as these lesser Victorian pieces are often bought not as antiques but simply on the basis of price as utilitarian furniture.

Reproduction furniture has been rising in price during the past five years, as has all secondhand furniture. These reproductions are not of fine Louis XV and Louis XVI pieces, but just reproductions of ordinary quality and good quality which can always be found at auctions in all parts of the country. This type of reproduction furniture, as well as all secondhand furniture, has been rising in price steadily, but relatively little. If we compare the simpler Victorian furniture with these two categories we may find that Victorian has risen about 5 percent more per year.

The degree of price rise in Victorian furniture is not as important as in earlier fine antique furniture because fewer dollars are involved in Victorian furniture. If a Victorian chair sold in 1964 for $15 (which it often did) and it now sells for $45, the price has tripled. Still, we are not talking about very many dollars, and a French commode that in the same period rose from $15,000 to $45,000 is far more noteworthy. In addition, the expensive piece was a better investment, since less space is required to store one such piece bought for $15,000 than 1,000 pieces of Victorian furniture costing a total of $15,000.

The outlook for Victorian

In general, Victorian furniture, while sturdy, is also heavy, and much of it is not very well proportioned. The frame members are often large, and on the large surfaces there is large ornamentation, a good deal of it done by machine—lacking the quality of hand-craftsmanship. Very often the wood is dark and dull, although polished rosewood and mahogany can be beautiful even on overly ornate Victorian pieces.

Artistic and connoisseur opinion has been against Victorian furniture. It has not been considered truly beautiful, or truly antique, or truly worthy of collecting. There is a tremendous amount of this furniture always available, so it does not have value as a rarity. The supply seems no smaller in 1974 than in 1964 or 1954.

In 1971, Sotheby's of London formed the Belgravia auction rooms to sell Victoriana—furniture, paintings, and objects of art. The British nineteenth-century paintings soon established new price records, and some other items, such as a Sèvres porcelain ormolu-mounted clock garniture in Louis XVI style (but made in the mid-nineteenth century), brought extremely high prices. The garniture sold for over $21,000! Desks and tables in the Louis XV style brought from $4,000 to $6,000 when they were of fine quality. Volume doubled at Sotheby's Belgravia gallery from the first season to the second—reaching over $7 million.

As certain collectibles go up in price, demand turns to those items which are available at reasonable prices, and then the prices of these latter items rise. This may be the future of Victorian furniture. As dealers and auction houses find it more and more difficult to acquire fine pre-1820 antiques, they may be forced into handling and publicizing Victoriana more than they have in the past, which will result in increased prices for these nineteenth-century "antiques," particularly those of finer quality.

PART FOUR

Investing in Ornaments

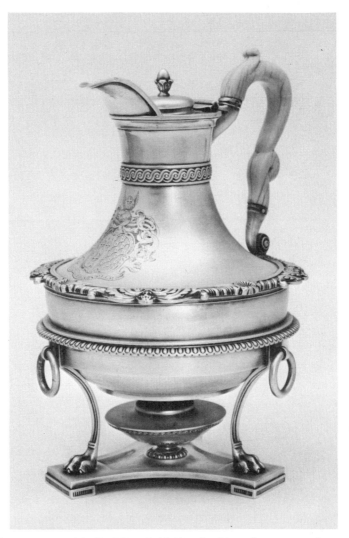

Silverware created by Paul Storr is highly prized by collectors, yet pieces sell at reasonable prices considering their quality. Storr made this coffee jug on a lampstand in London in 1808. In March, 1974, it was purchased at auction in New York for $2,600.

12

Georgian Silver

Georgian silver is particularly important as an investment collectible for several reasons:

• It can be purchased in dealers' shops and at auctions in many places.
• It is not expensive, and purchases can be tailored to the budget of almost anyone.
• It is going up in value, but at the beginning of the 1970s it took a severe price drop from which it has just now recovered.

Georgian silver was produced in the British Isles during the reigns of George I (1714 to 1727), George II (1727 to 1760), and George III (1760 to 1820). It is, for the most part, tableware. It includes coffee pots, teapots, candlesticks, flatware, sauce boats, creamers, sugar bowls, trays, salvers, serving dishes, and all manner of other pieces connected with the dining room and living room.

Fine silver was produced before the reign of George I of course. It was produced in the reign of Queen Anne (1702 to 1714), in the

reign of William and Mary (1689 to 1702), and back in Elizabethan times. Generally the older it is the more valuable the silver.

Silver produced in the reign of George IV (1820 to 1830) is
rapidly becoming as valuable as that of the earlier Georges. The
next period was the reign of William IV (1830 to 1837) and this
silver is also becoming a collectible. So is the enormous amount of
silver produced in the reign of Queen Victoria (1837 to 1901).
Since 1972, Victorian silver has acquired a good deal of the prestige and rising value of Georgian silver. The best Victorian silver
is by no means inferior to Georgian silver. It may be more ornate,
but it is still hand made.

The finest silver was made in London. Price, however, is often
determined not solely on the basis of quality but on rarity, and
some pieces of silver have more value simply because the remaining
supply of silver from their city of origin is smaller than the supply
from London or other cities. These are the main cities of origin of
Georgian silver: London, Birmingham, Chester, Dublin, Edin-
burgh, Exeter, Glasgow, Newcastle, Norwich, Sheffield, and York.
In addition, there are at least twenty-nine minor guilds of silversmiths.

Identifying Georgian silver

Georgian silver can be positively identified by the hallmark as
to when it was made, the city of origin, and the maker. Few other
collectibles in any field can be so positively identified.

The value of a piece of British silver depends more upon its hallmark than upon any other single factor. Hallmarks are stamped on
the silver by the silversmith as required by law, and regulation by
law has been applied to English silversmiths since the end of the
twelfth century. Toward the end of the fourteenth century a mark
showing the city of origin was required to be on every piece of silver, and this identification is required to this day. Since the latter
part of the seventeenth century the maker has also been identified
in the hallmark. Earlier makers can sometimes be identified, although the great London fire of 1666 destroyed the original plates
so that makers prior to that time are difficult to identify.

Prior to 1697 the law required that all silverware had to be 92.5
percent pure silver. Silverware was popular, and smiths found they
could melt down silver coins and turn them profitably into tableware. To discourage this practice, the government raised the standard for silverware to 95.8 percent in 1697. It thus became less profitable to melt down coins, as more coins were required to secure the
finer silver for tableware.

During the years of George I's reign there were four parts to a
hallmark. The first part of the mark—on the farthest left—was a

figure of the seated Britannia, which meant that the higher silver standard was in effect—95.8 percent silver. This Britannia mark was used until 1720, when the 92.5 percent standard was restored.

In 1719 and 1720 the crowned leopard's head reappeared as the first figure of a London hallmark. The lion passant figure in a hallmark indicates the 92.5 percent (sterling) silver content of the piece.

The third figure in the hallmark is extremely important as it represents the date of manufacture. It is necessary to have a directory of silver marks in order to identify the date.

The last figure in the hallmark identifies the maker—his mark or initials. These too can be identified by one of the silver directories. There are four highly important makers of Georgian silver among the hundreds of silversmiths: Paul de Lamerie, who worked in the early eighteenth century; Paul Storr, who worked in the late eighteenth and early nineteenth century; and Hester Bateman and John Schofield, who both worked in the latter eighteenth century. Hester Bateman was followed by a number of members of her family, all of whose names give their Georgian silverware pieces extra value.

On December 1, 1784, the tax mark—the head of the reigning sovereign, George III—was introduced on London silver. The head indicated that the tax had been paid on the particular piece of silver. This tax mark was continued until April 1, 1890.

A silver collector must have in his possession one or more of the following text and reference books:

Guide to Marks of Origin on British and Irish Silver Plate by Frederick Bradbury, J. W. Northend, Ltd., West Street, Sheffield 1, England.

English Goldsmiths and Their Marks by Sir Charles James Jackson, Macmillan and Co., Ltd., St. Martin's Street, London. This is a book of 747 pages containing over 13,000 marks.

The Book of Old Silver by Seymour B. Wyler, Crown Publishers, New York.

Silver Collecting for Amateurs by James Henderson, Frederick Muller, Ltd., Fleet Street, London.

Value determinants

The characteristics which determine the value of a piece of Georgian silver are:

1. *The date of the piece.* As a general rule, George I silver is more valuable than George II, and George II is more valuable than George III, which in turn is more valuable than George IV. While

the George III era extends from 1760 to 1820, the "magic date" is the year 1800. George III pieces made before 1800 are usually more valuable than those made after 1800—by perhaps as much as 25 percent.

2. *The quality of the piece.* Many valuable Georgian pieces of silver are by no means works of art. They are simply well-designed pieces of silver containing the "right" date. The finer the design of the piece, however, the greater its value.

3. *The maker.* Pieces by de Lamerie, Storr, Bateman, and Schofield are the most sought after.

4. *The condition of the hallmark.* A damaged hallmark or one that has been overcleaned reduces the value of the piece by as much as 50 percent or more. For any piece of silver to have investment value, the hallmark must be readable. Clear hallmarks definitely add to the value of any piece of Georgian silver.

5. *The condition of the piece.* A short time ago a teapot made by Hester Bateman was offered in London for $750. The price was so low because the piece had been elaborately repaired. Had it been perfect, the price might well have been several times $750.

6. *The weight of the piece.* This value-adding element applies particularly to the larger and heavier pieces. Good pieces without particular artistic merit should cost not over $30 an ounce.

7. *Where the piece is purchased.* The auction price tends to be less than the retail dealer price, but silver dealers buy at all silver auctions. They often outbid collector-buyers for the best pieces.

This George I silver teapot sold at auction in mid-1973 for $1,200 and the George II silver mug brought $4,000 in the same sale.

8. *The city of origin.* The rarity of pieces from a particular city will increase the value of those that are available.

9. *Excellent crests.* An ordinary family crest neither adds nor diminishes value, but an excellent crest, done sharply, does add to value.

10. *History.* The following add value to the finest pieces of silver—those which are purchased by prominent collectors and museums:

- An illustrious former owner, particularly a member of the nobility or royalty.
- Reference, and particularly illustration, in a book by an authority on silver.
- Display in an important exhibition of silver.

Forgeries perpetrated

Throughout history, penalties have been extremely severe for falsifying hallmarks, and punishments have compared with those for counterfeiting currency. Thus the hallmark is almost always authentic and correct. Still, there are forgeries, many of them perpetrated at the turn of this century when Georgian silver was selling at record prices. One function of the silver dealer and the silver department of an auction house is to spot fakes, and they are good at this job.

These three pieces of George II silver were sold in 1973. The cream boat brought $95; the sugar bowl, $620; and the spoon tray, $900.

One effective kind of fake is to take a piece of silver containing the "right" hallmark from a poor, simple, or worn piece of silver and graft it onto another piece. In Canterbury, England, there is a modern silversmith so skilled that he can graft one piece of silver to another piece leaving virtually no trace of the "operation."

There regularly appear at auction items that actually combine two pieces of silver—very often a Georgian tray with a Victorian rim of elaborate design. Frequently, one hallmark appears on the body of the tray and another is on the rim. At least one collector bought such a mismatched piece by not examining it carefully before he purchased it. Such a piece is worth not more than one-half of what it would be worth if it were entirely Georgian.

Very often marks are stamped over to produce an earlier and more valuable date, and the maker's initials are altered to "Hester Bateman," or "Paul Storr," or some other important name.

Later carving on a piece of silver diminishes its value by perhaps one-third, no matter how perfect or how ornamental the carving is. The same is true for repoussé work (patterns in relief), except that this type of later embellishment can reduce the price of the piece almost to the value of the silver in it. One very attractive teapot made by Richard Cooke, covered with repoussé flowers added in Victorian times, was offered a few years ago for $60. Had the teapot been absolutely plain, as it was originally, it would have been worth about $200.

The more a would-be collector looks at Georgian silver and the more he discusses it with silver dealers, the more expert he becomes in judging value and originality. As an example: An Elizabethan apostle spoon was offered to a collector by a silver dealer in Canterbury, England, a few years ago for $280. The collector looked it over very carefully. He then rejected it and announced to the dealer, "I think it's a fake." To his trained eye the piece somehow looked too good. The marks looked a little too sharp to have been done in the time of Queen Elizabeth. The color of the silver seemed more like that produced today than in Elizabethan times.

The dealer took the piece to Christie's silver department in London. There the experts found that the spoon was a fake produced in Victorian times.

Price trends

The study of the market price and investment value of Georgian silver is of importance not only to the collector of Georgian silver but to the person who acquires any type of collectible as an investment. It is too easy to draw price trends for past years and arrive at the conclusion that "everything has risen in price and therefore will continue to rise in price."

Georgian silver has certainly risen in price in the past, but it has also dropped in price. We might well draw a price trend beginning at a very low point for the Georgian silver market—the year 1956.

The John Kenneth Danby sale held at the Parke Bernet Galleries in New York on October 13, 1956, probably represents the lowest point in Georgian silver prices in recent years. The Georgian silver sold was of about the same grade as most of these pieces offered on the American and English markets today. It was by no means museum quality, nor was it poor silver. These are the pieces and the prices they brought:

- A George II teapot made by William Grundy, London, 1750, with repoussé: $110.
- Twenty-one spoons and serving instruments of various kinds, with date marks 1779 to 1829: $30 for the lot.
- Two candlesticks, dated 1718 and 1746, one by Jno. Gould, seven inches high: $45 for the two.
- Two more candlesticks by Taylor and Hamilton, Glasgow, c. 1785, 11¾ inches high: $55.
- A tea service consisting of teapot, sugar bowl, and creamer, by John Emes, London, 1801: $75 for the lot.
- A sugar basket by Hester Bateman, London, 1789: $90.

These prices were less than those paid for reproduction silver in that year.

By the 1960-61 season, prices had risen relatively little, possibly not over 25 percent. Prices may have doubled by 1965, which does not represent a great price increase when stretched over five years.

From 1965 on, however, prices began to rise rapidly. One event of considerable importance took place which had a positive effect on the Georgian silver market. In the fall of 1967 the pound sterling was devalued from $2.80 to $2.40—14.3 percent. A number of collector-investors came to the conclusion that the pound sterling was no longer a safe repository of wealth and that better repositories might be found. One such repository, they apparently felt, was Georgian silver. Such an investment was available almost everywhere. The items were small, useful, and decorative, and sold at prices suited to both the affluent and persons of medium income. By late 1969, when a peak was reached, prices had increased at least three times as compared with 1965.

Then what almost amounted to a crash took place. By the middle of 1970 prices had dropped about 40 percent from the peak of a year earlier. The larger, more expensive pieces dropped the most; simple flatware dropped the least. The great museum-quality pieces did not seem to decline in price at all. The Georgian silver market had risen to unrealistic heights under the impact of devaluation and inflation, which together threatened the savings of everyone in Britain.

By the end of 1971 about one-quarter of the loss from 1969 to 1970 had been made up. As of early 1974, prices of Georgian silver were still rising.

Recent prices

The further back we go from the time of George III the higher the price of silverware, as a general rule. Thus, for the medium-income and medium-capital investor, silver of the George III era is probably the category on which to concentrate at the present time. At times George II pieces can be secured at other than sky-high prices and so can George I pieces, but George III silver is both plentiful and reasonable in price as compared with other periods. It is, of course, true that the finest George III pieces sell for very high prices at times, but simpler pieces can be bought for sums ranging downward from a few thousand dollars, and also tend to have a fairly definite market price.

In discussing market prices, it might be helpful to select several standard, useful, and fairly reasonable pieces of silverware for a price survey.

One of the most "standard" of all pieces, and at the same time something of a measure of the Georgian silver market, is the teapot. This is an attractive piece of silver that can be used in any household. It can also be sold to a dealer or at auction at any time, and it is in constant demand.

In London in July of 1973 a small, plain, oval teapot, bright cut with bands of flowers and two cartouches, on a beaded base, made by the famed Hester Bateman, brought $1,050. In June, 1973, a similar Hester Bateman teapot on a stand, weighing a little more than the above pot, sold in New York at auction for $1,200. Had these two teapots not been made by Hester Bateman, they might have brought $600 to $700.

Earlier in that year, a similar plain oval teapot and stand by Hester Bateman sold for $960. The next lot in the sale, a pear-shaped coffee pot, 12½ inches high, a very ornamental and impressive piece of silver, but still a standard item on the market, even though made in 1784 by Hester Bateman, brought $1,920.

Pieces by Paul Storr are, to a great extent, works of art and yet still seem low in price for what they are. In March, 1973, in New York, a Paul Storr coffee jug, 8½ inches high, brought $1,900. It weighed 29 ounces, but for such items, price per ounce does not apply. In the same month in London, a Storr Regency vase-shaped jug, 11¼ inches high, went for $2,520. It weighed 41 ounces.

George III silver coffee pot made by the famed Hester Bateman was purchased in 1973 for $2,000.

In May of 1973 something of a rarity was sold in London: a George I plain octagonal coffee pot made in 1716 by Nelme. It was 9 inches high and weighed 21 ounces. It brought $1,150.

On November 1, 1973, an almost identical pot, 8¾ inches high and weighing 19 ounces, brought $5,250. Although the Georgian silver market was rising, it was not rising this fast, but the trend is certainly indicated.

In March of 1973 one could have purchased a cylindrical Queen Anne coffee pot, made in 1702 by Joseph Ward, 8⅞ inches high and weighing 17 ounces, for $3,120.

Two very ornamental and useful pieces of silver were sold in early 1973 at auction in New York. The first was a silver tea urn made by James Young in 1773. It was a large piece, 19½ inches high and weighing 101 ounces. It sold for $800. Had it been in perfect condition, it would have brought more. In the same sale there was a coffee urn, this one by Charles Hougham, London, 1789. It was 22 inches high, weighed 74 ounces, and sold for $800. These urns have considerable capacity for liquids and contain a spigot for filling cups.

Also in New York, in March, 1973, a coffee pot of inverted pear shape and a circular teapot, both by Alexander Johnston, London, 1762, sold for $1,700 for the two pieces.

A second significant piece of Georgian silver and a very useful and ornamental one, that generally sells for less per ounce than hollow ware, is the salver, or circular serving tray.

In early 1973 a beautiful salver with a beaded border on three feet of ball-and-claw design, 12¼ inches in diameter, made by Richard Rugg in 1779, sold for $1,200.

In the same sale something of a bargain was sold—a plain George I salver, 12 inches in diameter, made by David King, Dublin, 1719. It brought $1,392.

A plain salver with beaded edge, 13¾ inches in diameter and weighing 37 ounces brought $600—$16 an ounce—in New York in March, 1973. It was made by Robert Salmon, London, 1789.

Larger salvers tend to be less expensive per ounce, and sometimes the goal of $20 an ounce can be achieved. In 1972, a large oval tray (not a salver) with a gallery sold in Canterbury, England, at Worsfold's auction, for $744. It weighed 155 ounces and thus sold for $4.80 per ounce. It would bring over twice this price today.

Candlesticks are also of use and of ornamental value. They are usually sold in pairs, but sometimes a set of four is sold. In New York in March, 1973, a set of four George III candlesticks, 11¼ inches high, with reeded columns, made by J. Tibbitts of Sheffield in 1776, brought $1,800—about a standard price. In the same sale a pair of somewhat similar candlesticks which measured 11¾ inches high and were made by E. Coker, London, 1765, sold for $900.

Small pieces of hollow ware are generally within the price range of most collectors. In March, 1973, a creamer by Peter and Ann Bateman, 4 inches high, was sold for $210. Another creamer, 5½ inches high, by J. Angel, London, 1812, brought $150. Still another creamer, 4½ inches high, made by Smith and Hayter, London, 1783, brought $175.

Once in a while a magnificent and highly ornamental piece of silverware known as an epergne sells for a reasonable price. This is an elaborate piece for the dining table or sideboard. It has a broad base and arms which end in holders for glass liners. There is a large holder at the top of the piece. An epergne can be used to hold fruits, candy, nuts, and such. One such piece, 14¾ inches high and about twice as wide, weighing 105 ounces, and made in 1775 by Thomas Pitts of London, brought about $3,000 at auction in London in July, 1973. Sometimes simpler ones will sell for as little as $1,200.

In the same category of impressive pieces of tableware are silver serving dishes. In March, 1973, a set of a dozen serving dishes of the George II period, made by George Methuen in 1756, 9¾ inches in diameter and weighing a total of 195 ounces, sold for $5,760— about $500 a plate.

It is likely that in 1973 prices of Georgian silver increased by a minimum of 25 percent. Some pieces, such as teapots, rose more. The great pieces of silver rose by at least this percentage. The smaller pieces, such as spoons, showed less increase.

Early in 1974 there was some leveling of prices. Then the trend turned sharply and is paralleling the rise in the price of silver bullion.

Paul Revere made this silver teapot and covered sugar in 1791. In early 1974 they were sold at auction for $30,000. While Revere's silverware brings top prices, there are attractive and useful pieces by other silversmiths available for reasonable sums.

CHAPTER 13

Early
American
Silver

Early American silver is available to the collector almost wherever he looks, and at reasonable prices. Every antique exhibition and fair seems to have a good deal of antique American silver for sale, and there are over 2,000 such fairs held around the country each year.

This silver which is so plentiful and inexpensive consists mainly of spoons made in the early or middle nineteenth century. Teaspoons sell for under $10 each, and sometimes can be bought for $5 each. These spoons are of fiddleback design. They are for the most part thin, containing little silver. Many of them are worn or dented. Still, sets of such spoons are both ornamental and useful, but sets are very hard to find, and when they can be found the sets are often priced much higher than $10 a spoon.

There are some forks of the period, which may sell for $25 apiece. Pistol-handle knives that nicely complement the spoons and forks also come onto the market, but these knives in sets may cost as much as $50 each at the present time.

Teasets consisting of a teapot, a sugar, and a creamer, made in the early or middle nineteenth century are not at all rare. They are very well designed and well made, and sell for about $1,200 a set. A tray or a salver to carry such a set is something of a rarity and may also be purchased for about $1,200—if one can be located. These prices are low in the present silver market.

At the opposite end of the price spectrum in American silver are the fine pieces. A few years ago a set of twelve spoons made by Paul Revere in 1796, weighing a total of 24 ounces, sold at auction for $16,000—well over $1,000 a spoon.

In 1969 a Revere soup ladle weighing 5 ounces brought $7,500— $1,500 an ounce—compared with the standard purchase price of $20 an ounce for English Georgian silver.

A Paul Revere sauceboat, one of the most desirable and valuable pieces of silver, weighing 14 ounces and 7¾ inches long, brought the extremely high price of $53,000 at that time.

In the same sale a Revere sugar bowl and cover, not a very rare piece and not particularly impressive even when made by Revere, brought $18,000. It was 7½ inches long and weighed 14 ounces.

A Revere caster, an unimpressive piece of silver, 6 inches in diameter and weighing 4 ounces, was sold for $10,500—about $2,500 an ounce—in that October, 1969, sale at Sotheby Parke Bernet.

The history of American silver

In general, American silver is similar to English silver of the same period, many of the American designs having been based on the English. In fact the first American silversmiths came from England and began plying their trade in this country in about 1650.

From about 1650 to 1690, American silver was rectilinear and architectural in design. The pieces were relatively simple but did include heraldic designs and paneling. Leading silversmiths of this period were John Hull, Robert Sanderson, and Timothy Dwight.

About 1690 the simple design of American silver gave way to curves and floral patterns. This massive silver was produced by such leading smiths as Jeremiah Dummer, Jurian Blanck, Jr., Edward Winslow, and John Coney. This era continued until about 1720, when silver became far simpler in construction and ornamentation. Surfaces were simple, but form was beautiful. This era, with such leading silversmiths as Nathaniel Morse, Jacob Hurd, Simeon Soumain, and Peter van Dyck, continued until about 1750.

In the middle of the eighteenth century another basic change in style took place, emphasizing surface ornamentation. Leaves, flowers, and the shell motif were used, as were engraving and repoussé work. This was the period of Paul Revere. Myer Myers ranks just below the leader, Revere, and Joseph Richardson (whose sons,

Joseph Jr. and Nathaniel were talented silversmiths) ranks third among the preferred silversmiths of that time.

From 1775 to about 1810 there was another return to simplicity in design and ornamentation. It is silver of this period that the novice collector with some funds might purchase. Earlier silver does come onto the market and should be sought, but silver of the later eighteenth and early nineteenth centuries, with the exception of that made by the "greats," often can be purchased for moderate sums. The pieces are simple and beautifully proportioned. While this silverware is not plentiful, it can be found, even in the antique fairs held all over the United States.

From 1810 to about 1840 silverware became more monumental and of more or less Napoleonic, or Empire, design. The style was essentially Grecian, and all manner of classical ornamentation was used—sphinxes, paw feet, laurel leaves, blossoms, and elaborate moldings.

This silver is on the present market at fairly reasonable prices, and should be purchased by any silver collector for two main reasons: It is of fine design, and the thickness of the silver, particularly in the hollow ware, is often greater than in earlier pieces. These pieces often can be purchased for little money—little by the standards of almost all collectors.

Price trends

When the John Kenneth Danby sale of English and American silver took place on December 14, 1956, at the Parke Bernet Galleries in New York, the prices reached something of a low point. A good George II teapot, made by George Grundy, London, 1750, brought just $110. Twenty-one spoons of the late eighteenth and early nineteenth century brought $30 for the lot. A set of teapot, creamer, and sugar made in 1801 realized $75, and a Hester Bateman sugar basket brought $75. This was, of course, all English silver.

American antique silver offered in the same sale included several porringers. These quite common pieces of American silver are one-handled cereal bowls. The first porringer offered in the sale was made by Samuel Vernon of Newport (1683 to 1737). It was 8 inches in diameter. It brought $410—very much more than good English pieces in the same sale.

Another porringer offered was 6 inches in diameter and was made by John Tanner, who worked in Newport about 1740. It brought $260—another high price as compared with the prices of English silver in that sale.

A much later porringer by John Jones of Boston (1782 to 1854), 7¾ inches in diameter, brought $95, still a high price as compared with the prices reached by pieces of English silver of this late date.

In this sale a tea service of urn form, by William Ball, Jr., of Baltimore (1763 to 1815), consisting of a teapot, a sugar bowl with cover, and a helmet-shaped creamer, brought $475—an extremely high price as compared with an English teaset of the same late-eighteenth-century period. A matching coffee pot, 13½ inches high, brought the relatively high price of $325. On the other hand, the very common spoons sold in this sale for relatively little. Seventy-two tea and coffee spoons, made during the late eighteenth and the nineteenth centuries, brought $55 the lot—well under a dollar each. Today each spoon would probably sell for about $10.

Between 1956 and 1960 there was very little rise in the price of American silver. There was some rise between 1960 and 1965, and then a great rise took place between the middle of the decade and 1969. In the period from 1960 to 1969 the price of American silver rose about five times.

We might trace the price of porringers. Even good early porringers could be purchased in 1956 for about $250. By 1960, they were certainly not over $500 in price. By 1965, $1,000 was not an unusually high price, and by 1969 the gallery estimate in New York on one such item was $2,000. But the gallery estimates for silver proved to be too high, and the salesroom bids did not meet the reserves (the minimum prices acceptable to the sellers). By 1970, $1,000 would buy a good early porringer. The price level of 1965 had again been approximated. By the fall of 1971, about one-fourth of this drop had been overcome and the American silver market was well on the road to recovery.

Identifying American silver

Virtually all English silver is identifiable as to date, maker, and city of origin. The collector of American silver is not so fortunate. Only in Baltimore from 1814 to 1830 was the date required to be stamped on the piece. In those years Baltimore had an assay office which made this requirement.

Early in his collecting activities the investor in American silver should acquire some reference books, including:

Early American Silver for the Cautious Collector by Martha Gandy Fales, Funk and Wagnalls, New York.

The Book of Old Silver by Seymour B. Wyler, Crown Publishers, New York.

American Silversmiths and Their Marks by Stephen Ensko, Robert Ensko, Inc., New York.

American Silver in the Yale Collection by Buhler and Hood, Yale University Press.

Silver tea set made by William Thomson of New York in 1831 brought $1,700 at auction in late 1973.

The dates of birth and death of many silversmiths are given in these books. In some cases their "working dates" are given, which makes it possible to approximate the date when a piece was made.

In the nineteenth century the silversmith often stamped his entire name on a piece, and a reference book can be used to determine the period in which a piece was created by a particular maker.

Beginning in the middle of the nineteenth century some American silversmiths began to date their work. Some kept diaries of the pieces they made and for whom they were made, as well as the date of sale.

Family Bibles, records, and probate papers can be used to fix a date for a particular family piece of silver, provided the piece is initialed with the buyer's name.

Fortunately, much American silver contains the maker's mark or initials.

The word "Coin" on a piece of silver means that it was made between 1830 and 1860, but does not necessarily indicate that the piece was made of melted silver coins. It means simply that the piece was originally made of a good grade of silver. The word "Sterling" was used from about 1850 onward, and this word generally (though not always) means that the piece is not of great importance from the point of view of a collector-investor.

The silversmith had a die which he cut to contain his name, his initials, or his mark. This die he applied to his work as his signature. The finer and sharper this mark the finer and more valuable the piece of silver. The quality of a piece of silver appears in the piece itself and in the maker's mark. In a sense the quality of the mark is an indication of the quality of the silversmith's work on the piece itself. A good student of silver can, from an examination of the maker's mark, determine whether or not the piece is authentic or fake, as the mark is a type of signature. Upon the death of the silversmith, the die was usually destroyed so that it could not be used fraudulently.

Best buys at present

The early to middle nineteenth-century teaset is an item that the American silver investor might seek in the present market. It is impressive looking, well made, ornamental, and useful. It is also rising in value fairly steadily. One such typical set of four pieces was sold in March, 1973, at auction in New York. It was made in New York about 1830 by J.J. Monell, and consisted of a teapot, a covered sugar bowl, a waste bowl, and a creamer. The total weight of the four pieces was 95 ounces, and the set brought $1,200—under $13 an ounce. The set was initialed for Fanny A. Washington, granddaughter of Samuel Washington, brother of George Washington. The pieces were vase shaped, with borders of shells, flowers, and foliage.

If late eighteenth-century American pieces can be found at anything like reasonable sums, they should be purchased, as they are fairly rare and there is at the present time something of a buying opportunity.

In the summer of 1973 a tall silver teapot, 11⅜ inches high and weighing 24 ounces, brought $3,200 in New York. It was made by Christian Wiltberger of Philadelphia, circa 1790. A sugar bowl and cover by the same maker, 10⅜ inches high and weighing 14 ounces, sold for $1,500, and a Wiltberger creamer, weighing 6 ounces and 6⅞ inches high, brought $950.

To compare American silver prices with similar English Georgian silver prices, a plain oval teapot made by John Jenkins of Philadelphia, circa 1785, brought $1,700. It was 4⅜ inches high and weighed 15 ounces. The price was probably over what a Hester Bateman teapot without a stand would have brought and well over the price of a teapot by an ordinary London silversmith.

A rectangular American silver teapot, 6¾ inches high and weighing 32 ounces, made by Anthony Rasch of Philadelphia, circa 1820 —not an early piece—brought $900.

A fine silver bowl, 6⅞ inches in diameter and weighing 15 ounces, by Alexander Gordon of New York, circa 1790, brought $700. The same price was realized for a silver bowl of almost the same size made in New York, circa 1800.

American silver is far more expensive than English silver of the same period and of the same quality. It may now have reached so high a price as to reduce the demand and thus stem the price rise.

Prices for the work of the very best and most sought after American silversmith, Paul Revere, appear to have peaked, at least temporarily. These prices in recent years have been almost unbelievable. In a recent sale, a little teaspoon—no great work of art but with a fairly illustrious history—brought $600. In the same sale a fine and rare pair of Revere silver sauceboats, 8 inches long and weighing 27 ounces, did not find a buyer at the reserve price. Neither did a silver can, $2\frac{5}{8}$ inches high and weighing 3 ounces. However, a fine silver coffee pot by Revere, $13\frac{1}{4}$ inches high and weighing 34 ounces, brought $11,000—perhaps not too high a price for a large piece of his silver with a letter from the Yale University Gallery of Fine Arts giving details of the original order placed with Revere to make the piece.

It would seem wise in the present market to concentrate on early nineteenth-century pieces of good design, but not masterpieces. At times it is also possible to buy good late eighteenth-century pieces at reasonable prices. It would probably be best to avoid both ends of the spectrum: the great pieces that bring high prices and the extremely minor pieces, such as fiddleback spoons, which are at best no great treasures for any collector. It is the middle group of American silver which has been rising and which is still rising in price.

This Tiffany lamp, 16½ inches high, sold for $16,000 at auction in early 1974. Many lamps of this type were discarded in the 1930s and 1940s when they were out of fashion. Lamps which sold for $400 to $500 when new are now bringing prices in the range of $15,000 to $27,000.

CHAPTER 14

Artistic Glassware

Glassware as a collectible is almost limitless in scope. One can occasionally find an ancient piece of extremely fine Roman glass for upwards of $10,000. It is also possible occasionally to find a piece of Heisey glass for $10.

There is one type of glass that offers "something for everybody," no matter what his collecting budget, and this is Art Nouveau glassware. This type of glass was developed in the later nineteenth and early twentieth century as a kind of protest against the machine age, which, many felt, eliminated individuality, beauty, and creativity.

Art Nouveau glass is ornamental. It has little or no use other than for decoration, and its value depends first on its artistry and second on its rarity. It is above all not uniform, and it cannot be judged on the basis of its regularity, as can a good deal of other glass.

As its name implies, Art Nouveau glassware is to be judged as a work of art, which much of it is. It represents a degree of artistry rarely achieved in glass made anywhere in the world prior to its advent. The fashion for things Oriental no doubt was a great source of inspiration.

Usually the pieces of this art glass are small, often less than a foot in height. Probably the most common piece is the vase. The many other forms include snuff boxes, lamps, lamp shades, pitchers, dishes, flasks, chandeliers, atomizers, bottles, bowls, and inkwells. Some of the vases are very large and impressive—three feet high or more—and some are under six inches in height.

One of the greatest innovations in this ornamental glassware is that the glass was often given the appearance of ancient glass or of other materials: ceramic, lava, onyx, satin, mother-of-pearl, jade, wood, gold, or silver. It was almost never clear and colorless. It was either translucent or opaque. Some transparent glass was produced in the Art Nouveau manner but it was almost always colored or decorated.

A second innovation is that nature was the inspiration of the glassware makers. Most Art Nouveau glass was based on botanical forms, and sometimes on animalistic forms. The flower, the bud, the vine, the stem, and the leaf were all used extensively both as ornaments and as basic designs.

A third innovation was the application of glass on glass as an overlay or an insert, or simply as a surface piece of ornamentation.

A fourth innovation was the carving and grinding of the surface to secure desired textures or to reveal an underlying layer of glass. This process could be duplicated to some extent more cheaply and more easily by the application of an acid which would remove some of the surface of the topmost layer of glass.

Tracing its history

When Art Nouveau glass appeared in the late nineteenth century it was an almost instantaneous success, both from the artistic and the commercial points of view, and the relatively few factories and shops turning it out were hard put to meet demand.

In the 1930s and 1940s, Art Nouveau glass hit its low point as far as demand and price were concerned, and even artistically it was considered to be "old-fashioned."

The ornateness of the glass and its uselessness ran counter to the dominant artistic attitude of the time: functionalism. The believers in functionalism said that the best way to judge design was to see how well it served the use of the object. This theory discarded carved gilt picture frames and most ornamentation. It did not favor large, chrome-covered cars such as the Duesenberg. For the interior of homes, it favored simplicity of furniture design, no ornamentation, and unadorned walls.

At this time Art Nouveau glass was either discarded or sold for very little money. One very fine flower-shaped Tiffany vase on a metal base sold for $2.50, and before the collector parted with his $2.50 for it in 1939 there was considerable discussion about both the merits of the piece and its price. Today this same piece might bring $200, not a fortune but eighty times the cost nevertheless.

The collecting of art glass picked up a little in the 1950s, but it was not until about 1966 that prices for this glass began to "take off" in earnest.

In 1966 the London galleries began to feature Art Nouveau of all kinds at auction. Since that time prices of the commercial-grade and quality Nancy glass have approximately quadrupled. In 1972 prices of the commercial-grade glass increased about 15 percent. Since then prices have increased about 25 percent. The rise has been steady but not spectacular. On the other hand, when the prices of many collectibles declined in 1969 and 1970, the price of art glass did not. It continued its gradual rise in price.

The two leaders

Of all of the Art Nouveau items on the market, glassware is probably the most sought after and two of its makers are in greatest demand—Emile Gallé and Louis Comfort Tiffany. Gallé was the great innovator of an era slightly ahead of Tiffany and also probably the greatest craftsman as well as the greatest artist in glassware of his era. This leader in the entire field of French Art Nouveau as well as in all French decorative glass of the later nineteenth century lived from 1846 to 1904.

Gallé was the son of a French glassmaker. By the time he was nineteen he was designing glass for his father. Nine years later he had established his own factory in Nancy.

During Gallé's time, the general reaction against the lack of artistry after the industrial revolution, particularly in the field of mass production, led to a situation in which a new school of art might arise. There was a return to the art of the Renaissance, including glassware designs of that period. There also began to be an interest in Far Eastern designs. Finally, the forms of nature began to be emphasized, and above all original, hand artistry.

All of these influences led to the formation of L'Union Centrale des Arts Décoratifs. This organization helped to form the Musée des Arts Decoratifs and also organized exhibitions of current art of various kinds. At one of these exhibitions, held in 1878, Emile Gallé first became known as a designer and craftsman in glass. Gallé founded the Ecole de Nancy and established the entire art glass industry of his native city.

It was at the Paris International Exposition of 1900 that the entire field of Nancy glass, and Gallé glass in particular, became recognized as the foremost school of glassware created in Europe.

The four periods of Gallé glass

Gallé's first period began with the establishment of his glassworks in 1874. The base material that Gallé used in this period was transparent glass, not translucent or opaque glass, and the transparent glass was generally colored brown or green. On top of this transparent glass were placed ornamental forms, such as decorative enameling and gilt. He used some classical forms such as the ewer.

These are in general not his innovative pieces and they are very different from those which came later. They were also much easier to produce than the complex forms and materials of his later work.

By 1878, Gallé's style had changed and he began to produce some of his finer work. In this second period, which lasted until 1884, his style became freer and he depended much less on classical forms. Nature was now his primary inspiration for form and embellishment. Glass became simply a means of his artistic expression, regardless of whether the resulting piece was useful or not. He developed cutting, engraving, and enameling, and a glass marquetry process in which he fused various masses of colored glass. His "signature" on the glass became a part of the decoration.

It might seem that the pieces of Gallé's first period would be worth very much less than those of his second period. In general, pieces of his first period tend to sell for not very much less, and a fine first-period piece can bring far more than an ordinary second-period piece. It would appear, from a survey of what shops and auctions have to offer, that Gallé first-period pieces are scarcer than second-period pieces. Thus rarity tends to raise the prices of the earlier simple and less artistic pieces.

In 1884 Gallé entered his third period, which lasted until his death in 1904. This was the period of his greatest work, and is sometimes known as his opaque or colored period. In this period he developed moonlight glass by adding cobalt oxide to molten glass.

So great was the demand for his wares during this time that he developed a method of "quick cutting" by the use of hydrofluoric acid. The acid, rather than a grinding wheel, produced the patterns on the surface of the glass.

In this period the basic piece consisted of an opaque glass body which was overlaid with layers of translucent glass. These overlays were then cut back to reveal earlier layers of glass.

Engraved or carved signatures appeared on the plainer parts of the surface. Some of the signatures were Oriental in style. A much-sought-after piece has what is called "the macaroni signature." Gallé, however, did not sign all of his pieces himself.

Pale mauve, purple, and greenish tones were characteristic of

Gallé vase that sold for $750 at auction in mid-1973. This price is reasonable for good pieces of Gallé or Tiffany glass on the present market.

Gallé's third period, and he tended to produce repetitive designs in view of the great demand for his works at this time.

In this period he created his masterpieces of hand work that are almost never seen in the shops of dealers or at auction sales.

The last "Gallé" period begins with his death in 1904 and runs to 1935, during which time the factory was under the direction of Gallé's friend, Victor Prouvé. The Gallé glass produced in this period generally has a star just before the signature, and is, in general, the least sought after by knowledgeable collectors and the lowest in price.

Gallé's followers

There were not only other makers of Nancy glass of the same general type that Gallé produced, but there were makers of the Gallé type of glass in other parts of France, in other parts of Europe, and in other parts of the world, including the United States. These other makers had been associates of Gallé or were simply glassmakers impressed with his style. There was also a great deal of later copying of Gallé glass and also faking of the glass.

The most famous followers of Gallé were the Daum brothers, Auguste and Antonin. They created glass in more or less the Gallé manner from 1900 onward. The brothers had been Gallé's assistants and were associated with him when he organized the Ecole de Nancy, an organization of glass designers. Much glass produced by the Daum brothers' factory is on the market and is marked "Daum Nancy." This glass does not sell for much less today than comparable Gallé glass.

Joseph Brocard, who attempted a revival of enameling, was greatly influenced by Gallé in his later work. Another follower, Eugène Rousseau, used enameling as well as the cased glass process, indicating the Oriental influence.

Until the mid-1920s a younger group manufactured in the Gallé manner. The most outstanding of these later workers was G. Argy-Rousseau. Dammouse and Decorchement also made glass in this period in the same general style. DeVez and Walter worked in this style, and their glass appears on the present market in fairly substantial quantities.

DeGuy is on a lower price level, and much of his glass could be purchased recently for as little as $100 a piece. Some of his pieces are large, fairly elaborate, and signed. La Verre Français is similar glass to deGuy's, but the price range of La Verre Français is higher. The glass known as Richard is plentiful and in the lowest price range.

At the present time $250 will buy a good piece of Gallé glass, such as a vase eight to ten inches high. The same sum will also buy

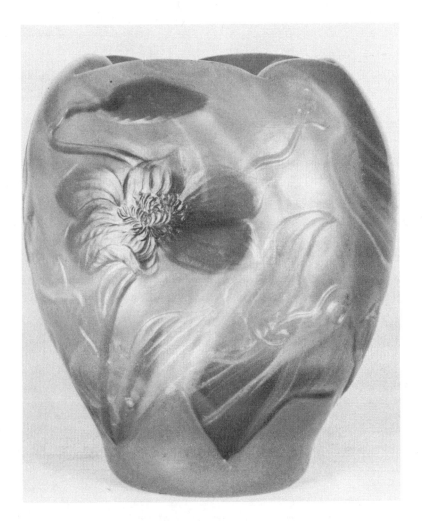

Wheel-carved, inlaid, free-form glass vase made by Emile Gallé about 1900 sold for $5,500 in 1973.

a perfume bottle or other uncomplicated piece of this size. A Gallé lamp can bring a little over $1,000. Generally, the bigger and more elaborate the piece the greater its value.

Gallé prices are scaled down somewhat in the case of the other makers. It is possible to get a deGuy or Richard piece of glass on occasion for as little as $150. In 1972 it was not difficult to find very attractive pieces by these lesser masters for as little as $100.

A Daum Nancy bowl, bottle, or vase may be purchased at auction for as little as $200 and sometimes for sums slightly under this figure. Larger pieces can cost up to $1,000.

The Gallé masterpieces

The very finest pieces of Gallé glass almost never appear on the market, not even in London or Paris. When it is known that a fine piece of handmade Gallé may be sold, it is generally purchased by a ring of Paris dealers. Such pieces almost always come from private sellers in France. The Gallé dealers then offer the pieces privately at suitable prices. When the Parisian dealers come to London, they purchase commercial-grade pieces, usually buying individually and competitively, not as a group.

The very finest Gallé glass is the sculptured or marquetry pieces that have a waxlike finish. These must be in perfect condition for the leading dealers to be interested in them. There is no acid cutting on such pieces. Gallé's signature is cut into the glass; it is never the common raised (cameo cut) variety of signature. The very best signatures are vertical, not horizontal. The price of one of these pieces can run to well over $10,000.

Most Gallé glass, as well as the other glass of Nancy, is for sale at dealers' establishments, not at auction. The distribution channel is from collector to art shop, and this movement takes place mainly in Paris. From Paris, and from a few other parts of France, the glass moves to America via wholesale dealers or directly to retail dealers. One wholesaler regularly brings to the United States for resale to dealers thousands of pieces each year. He also sells to retail customers.

Once in a while the major dealers do have a Gallé masterpiece for sale to the public, but this is unlikely to be one of the largest or most elaborate pieces. The masterpieces that occasionally come onto the market seem to end up in the collections of Alain Lesieutre and Robert Walker of Paris.

Tiffany glass

The greatest exponent by far of Art Nouveau in America was Louis Comfort Tiffany, son of the founder of Tiffany and Company. He lived from 1848 to 1933, and was a contemporary of Emile Gallé.

Tiffany, a trained artist and decorator, made numerous trips to London and there came under the influence of the William Morris group, which was trying, among other things, to revive the art of stained-glass windows. Tiffany produced such windows in America at his Tiffany Glass Company, organized in 1885.

In 1889 he visited the shop of S. Bing in Paris and was impressed by the work of the designers and producers of ornamental table pieces—among them Emile Gallé. In 1893, Tiffany established a glassworks in Corona, New York, and produced the decorative glass known as Favrile.

Tiffany's glass did not have as much surface decoration as Gallé's. The Tiffany glass was decorative in itself and needed little other embellishment. What he achieved was a glass that was artistic because of its color, design, and density. Tiffany used all of the typical Art Nouveau forms—flowers, peacocks, Japanese motifs— and particularly the iridescent colors that have come to be closely associated with Favrile glass.

The collector who made his first purchase in 1939 of a Tiffany Favrile glass vase set in a bronze base for $2.50 was not alone. An authority whose doctoral dissertation was on Louis C. Tiffany and his work, wrote in 1964:

"Ten years ago (in 1954) I stumbled on my first reference to the work of Louis Comfort Tiffany. I was studying architecture at Yale University. . . . The following semester, during a course with Professor William Jordy, I presented a seminar report on Tiffany as the leading American exponent of Art Nouveau and, just for fun, I purchased a Favrile glass bowl made by Tiffany as a demonstration of the quality of his work. It cost four dollars, and I thought it was expensive. . . . When I brought it home my wife asked, 'How long do we have to keep it?' "[1]

In contrast, Robert Koch stated in 1974: "As Louis C. Tiffany is becoming recognized as one of the most important artists in America, the market on objects designed by him has been very strong in the past few years, and important Tiffany objects will not only hold their value but increase in the years to come." Since Mr. Koch is now a leading dealer in Tiffany glass, he is in something of a position to know the market and its trend.

In Tiffany's sales catalog of 1911 the statement is made:

"As this unique glass is being imitated, and inferior products represented as 'Favrile Glass' or 'Tiffany Glass,' patrons are cautioned to look for the distinguishing mark on every piece of Tiffany Favrile Glass, the large and medium size pieces being signed

---

1. Robert Koch, *Louis C. Tiffany, Rebel in Glass*, Crown Publishers, Inc., New York, 1964, preface to the first edition, p. 2.

with the full name, 'Louis C. Tiffany' or 'L. C. Tiffany-Favrile,' the smaller with the initials 'L.C.T.'

"In New York the genuine 'Tiffany Favrile Glass' is sold only by Tiffany & Co., and at the Tiffany Studios, Madison Ave., corner of 45th Street."

Some prices in this 1911 sales catalog are:

Nut bowls	$8, $10, $12
Almond dishes	$1 and $1.50
Berry bowls	$8 to $18
Bonbon dishes	$1 and $1.50
Shades, oil and electric	$15 to $60
Desk lamps	$18
Fruit bowls	$8 to $18
Vases, luster, gold and blue	$6 to $35

At the present time the most sought after and most valuable Tiffany item is the leaded lamp shade—which was thrown away in great numbers when it went completely out of fashion in the 1930s and 1940s. These are the prices of some of these lamp shades from Tiffany's price list of 1906:

Azalea dome	$40
Apple blossom dome	$50
Woodbine dome	$55
Dragon fly dome	$80
Dogwood dome	$85
Dogwood low dome	$115

In 1973 a Tiffany wisteria dome lamp brought $10,000 at auction in Philadelphia. In January, 1974, Sotheby Parke Bernet in New York sold an identical Tiffany wisteria lamp for $16,000.

Tiffany's price list of 1933 includes a glass and bronze twelve-light lily lamp for $150. In October, 1973, the identical model was sold at auction for $4,500. In January, 1974, another identical lamp brought $5,500 in New York.

The first major sale of Tiffany glass in recent years was held in New York on October 21, 1966, at the Sotheby Parke Bernet Galleries. In that sale a Tiffany agate vase brought $350, a fine price at that time. A similar agate vase, but larger, recently sold for $5,500. The same $350 vase would bring $3,500 today, according to the best estimate of Barbara Deisroth, head of the Art Nouveau and Art Deco department of Sotheby Parke Bernet.

Of all art glass, Tiffany appears to have been the first to increase pricewise and to have risen the most. Between the years 1966 and

Twelve-light lily lamps that Tiffany sold for $150 in 1933 now bring thousands of dollars. This one was purchased for $5,500 in early 1974.

1974 the prices paid for Tiffany glass increased at least ten times.

Examples of recent prices

One of the most expensive dome-shaped lamps made by Tiffany cost, when new, approximately $485. The head of the Tiffany glass department of Sotheby Parke Bernet discovered one such wisteria lamp in a home in Jersey City. It was recently auctioned off in New York for $27,000—to the delight of the owners, who were in great need of money.

A young girl inherited an apple blossom lamp from her grandmother. She had just married and wanted to furnish her new apartment. She auctioned the lamp in New York. It brought $17,000. This lamp appears to have been listed for $400 when new.

A housewife recently brought into Sotheby Parke Bernet some pieces of Tiffany glass which she had purchased while she was employed in Tiffany's plant in Corona. Among other glass, she had three unsigned pieces (although the Tiffany catalog stated that all Tiffany pieces should be signed, which most are). The gallery estimated that these unsigned pieces would bring from $1,500 to $3,000 each. They brought $5,500, $5,000, and $2,000. For all the pieces she sold at auction the woman received $20,000.

One of the best ways to determine the range of Tiffany glass is to examine the list contained in the appendix of Robert Koch's book, *Louis C. Tiffany's Glass—Bronzes—Lamps*.[2] All items for sale are numbered and the numbers begin at 101 and go to 1581, each item completely different from the others. There are also twelve more items—candlestick tops. In addition, the book contains a 1933 price list with photographs of the items offered by Tiffany, and in many instances these can be matched with the illustrations contained in present-day Sotheby Parke Bernet sales catalogs.

Tiffany's sales catalogs were divided along strictly commercial rather than artistic lines. These were the categories of wares for sale: oil lamps, electric lamps, hanging shades, fancy goods (boxes, inkstands, paperweights, etc.), candlesticks, leaded shades, and candlestick tops. Over the years, Tiffany glass became less and less of a commercial item and more and more of an art object. The present classifications are:

Tiffany Favrile Iridescent. Iridescence is more or less the distinguishing characteristic of about 95 percent of Tiffany glass.

---

2. Crown Publishers, Inc., New York, 1971.

Paperweight. This glass has the appearance of a blown-up antique French paperweight flower.

Lava. This glass looks like its name.

Agate. This consists of several layers of glass cut back to show the various layers, as in many of the pieces of Gallé glass.

Cypriote. Glass with an irregular surface and iridescent qualities.

Two prime pieces of Tiffany glass are illustrated in *Art at Auction: The Year at Sotheby's and Sotheby Parke Bernet—1972-1973.* The first is a free-form Tiffany lava vase 3¾ inches high, the base engraved "R1837, LCT." This piece was sold in London in June, 1973, for $2,500. The second piece is a gold and luster vase, height 7⅞ inches, the base engraved "07805" and with original paper label, circa 1900. This piece was sold in the same London sale for $2,300.

In January, 1974, seventy pieces of Tiffany glass were sold in one New York auction. These are some of the items and the prices realized:

• Glass vase, baluster form with sloping sides, of iridescent midnight blue shading to black and splashes of aquamarine, 20 inches high: $1,300.

• Pair of glass oil lamps, with kerosene lamp inserts and chimneys, iridescent amber, 15¼ inches high: $450.

• Glass finger bowl, 2½ inches high: $100.

• Glass jack-in-the-pulpit vase with wide flaring rim, iridescent amber, 18½ inches high: $2,000.

• Glass vase in trumpet form, iridescent amber with intaglio cut, 16 inches high: $600.

• Glass vase, unusually large baluster form, iridescent amber and colors shading from aquamarine to deep blue, 21 inches high: $1,050.

On the present market the cameo-cut piece is much sought after and high priced. One such glass vase was sold in January, 1974. It was 13½ inches high, and had a slender cylindrical body cut with stylized blossoms and leaves. The dominant body color was amber. It realized $000.

Art Nouveau glass, while it can be purchased by collectors with even the most limited budgets, is definitely going up in price and shows no sign of nearing its peak.

Certain types of Art Nouveau glass have a more definite world market and a more definite world price than almost any other collectible. A Gallé piece varies very little in price whether it is sold at Sotheby's Belgravia gallery in London, at the Plaza Art Galleries in New York, at the Paris shop called Yesterday, or at a Saturday afternoon street exhibition and sale in The Hague.

The auction market for Art Nouveau glass has been developing and more is put up for sale each year. Still, there are few if any auctions devoted to the glass of Nancy or to Tiffany glass. These two main categories of Art Nouveau glass are included in sales of Art Nouveau, Art Deco, and nineteenth-century porcelain and ceramics. One day this glass may merit auctions of its own.

Guidelines for collecting

When purchasing art glass the collector should keep these points in mind:

1. Pieces with damages of any kind should be avoided. In some other areas of collecting, such as old master paintings, small imperfections do not decrease value. In art glass, chipped pieces should not be purchased as investments. Neither should cracked pieces, even those with small hairline cracks. The examination of each piece should be extremely thorough. Some day imperfect pieces may be in demand—as prices rise and supplies do not appear in such volume on the market—but at the present time only perfect pieces should be purchased. Breaks which have been ground down may be hard to detect. For that reason, styles should be understood fully.

2. The "big names" are available in quantity and at fairly reasonable prices on the present market, and are not much more expensive than the lesser artists. These big names, Gallé and Tiffany, can be concentrated on—while they are still available.

3. Values for each type of piece should be learned by reading the texts in the field and by securing the priced catalogs of Christie's, Sotheby's, and Sotheby Parke Bernet.

4. Demand—rather than scarcity of supply—is all important in determining price. See which pieces are in great and rising demand, such as cameo-cut pieces, as their price is likely to rise.

5. Do not buy at the top or at the bottom of the price range. The $25,000 lamps may not easily rise to $50,000, and the $100 vase may not be an item in much demand. In the present market $1,000, or even a little less, should purchase a good piece of Gallé or Tiffany glass.

6. Patronize dealers primarily, as art glass is dominated by dealers rather than the auction houses, and thus dealers tend to have the better pieces.

7. In the United States, Sotheby Parke Bernet is at last offering some Gallé glass, although generally the lesser pieces. However,

this firm is handling a great deal of Tiffany glass, and in its January, 1974, auction offered seventy Tiffany pieces, some of which reached prices well into five figures.

8. The collector of Nancy glass should buy on the Paris market, if possible, as Paris has a better selection than either London or New York, and the Paris prices are not higher than those of other markets.

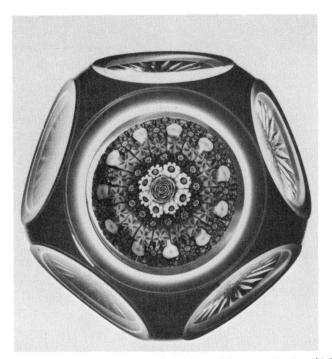

This rare Clichy turquoise double-overlay paperweight was valued at $1,000 in 1964. By 1974 its value had risen to nearly $5,000.

CHAPTER 15

French Glass Paperweights

French glass paperweights of the mid-nineteenth century are among the highest artistic achievements in the entire field of ornamental glassware. The intricate workmanship required to create these little masterpieces is remarkable in itself. It is no wonder that they have become such popular collectibles, showing in some cases tremendous price rises.

These paperweights are highly decorative objects for the collector's cabinet, and are not so expensive as to preclude a large number of potential collectors. Nor are they so inexpensive as to require a large storage space to house an investment costing only a relatively small sum of money.

One important characteristic of these paperweights is that they are absolutely limited in the number extant, having been produced during a relatively few years in the middle of the nineteenth century. As their supply is small, any increase in demand tends to raise prices greatly. In the mid-1960s the demand for French paperweights soared, and so did the price. At the end of the 1960s the boom leveled off and then prices dropped. Since the beginning of the 1970s prices have been rising steadily, but less spectacularly.

The important French factories

There were only three well-known factories which made French paperweights—Baccarat, Saint Louis, and Clichy. These three (together with a possible "unknown factory") created the most sought after paperweights in the world. The majority of these fine paperweights, a lasting tribute to the art of glassmaking, were produced in France between the years 1845 and 1860.

The Baccarat factory, located 200 miles east of Paris in the Vosges Mountains, began to make glass paperweights in 1846. The weights manufactured during this period are dated 1846, 1847, 1848, and 1849—the last being the rarest. After 1849, dates apparently were used on commemorative weights only.

The Saint Louis factory was located not far from the Baccarat glassworks, and records indicate that this was the first to make French glass paperweights. There is at least one Saint Louis piece dated 1845.

The third great glassworks was established at Clichy-la-Garenne just outside Paris. Clichy weights are rarely signed and are not known to be dated. It is believed that most Clichy paperweights were made about 1849. The factory operated until 1870.

The Baccarat and the Saint Louis glass factories make paperweights of excellent quality today. They are almost indistinguishable from the nineteenth-century weights, at least to the nonexpert, except for the fact that they are now being dated.

Baccarat continued to make its famous pansy weight until 1920, although it was a different version in the 1890-1920 era than those made in the mid-nineteenth century. Although the early paperweights were made from 1845 until the late 1860s in France, the great vogue for paperweights waned in the 1850s.

How a paperweight is made

Millefiori (a thousand flowers) is the paperweight design most often used, and the earliest known. Baccarat, Saint Louis, and Clichy all used this design, which was originated by the Egyptians in the fifteenth century B.C.

In order to create millefiori canes, the glassblower makes a rod of glass. He then rolls another colored glass or two onto the rod. He may then plunge the rod into a mold to give it an unusual shape, or he may have earlier used a mold to make a small design in the center and then rolled the colored glass over it.

At this point in the operation the rod is about six inches long and three inches in diameter. The mass is heated and drawn out by two glassblowers moving away from each other. The farther they

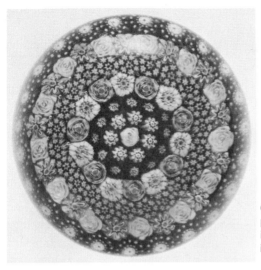

Clichy concentric *millefiori* paperweight, 2-9/16 inches in diameter, sold for $1,200 in early 1974.

move from each other, the thinner and longer is the cylinder with its several colors of glass, but all of the layers of color and the center design remain the same—they just become smaller.

Then the cylinder, or cane, of glass is laid aside to cool so that it can be cut into small sections, or "lozenges." These lozenges look something like hard candies with multicolored centers that, no doubt, are made by a somewhat similar process.

After being cut, the lozenges are placed together in attractively arranged bunches, and the entire mass is dipped into molten glass and cooled several times. This molten glass forms the clear glass ball which houses the millefiori bouquet in the center. The bottom is flattened and sometimes cut in an attractive pattern. The top is polished so that it has a clear, round surface through which the flowers can be seen.

Very often millefiori paperweights contain canes with centers in the shape of animals, a butterfly, a dancer, and so forth. These are called silhouettes, and a single millefiori paperweight may contain over twenty-five different silhouettes.

Although the millefiori paperweight design is the most common, there are, of course, others—a flower, a bunch of flowers, a butterfly, a snake, as examples. These designs are usually made for the center of the weight by a blow torch. After the design is fashioned by the glassmaker, using a blow torch (and a well-guarded secret process), it is encased in glass as described above, by successive dippings and coolings until it is the desired size of glass ball. Sometimes it is covered with a coating of opaque or translucent glass, and sometimes with two coatings—one opaque white and the second a color such as turquoise. When this process of overlaying is used, windows, called "printies," are then cut out of the sides and top of the overlay so that the interior design can be seen through the clear glass openings. Overlay definitely adds to the value of a paperweight, and the color of the overlay is also of importance— the rarest color being yellow. A record price was achieved for a weight with a yellow overlay—the only early weight known to have that color.

The finished paperweight is a piece of highly decorative glass three, three and a quarter, or three and a half inches in diameter. There is also a "magnum" weight four or more inches in diameter and a "miniature" weight approximately two inches in diameter.

The collector soon becomes aware of value-adding qualities. The most important of these are rarity of subject or design and the quality of the workmanship. A rare color of glass overlay adds value, as does an unusual color of the ground. The smaller weights generally have less value than the ones of standard size, other features being equal.

Classifying paperweights

These are the most important classifications of paperweights:

Millefiori	Bouquets
Flowers	Sulfides (having a cameo-like
Rare subjects	appearance)
Tufts (mushroom	Fruits and vegetables
weights)	Swirls
Crowns	Faceted (weights cut somewhat
Overlays	like a diamond)
Butterflies	Pedestal (weights on a glass
Carpets	pedestal)
Color grounds	Checkers
Snakes and reptiles	

The making of paperweights probably originated in Italy. In a book written in Venice by Marcantonio Sabellico, circa 1495, there is mention of little glass balls filled with spring flowers. These might well be similar to the paperweight as we know it. We do know that the Italians were making glass paperweights before 1845. An exhibition of some of their weights was held in Vienna in that year. The work of Venetian glassmaker Pietro Bigaglia was admired at the Vienna exhibition by M. Peligot, a member of the French Chamber of Commerce, who later reported glowingly and in detail about these millefiori paperweights. It was probably this enthusiastic report that brought the idea of creating ornamental paperweights to France.

In the same year, 1845, a vase with a crude millefiori base and with the date inscribed backwards, was produced in France. The French then went ahead full steam in this new industry, and by 1848 the paperweight craze reached England. English glass factories followed French paperweight designs and the Exhibition of 1851 held at the Crystal Palace in London featured paperweights, bringing this ornamental product even wider attention and acclaim.

The New England Glass Company of East Cambridge, Massachusetts, produced the first dated American paperweight in 1851, and continued to produce them into the 1870s. Other factories turning out American paperweights were the glassworks of Sandwich, Dorflinger, Gillinder, Millville, and Mt. Washington. Over the years paperweights were turned out from time to time in other locations. Today the industry seems to be reviving. Charles Kazium and François Whittemore are considered to be the leading makers in America today.

There are a few artists abroad who continue to make paperweights, in addition to those at the Saint Louis and Baccarat factories. Cristal d'Albret specializes in sulfide weights. Paul Ysart, a third-generation glassmaker who is considered to be the best in his field, creates designs for the Caithness factory in Wick, Scotland, and has started his own glassworks to specialize in limited-edition paperweights.

Determining value

The most important element determining the value of a paperweight, all other things being equal, is its rarity. The second value-determining characteristic is the quality of workmanship. The third is the piece's condition.

In 1972, Spink and Son of London, one of the leading dealers in paperweights, held the first major London exhibition of paperweights in recent years. On display were 426 weights and related objects. One item was a Clichy lily of the valley weight with a translucent pink ground—the color of vin rosé. This weight had sold at auction for $22,000. In the same exhibition, however, was another Clichy paperweight, slightly smaller but made in the same period. This one was priced at $130. It contained the typical Clichy rose and several cut canes in a simple pattern. The sharp difference in price between the two weights was due to the fact that the second weight lacked rarity and intricacy of design. The lily of the valley weight was the only known example of this type in existence.

Price history

In the last sixty years, and certainly since the turn of the century, the prices of fine antique French glass paperweights have gone from less than $5 to over $5,000. Even as late as the period

Baccarat turquoise double-overlay paperweight brought $2,000 at auction in 1974. Paperweights with rare overlays usually bring top prices.

just prior to World War II, a dated Baccarat millefiori weight could be purchased for about $40, and one with an overlay could be bought for not much more. In the 1940s there were very few paperweights priced at more than $1,000. However, in 1943, collector Estelle Dohenny paid $1,200 for a very rare Clichy lavender overlay weight, which Paul Jokelson, head of the International Paperweight Collectors Association, values at about ten times that amount today.

In the early 1950s, prices for ordinary Baccarat millefiori weights were in the $200 category, and some brought less. Paperweights with overlays brought about $300, as did those with rare subjects and grounds. Then in the late 1950s prices began to rise, and almost skyrocketed in the 1960s. A Clichy flower weight which had sold at Sotheby's in London for $245 in 1963 sold in 1968 for $6,120. A very rare liver-red salamander weight, 4½ inches in diameter, by an unknown maker, reached $9,360 in 1963. It sold at Sotheby's in 1968 for $14,400.

In the rising tide of prices over the past few decades, there have been some very high waves of special interest in the rarer weights. Prices of the more ordinary weights rose about two and a half times in the period from the 1950s to today, but the rare subjects, such as the liver-red salamander, or the rare overlay, or the rare flowers such as the Clichy lily of the valley weight, have gone up ten times or more in price.

The rare lavender overlay which was purchased in 1943 for $1,200 is now valued at over ten times that amount while an American-made Millville rose paperweight, which the same buyer purchased in the same year for $1,300, is now worth about the same amount as when it was purchased. The popularity of Millville pieces has not been great over recent decades, but that is not to say that these will not be of interest to collectors in the future. At the moment, interest centers on French glass paperweights of the mid-nineteenth century. It is these weights which have commanded the highest prices, and which are preferred by most knowledgeable collectors.

Baccarat weights and their prices

Dated canes in Baccarat weights will usually bear dates between 1846 and 1849, the most common date being 1848. The "B" signature in the cane and the dated cane, although desirable, are not the most important value-adding elements. Rarity of design and quality of craftsmanship are of greatest importance to the connoisseur and give the weight its commercial value.

Rare subjects are possibly the most important group—salamander, reptile, caterpillar, and so forth. Perhaps only one or two specimens of some of these rare subjects are known—such as the unique caterpillar weight which sold for $4,800 in London in 1952. It was purchased by Spink and Son's paperweight specialist, Patricia McCawley, for King Farouk.

Weights featuring a snake are not so rare and represent about one out of 100 weights, but they have become very popular in recent years and can bring $3,000 to $4,000 at auction. In the 1950s, snake weights brought about $400 to $1,200 each.

A Baccarat blue carpet ground weight dated 1848 and signed "B," with the millefiori design and animal silhouettes, sold for $2,400 at Sotheby's in 1968—a 500 percent rise over its 1960 price.

The butterfly weight without a flower usually brings less than one with a flower. A fine butterfly weight with a flower brings about $2,000 at auction today. In March, 1973, a butterfly over a white pompon brought $1,900 in New York.

Sulfides (encrustations), which are weights incorporating cameo-like heads of famous persons, did not usually bring as much as $400 in the early 1950s, and sporting scenes brought even less in London auctions at the time. These still can sometimes be purchased reasonably. They have not shown the great rise of some of the other types of weights.

Other things being equal, an overlay will bring a premium price. A Baccarat weight with translucent green overlay and seven "printies" (windows), with garlands of millefiori flowers, some with silhouettes, diameter $3\frac{1}{8}$ inches, brought $2,500 at auction in 1973.

Saint Louis weights and their prices

The millefiori design was used by the Saint Louis factory for perhaps one-quarter of its output, and it combined these millefiori canes quite often with green leaves to make a small bouquet design. Saint Louis also made beautiful weights with flowers, fruit, vegetables, and reptiles. A Saint Louis dahlia weight, which sold in 1963 at Sotheby's for $800, sold again in 1968 at the same auction house for $4,800. Prices were reaching a peak at that time. In the same sale, in the summer of 1968, a Saint Louis bouquet weight brought over $8,000.

Saint Louis, like Baccarat, used overlay at times and made various sizes from miniature to magnum. The colors are considered to be more delicate than Baccarat colors. The weights are seldom signed. When dated, the year 1848 is most often found. The year 1847 is considered a very rare date. Some weights are signed "SL" and have no date. There is said to be one Saint Louis weight, signed "SL" and dated 1845, in the Baccarat museum. This would be the earliest known Saint Louis weight.

In 1972, a signed ("SL") millefiori weight—with the rare 1847 date—brought $1,500. A similar weight, also signed "SL" but undated, brought $1,000.

Grounds can double or triple the price of weights. There are many opaque and translucent types of grounds, ranging from a carpet of canes to a latticinio decoration, which is like fine threads of glass, sometimes latticed and sometimes swirled.

A Saint Louis white pompon weight set on a pink latticinio basket, 2⅞ inches in diameter, brought $650 in 1972. The same sale featured a rare Saint Louis pompon weight on a rich tomato-red ground of swirling threads. The weight, 3⅛ inches in diameter, brought the highest price of the sale—$3,900. It was the tomato-red ground that gave it rarity and high value. The beauty and quality of workmanship were also outstanding. Another value-adding element—a dark blue double overlay—encased a Saint Louis weight of the same 3⅛-inch size which was sold that year for $6,500.

A rare Saint Louis flat bouquet weight, also 3⅛ inches in diameter, sold for $10,000 in New York at Sotheby Parke Bernet in 1973. As noted in the catalog, it consisted of an unrecorded combination of flowers, and was extremely attractive as well as very rare. It brought the top price of the sale that day.

Clichy weights and their prices

The signature "C" or "Clichy" is seldom to be found on Clichy weights and they are also undated. The signature for most collectors is the "Clichy rose," which is a distinguishing feature of many of the Clichy weights. The "rose" is more like a miniature artichoke with the leaves cut at the tips, and is often pink with green leaves, although white roses are also common. Clichy made a higher percentage of millefiori weights than any other factory, and the rose is usually in evidence in these weights.

Clichy colors are considered to be more brilliant than those of

Saint Louis pink pompon paperweight was purchased at auction in early 1974 for $1,300.

either Baccarat or Saint Louis. The difference is not very noticeable to the average viewer, as the colors are brilliant and beautiful in all of the weights made by the three firms.

Clichy overlays are sought by collectors as they represent a very low percentage of the output. A Clichy red overlay weight sold at Sotheby's in London in 1968 for $5,760, almost double its 1965 price.

A Clichy bouquet weight, $2\frac{7}{8}$ inches in diameter, of three flowers with leaves and a swirled latticinio background, sold in 1960 for $500 at auction. In 1968, it brought $5,040. It had risen ten times in price in less than ten years—a rise of 1,000 percent.

Tips for potential collectors

Although prices of paperweights rose rapidly during the 1960s, only to fall off in many cases at the end of the decade and reach a low point in 1969, they are climbing again and have caught up with former highs in a number of cases.

It has been the top-quality weights of rare design and superb craftsmanship that have held most of their value and again begun to rise. The lesser weights, which rose more than they should have on the price tidal wave of the 1960s, in some cases sank to as low as 50 percent of their 1968 value. As is often the case in the field of collecting, in the long run it is quality that counts.

To study quality, potential collectors may wish to visit the public collections of paperweights, among them the superb Sinclair collection at the New York Historical Society. In Washington, D.C., there is a small collection at the Smithsonian Institution, and in Massachusetts, there is the attractive J. Cheney Wells collection in Old Sturbridge Village. The largest of all is the Bergstrom collection at Neenah, Wisconsin, and it is worth a visit for those seriously interested in collecting paperweights.

Rare "Medici" porcelain bowl that rose in price from $200 in 1916 to $180,000 in 1973. Fine European porcelain and pottery of lesser rarity can still be purchased at modest prices, but expertise is needed to select pieces of investment quality.

CHAPTER 16

European Porcelain and Pottery

Francesco de' Medici made the first European version of fine Chinese porcelain in his Florentine factory in 1575. Few—perhaps less than sixty—of these de' Medici pieces are known to exist. One was recently discovered in the possession of the nuns at Elizabeth Seton College in Yonkers, New York, who had received it as part of a gift of a house and its contents.

Sotheby Parke Bernet's Joseph Kuntz discovered this Medici bowl while making an appraisal and was able to trace its history. It had sold in 1916 for $200. In 1949 a similar piece was auctioned for $4,400. When the nuns sold their Medici bowl at Sotheby Parke Bernet in 1973, it realized $180,000—a record price for a single piece of European porcelain sold at auction.

Porcelain and pottery are regularly offered for sale at almost every auction house in this country and in Europe, and are also available for purchase at probably all of the more than 2,000 antique exhibitions held in the United States each year. Ceramics of some sort are also available in most sales of estates.

It is very difficult to separate valuable and highly collectible pottery and porcelain from that which may have little value. Also difficult is to distinguish, among the immense variety of porcelain and pottery, what is genuine and what is a fake or a later copy. This is one field in which expertise is essential for profitable collecting.

From a more optimistic view, the would-be collector of porcelain and pottery should be aware that extremely fine pieces can be bought for a few hundred dollars, and that these pieces have great decorative value. This chapter, therefore, will concentrate on fine, antique, European pieces of investment quality which can be purchased at fairly reasonable prices. Almost all of the investment-quality European porcelain and pottery are of the eighteenth century, with the earlier eighteenth century products generally being more valuable than those of the later eighteenth century.

Porcelain and pottery defined

The entire field of ornamental porcelain and pottery is sometimes called ceramics, and in view of the fact that most of the porcelain and pottery pieces are from Europe, the sales catalogs in this country are labeled "Fine European Ceramics." By definition, ceramics are articles made wholly or in part of clay and fired in an oven.

Porcelain is of two types: soft paste and hard paste. Hard paste porcelain is true porcelain and is made of a mixture which includes pure clay, feldspar with mica, and sand or quartz. The hardness of the paste depends on the mixture of clay and feldspar—the more clay in the paste, the harder the final product. Once molded or shaped, the piece is fired in a kiln twice, before glazing and after glazing. The glaze is made of the same substances as the body but in a different proportion, so that the fusion is complete and the surface is extremely durable.

Hard paste porcelain has a transparent quality and a beautiful "ring" when gently tapped. The hard paste formula was "discovered" in Meissen, Germany, in 1708, but was actually discovered (and kept as a well-guarded secret) in China centuries earlier.

Soft paste porcelain is made of sand, saltpeter, alum, salt, soda, and alabaster. Gypsum and clay are added to this mixture. This substance is fired and what is produced is a porous piece. A glaze is then added to the outside. This glaze is mainly glass, which upon heating fuses with the basic substance of the piece to form a hard and decorative finish. This was the type of porcelain made by the Medicis in the sixteenth century.

Pottery was made many centuries before the birth of Christ. It is essentially clay which is shaped and hardened by heat after coloring elements are added. It is generally coarser than porcelain. Essentially, faience is pottery, and the terms to a considerable extent are interchangeable. Pottery is fired as porcelain is. It is sometimes unglazed but, like porcelain, pottery usually has an outside glaze, and this is often of tin or lead admixtures.

The entire field of ceramics is divided for sales purposes into porcelain and pottery or into porcelain and faience. An important sale of fine European ceramics is likely to include hard paste porcelain, soft paste porcelain, and faience (pottery).

The English factories

Almost every type of porcelain and pottery is identified by the name of the town in which the originating factory was located.

Worcester. This factory was organized in 1751 by John Wall. Porcelain buyers up to that time preferred imported Chinese porcelain because it was superior to the English product. In the Worcester plant, major objectives were to make a harder porcelain and to imitate Chinese porcelain shapes and decorations.

At the end of the eighteenth century and the beginning of the nineteenth, neoclassical design was used for Worcester porcelain, often employing paintings by such artists as Swiss-born Angelica Kauffmann.

Worcester marks. During the "Dr. Wall period" and until 1783, the factory mark was a "W," a half moon, or a kind of Chinese square. The half moon was used after 1783 but with the name "Flight" added to indicate the new owner, Thomas Flight, and his sons, Joseph and John. From 1793 to 1807, "Flight and Barr" was used as the mark to include the name of the new partner, Martin Barr. An incised "B" was also used as a mark at this time. In the mid-1780s, Robert Chamberlain, who had worked in the plant, left to form his own factory and he used the name "Chamberlain's" and "Chamberlain's Worcester." In 1840, the two plants combined. In 1862, under W. H. Kerr, it became the Worcester Royal Porcelain Company.

Rarity and the attractiveness of the pattern are the chief value-giving elements of Worcester porcelain. Worcester buyers often collect by "pattern." Its color ground can also greatly influence a piece's value. The blue scale color ground is fashionable today with collectors, as is the apple green color ground, followed by the yellow, or yellow scale.

In the early part of the 1973 season, Christie's of London sold a small, blue, decorated bowl, 6½ inches in diameter, of the earlier (Dr. Wall) period at a record price for a piece of English porcelain —$22,680. They also sold a pair of Dr. Wall period porcelain figures in pure white, 7¼ inches high, for $12,600.

However, a pair of Worcester leaf dishes with green edges and raised veins, 8¼ inches in length, sold in New York in late 1973 at Sotheby Parke Bernet for $400. These were also of the first period of Worcester. Another lot was a "Collection of Table Articles" consisting of the bottom section of a partridge tureen painted in colorful enamels, a teabowl and saucer painted with Oriental flowers, and a fluted saucer decorated with flowers—all of the first period. The lot brought $80—not important pieces, but within the range of modest collectors.

Bow. This factory was founded around 1745. In general, those pieces made before 1750 were not of high quality. In the 1750s, the influence of Meissen and Chinese porcelain was dominant. In 1760 carmine red figures were made on four-legged bases. In 1763 the last of the three owners found himself in financial difficulties and sold the plant to William Duesbury, who moved the operation from Bow to Derby.

Bow marks. In early years the marks were indeterminate, but an anchor and a red dagger were employed from 1760 to 1765. The signature of the maker of each piece was often placed under the overall Bow mark.

In October, 1973, a pair of potted "flowering trees" 6¾ inches high, made about 1760, realized $230 at a New York auction. A slightly larger "flowering plant" brought $325. A Bow figure group which had been repaired brought $1,200 at auction in early 1974.

Chelsea. This factory was in existence probably as early as 1745. After changing owners several times, it was sold in 1770 to William Duesbury and J. Heath of Derby. Soft paste porcelain was made at first and then hard paste porcelain, and in the final years bone ash was added to make bone china. The factory used Oriental shapes and decoration, as well as painted decorations and figures of Meissen, and Sèvres tableware shapes with grounds of blue, red, yellow, carmine, turquoise, pea green, and sea green. Paintings were reproduced on some pieces.

Chelsea marks. The early mark was a triangle. An oval medallion and an anchor in low relief was the next mark. Later the anchor was painted in red or red-brown and sometimes in blue or gold.

In one of the late sales of the 1973 season, Christie's of London sold a rare pair of painted Chelsea finger bowls and stands for $2,645. In October of the same year, a beautiful Chelsea peony dish of the red anchor period, 8⅞ inches long, in apple green and dark green, was sold at auction in New York for $600, and for the same sum an octagonal decorated bowl, in the Oriental manner, 6¼ inches wide, was sold. A rare, but repaired, Chelsea dove tureen brought $13,000 at auction in February, 1974.

Derby. In the early 1750s William Duesbury founded a plant in Derby. In 1770 he bought the Chelsea plant, which continued until 1784. In 1776, Duesbury bought the Bow plant and closed it, taking the molds to Derby. In 1848 the Derby plant was closed.

Early Worcester bowl of the Dr. Wall period brought $22,680 in 1973.

Chelsea plate with the red anchor mark was purchased in 1973 for $1,900.

Bow potted flowering plant, circa 1760, sold in 1973 for $325.

In the early years of operation, the Derby plant made small figures and tableware and other utilitarian pieces. After the Chelsea plant was taken over, both plants made about the same line of products. Japanese motifs were used, and from the middle of the 1780s to the middle of the 1790s flowers and other decorations were executed, as were biscuit (unglazed) figures and medallions.

Derby marks. Before 1769 a "D" or "Derby" was used. After 1769 "D" with an anchor was the mark, the anchor intersecting the "D." After 1782, there were crossed batons plus six dots plus the crown and the "D." Robert Bloor purchased the plant in 1811 and from 1830 the mark "Bloor Derby" with or without the crown was used.

In late 1973 a good pair of Derby figures of dwarfs, made about 1785, was sold in New York at auction. The figures were 7 inches high and the colors were green and brown. They brought $2,200. A fine "Japan pattern" tureen and cover, 14 inches in length, early nineteenth century, signed with crowned crossed batons and "D," brought $1,250 at auction in early 1974.

A pair of useful and decorative figural candlesticks, 6¾ inches high, made circa 1770-80, brought $300 in late 1973, and a larger pair, 8¾ inches high, made circa 1770, sold for $425.

In general, collectors of Worcester stress decoration and pattern in determining value. The early period of manufacture is the element that is stressed by the collectors of Bow, Chelsea, and Derby porcelain.

The entire English porcelain market has experienced an upward trend for the past decade or two. A hexagonal Worcester vase with "Jabberwocky" pattern, a decoration derived from *Alice in Wonderland*—basically an Oriental piece, however—11½ inches high, sold at Sotheby's in London in 1958 for $210. Twelve years later a very similar piece, but smaller, 10¼ inches high, also of the first period, brought $5,280 at the same auction house in a poor year for the art and antique market.

We have discussed only those English porcelain factories which are most important from the viewpoints of artistry and position in today's porcelain market. We shall use the same standards in discussing the factories of other countries.

The French factories

Sèvres. With regard to elegance, prestige in the world market, and collector interest, Sèvres porcelain may very likely rank at the top.

In 1745 a factory was organized to make porcelain at Vincennes. This factory secured the support of the king, who in 1753 actually became a partner in the firm. From that time on, the name of the firm was Manufacture Royale de Porcelaine. The artistic operations of the company were in charge of Bachelier, who in effect became the true developer of fine French porcelain. This porcelain was soft paste. In 1756 the plant was moved from Vincennes to Sèvres, and by 1759 the king assumed full financial responsibility for the company. We thus have two porcelains, the earlier one known as Vincennes and the later known as Sèvres.

The Vincennes plant concentrated on tableware, and emphasized ground color, particularly a color known as *bleu de roi*, made from 1749 onward. From 1752 on, *bleu celeste* (turquoise) became typical, with panels on which pictures were painted.

After the factory was moved to Sèvres in 1756 it continued to make soft paste, but in 1769 began to make hard paste. The soft paste porcelain was discontinued in 1800. The hard paste porcelain made after 1800 lost much of the artistic excellence of the earlier porcelain and is less preferred on the market today.

The new Sèvres factory made dinner, tea, coffee, and chocolate services, boxes, dishes, fruit baskets, clock cases, candlesticks, vases, and many other items. Figures were made in great quantities, almost exclusively in biscuit. Colors were richer and more ornate than at the old plant. Pure pink was added as a ground, or base, color, and panels were gilded and polychromed. After 1770, rococo styles were replaced by classical or neoclassical, and the classical style spread to other European plants.

Sèvres marks. No factory marks were used from 1745 to 1753. From 1753 two crossed "L"s facing each other were used. Royal pieces sometimes had lilies above these letters. After 1753 a letter was placed between the "L"s, indicating the year of manufacture. From 1793 to 1800 no year was indicated—only "RF Sèvres" (for République Française). Hard paste porcelain made between 1769 and 1793 usually had a king's crown above the "L"s. Impressed writing was used in the nineteenth century.

Today's collectors prefer the rare yellow pieces, the pink or *rose Pompadour* pieces, the apple green, and the blue. Prices of Sèvres are usually higher in America than they are in Europe. All the markets seem to prefer the pieces made prior to 1760. Royal services such as those made for Catherine the Great and Madame du Barry are treasured by collectors.

In 1973 a very fine and large (55½ inches high) ormolu-mounted vase and cover with a picture painted on the side brought $10,000 in London. A fine rose and apple green dish, 9 inches in diameter, made circa 1755-65, brought $2,750 at auction in late 1973. An impressive Vincennes *bleu celeste* tray with flowers, 12 inches in diameter, made in 1754, sold for $2,400. A fine Vincennes *bleu celeste* teapot and cover made in the same year brought $1,500, but an early dish, made in 1756, 8⅝ inches in diameter, realized only

La Baigneuse, a Sèvres biscuit figure by Falconet, circa 1758, was bought in 1973 for $1,700.

One of a pair of Chantilly porcelain and ormolu figures bought in 1938 for $3,500 and sold in 1973 for $189,000.

$250—a price within the means of many collectors. A set consisting of a tray, teapot and cover, sugar bowl and cover, and two coffee cups and saucers, dated 1773, brought $1,150, and a biscuit figure of a gardener, circa 1755, 9 inches high, sold for $350.

Mennecy. This plant is also known as Mennecy-Villeroy. It was founded in Paris in 1734 and moved to Mennecy in 1748, and moved again in 1773 to Bourg-la-Reine. Meissen flowers were used as models for early decorations and the Chinese influence was evident. The plant also followed the patterns of the leading French factory —Sèvres. Biscuit figures were produced after 1751.

Mennecy marks. The earliest mark was "DV" (for the Duc de Villeroy, patron of the founder) and from 1773 on "BR" was used (for Bourg-la-Reine).

In late 1973 a pair of Mennecy vases on pedestals, circa 1750, 5½ inches high, sold for $300, and a cylindrical jar, 7¼ inches high, brought the same price.

Saint Cloud. In 1679, Pierre Chicanneau discovered how to make soft paste porcelain, and his family secured permission to manufacture such porcelain in 1702. Tableware was based on Chinese designs. Flowers, sprigs, and rosettes were often decorations. Blue, turquoise, yellow, red, and green were used on the glaze. The factory was closed by 1766.

Saint Cloud marks. The early Saint Cloud was marked "SC" or "STC" in underglaze blue. In 1695-96 a sun in underglaze blue was designed as the mark. From about 1722, "SC" was used with a cross above and a "T" below.

In the autumn of 1973, a Saint Cloud cylindrical pot and a teapot, circa 1725-50, sold for $200 at auction. Four blue and white knife and fork handles brought $125, and a white potpourri jar, 5 inches high, circa 1730-50, went for $175.

Chantilly. The Chantilly plant, which operated from the 1720s through the 1780s, used opaque tin glazes on the early pieces and after 1750 a clear lead glaze was used. The pieces made before 1750 are the ones preferred by collectors. The products turned out were in many ways similar to those made at Saint Cloud.

Chantilly marks. The mark of the Chantilly factory is usually an iron-red hunting horn. The word "Chantilly" with a blue hunting horn was used in the late eighteenth century.

A great deal of Chantilly porcelain appears on the market. In late 1973 a very rare Chantilly double salt and pepper box, with armorial and floral designs, circa 1725-35, 6¼ inches high, sold for $800. A covered dish with floral decoration, 7½ inches wide, brought $500, and a tin glazed cachepot—a large cup with two handles—3⅞ inches high, realized $325.

On most early pieces there are Japanese, or "Kakiemon," decorations. At a recent Christie's auction in London, a pair of pagoda figures with Kakiemon decoration and ormolu, brought the enormous sum of 75,000 guineas—about $200,000.

The German factories

Meissen. This factory is comparable in importance to the Sèvres factory in France. Johann Friedrich Böttger developed hard paste porcelain in 1708 or 1709, and the plant began operating in 1710 just outside Dresden. It was the first porcelain factory in Europe. In its earliest period it produced a dark brown stoneware which was polished. Then it developed a white undecorated ware employing Oriental shapes. Later, enamels were employed, using Chinese and Kakiemon designs, and these sell at the highest prices. Yellow and turquoise color grounds are in great demand today.

Meissen marks. In the Böttger era there were no systematic marks. Chinese inscriptions and drawings were used as marks between 1720 and 1722. After 1722 the marks were in underglaze blue and were either a drawing of the caduceus or the letters "KPM" or "MPM." Large Oriental pieces made between 1725 and 1730 bear the letters "AR," as do later pieces made for the royal court. Beginning in 1720 the mark became the crossed swords of the House of Saxony and this mark has been used ever since.

The earliest pieces turned out by the plant are in great demand. In the figure pieces, rarity of the model and brilliance of color determine value, the brightest colors bringing the highest prices.

The plant turned out many figures. Few of the Böttger figures remain, but there are many of the excellent figures done by J.J. Kändler. Bird (parrot and swan) figures are the most valuable. Human figures depicting the Italian comedy (commedia dell'arte) are also sought after and at the highest prices. On October 12, 1973, a fine Kändler Meissen Italian comedy figure (with playing cards on the jacket of the figure), circa 1739, 7¼ inches high, brought $21,500.

In 1973, a good, but late, figure of a dancing peasant modeled by Kändler, circa 1740-60, 6⅝ inches high, brought $800. In the same sale a pair of Meissen figures mounted in ormolu as candelabra, 11 inches high, of the mid-eighteenth century, brought $2,000. For $1,200 one could have purchased a beautiful Meissen tea kettle with cover and stand, circa 1745-55, 15½ inches high.

In early 1974 an attractive pair of ormolu-mounted Meissen bullfinch candelabra, each bird modeled by Kändler, circa 1740, brought $16,000 in New York. In the same sale a pair of Meissen ormolu-mounted Kakiemon vases, 14 inches high, went for $10,000. Had they not been slightly damaged, they would have brought a great deal more.

If a figure piece is perfect, the value is disproportionately great-

This eighteenth-century Meissen dog group by Kändler, from the collection of the Duke of Windsor, is valued at $15,000.

Meissen double-handled beaker and saucer, circa 1730-35, brought $300 at auction in New York in 1973.

er. If the head at one time was broken off the body, the value is reduced tremendously. Such damage can reduce the value from
$15,000 to $2,000 or even less. Loss of a figure's hand or a foot is not
so serious as a value-reducing element.

Frankenthal. Paul Hannong received permission in 1755 from
the elector palatine to found a porcelain factory at Frankenthal. In
1762 the elector himself bought the factory. It was closed down in
1800. Between 1755 and 1761, modelmaster Johann Lanz developed
excellent designs, and he was followed by Franz Konrad Linck. Karl
Lück took Linck's place in 1766. From 1779 to 1793, J.P. Melchior
was the modelmaster. He introduced and developed a neoclassical
style at the Frankenthal factory before he left to become the modelmaster at Nymphenburg.

Frankenthal marks. From 1755 to 1762, "PH" or "PHF" were
used as marks. From 1755 to 1759 a rampant lion was also the
mark, and from 1757 to 1762 intertwined initials "JAH." From
1762 on, the elector's monogram, "CT," was employed, with the
crown in underglaze blue. From 1770 to 1788, year numbers were
used, and from 1795 the letters "VR."

In late 1973 a fine Frankenthal group of a shepherd and shepherdess, 4¾ inches high, made circa 1770, sold for $750, and a fine tea-
pot and cover, dated 1773, 4¾ inches high, brought $425. A rare
pair of figural groups modeled by Lanz, with minor repairs, brought
$4,000 in early 1974.

Fürstenberg. Many of the great European porcelain factories
were either founded or sponsored by members of the royalty or high
nobility. The Fürstenberg plant was no exception. It was founded
by Duke Carl I of Brunswick and successfully began producing true
porcelain in 1753. The tableware showed the influence of Meissen.
Rich reliefs were employed in the 1750s and 1760s. Colorful, painted
decorations were characteristic of Fürstenberg. In 1795 the opera-
tor of the plant, Louis Gerverot, developed the Empire style, as did
many European factories.

Fürstenberg marks. The mark was an "F" in underglaze blue.
At the beginning of the nineteenth century, the running horse of
Brunswick was stamped on the biscuit pieces.

In New York in 1973, a Fürstenberg plate and tea caddy of the
eighteenth century, 9¼ inches high, brought just $70. In the sale
there were very few Fürstenberg pieces but a great many Meissen
pieces. The Meissen pieces brought very high prices, so that rarity
or scarcity cannot always be considered the main value element.
However, early 1974 saw a strengthening in Fürstenberg prices.
A coffee cup and saucer brought $450 and most pieces sold for more
than the pre-sale estimates.

Nymphenburg. Franz Niedermayer founded a factory for the

manufacture of porcelain at Neudeck, near Munich, in 1747. The government assumed ownership of the plant in 1761 and moved it to Nymphenburg. Not until 1862 was it again owned privately.

The porcelain sculpture of this plant was very much more important than its tableware. Modelmaster Franz Bustelli made the factory famous because of his figures, including those of the Italian comedy. Dominikus Auliczek succeeded Bustelli and tended to emphasize neoclassicism. This modelmaster was succeeded by J.P. Melchior, who retired in 1822.

Nymphenburg marks. The early Neudeck work is marked with a hexagram in underglaze blue plus a letter. In addition, a checkered shield was impressed and this mark continued to be used. Between 1754 and 1763, Bustelli used his initials "F.B."

In late 1973 a pair of figures of a shepherd and shepherdess, 6¾ inches high, circa 1763-67, with hexagram marks in underglaze blue sold for $450, and a coffee cup and saucer, circa 1760, went for $120.

Höchst. The factory had been well organized by 1746 by two financiers and porcelain artist A.F. von Löwenfinck, who had arrived from Meissen. In 1778 the elector took over the plant. After the French occupation, it closed down in 1798. The main influence on the work of this plant was Meissen, but it also used rococo design. J.P. Melchior became modelmaster in 1769 and remained in that position until 1779. He did a great deal of figural design work, including mythological forms.

Höchst marks. Before 1763 the mark generally consisted of a wheel with six spokes in red or gold impressed or just placed over the glaze. From 1762 on, the mark was painted in blue. Between 1765 and 1774 the crown of the elector appeared above the wheel.

In the fall of 1973 a rare Höchst figure of a print seller, circa 1775, 7¼ inches tall, was sold at auction in New York for $2,600. The colors were green, lavender, pale blue, yellow, and white, with gilt. For $250 one could have purchased an early Höchst cream jug, circa 1750-65, 3½ inches high.

A coffee pot, circa 1765, brought $1,050 in February, 1974, although the pre-sale estimate was $250 to $450. It was bought by a Swiss dealer.

Ludwigsburg. This factory was established in 1756 but, like so many of the European porcelain factories, was appropriated by the government. Duke Carl Eugen of Württemberg appropriated it in 1758. In 1759 he asked J. J. Ringler, who had a great deal of experience in porcelain plants, to take over its management. Between 1760 and 1767 the products were of a high degree of excellence. Later they declined, and in 1824 the plant was closed.

Ludwigsburg porcelain sculptures were of a high order under

J.J. Louis, J.C. Beyer, and P.F. Lejeune. In the 1760s, Beyer converted the motifs to classicism. He made contemporary and allegorical figures.

Ludwigsburg marks. From 1758 to 1793 intertwined "C"s were the mark. Sometimes a blue crown was used. From 1793 to 1795, there was an "L" below the crown; from 1806 to 1816, an "FR" below the crown; and from 1816 to 1824, "WR" was used. From the last quarter of the eighteenth century antlers were in the mark.

The simpler Ludwigsburg pieces are not expensive. An oval basket, circa 1765, 6⅞ inches in diameter, sold in late 1973 for $300, and in the same sale a plate, circa 1770, with floral and sprig designs in red, yellow, blue, purple, and green, 10 inches in diameter, brought $120.

In December, 1973, Sotheby's of London sold a fine Ludwigsburg group modeled by J. J. Louis. The group consisted of three figures and numerous objects. It was 7½ inches high and brought a little under $2,000.

There has been a fairly substantial price rise in recent years for the work of this entire group of German factories. The earliest pieces have tended to rise the most and to the highest figures. Brilliantly colored pieces have been especially coveted. Of all figures and figural groups, the Italian comedy theme is the most sought after and the highest in price.

Austrian porcelain

Vienna. The Vienna factory was founded in 1718 by Claudius du Paquier, assisted by Samuel Stölzel, the manufacturing specialist, and by Christoph Hunger. Both assistants came from the Meissen plant. In 1744, du Paquier sold the factory to the state. It was due to the ability of the new manager, Konrad von Sorgenthal, that the Vienna factory achieved the highest standing in Europe. In the nineteenth century the factory declined in importance and was closed in 1864.

The du Paquier period (1718 to 1744) was confined to the manufacture of tableware. From 1720 to 1730 polychrome chinoiseries predominated. Japanese motifs were also used. Iron red and purple were favored. From 1730 to 1740, Oriental designs were replaced by the baroque—shells, flowers, fruits, and landscapes.

The pre-Sorgenthal period (1744 to 1784) employed new shapes, motifs, and colors in the rococo style, and in the 1740s sculpture was developed, with Niedermeyer leading in the creation of these figures and figural groups.

The Sorgenthal period (1784 to 1805) was marked by an increase in dinner, tea, and coffee services. More painting, and in better colors, was done.

Vienna marks. From 1744 to 1749 a shield with two bars was the mark, and it was impressed. From 1749 to 1827 the same mark was used but in underglaze blue. From 1783 the year of manufacture was indicated.

Prices are very close to Meissen prices, as is the quality of some of the work of the Vienna plant. Collecting of Viennese porcelain is done rather quietly, with early pieces stressed. Chinese styles are in demand, as are hunting scenes. The 1744 to 1784 pre-Sorgenthal period is not in such great demand, as the pieces are considered by collectors to be somewhat uninteresting.

The decorated pieces of the Sorgenthal period are beginning to rise in price. In this period the painting and the gilding were at a peak in quality. The work of K.A. Kothgasser, the porcelain painter, is in tremendous demand, and a cup and saucer painted by him will bring from $700 to $1,050.

In late 1973 a cup and saucer, circa 1822, painted in a sun-and-moon motif, brought $550, and a pair of chinoiserie figures brought $650.

The Italian factories

Vezzi and Cozzi. The Vezzi factory operated in Venice from 1720 to 1740, making hard paste porcelain. The manufacturing process was made known there by Christoph Hunger, who had worked at the Vienna and Meissen factories.

Vienna cabinet cup and saucer with sun-and-moon decoration, circa 1822, sold at auction in 1973 for $550.

The Cozzi factory was established in Venice in 1764 and continued to make soft paste porcelain until 1812.

The Vezzi plant made tableware with painting and piercing, as well as modeled or impressed ornaments. Blue dominated at first, and later iron red. The Cozzi factory turned out similar products although, because it operated later, it turned more to neoclassicism.

The products of the Vezzi factory are extremely valuable. A teapot sold for $5,000 in 1972. A rare Cozzi teapot brought $3,262, and a very rare Vezzi beaker, 3⅜ inches high, brought $1,687 in December, 1973.

Ginori. The Ginori, or Doccia, plant began operations in Florence in 1735 and turned out hard paste porcelain. The motifs were Chinese and there was considerable imitation of other European factories. Some tableware made up to the year 1765 was unpainted or painted in underglaze blue. Beginning in 1780, Pompeian motifs were used, as were neoclassical styles. Recently a covered tureen from this factory brought $7,500 at auction. However, six Doccia custard cups and covers sold for only $100 at auction in late 1973.

Capodimonte. King Charles III founded the Capodimonte factory in Naples in 1743. It specialized in soft paste products. Charles moved the operation to Madrid in 1759 when he became king of Spain. In 1773 the factory was moved back to Naples and hard paste porcelain was made for the first time. The plant was closed in 1821.

Fine relief decoration with figural motifs is characteristic of some of the porcelain of this plant. The rococo style finally gave way to the classical, as it did in most European factories. Scenes from everyday life often were used, in pale and subtle colors. Figures of merchants and fishmongers were popular. The figures modeled by Gricci are extremely important to collectors and will bring from $10,000 to $20,000.

A simple plate will sell for $700 to $1,000 at the present time. A good Capodimonte teabowl and saucer, painted by Giuseppe della Torre, brought $7,200 in December, 1973, in London.

Faience or pottery

Pottery, or faience, consists of products made for the most part of clay. Lime, feldspar, or quartz are added and worked into a paste which is then formed into desired shapes by hand or by machine and then fired. These products are known as pottery or faience, and, in Italy, as majolica, or maiolica.

As far as collectors are concerned, this is a new and important area of interest. There has been a recent general rise in price in the entire pottery field.

From a manufacturing point of view, porcelain represents a more advanced product than faience or pottery, but hardly from a market and price point of view. In mid-1973 a sale of French faience was held by Sotheby's in Zurich. A pair of Niderviller figures of dwarfs, about 6 inches high, made circa 1755-60, sold for $14,000. A pair of Strasbourg candlestick figures, about 10 inches high, brought $17,500, as did a pair of Strasbourg tureens with covers in the form of ducks. A pair of Strasbourg wild boars, about 8 inches long, realized $18,500, and a pair of Strasbourg tureens and covers in the form of pigeons brought $70,000.

French faience

The greatest French factory is *Strasbourg*, both in quality of work and market price, and those pieces in the greatest demand are pigeon, duck, and goose tureens in accurate, life-size copies of the birds. These forms were, however, copied in the nineteenth century and these later pieces are not remotely comparable to the earlier pieces in collector interest or value.

Not all Strasbourg pieces are sky-high in price, however, and in the same sale that realized the very high prices mentioned above, a spice box and cover with three compartments and decorated with flowers brought about $700. A knife handle with similar painting realized about $200.

The French faience plant next in importance is *Marseilles*. The products of this factory are rising sharply in price. All of the pieces are tin glazed and colored. Decorations are flowers and chinoiserie.

Another plant of importance is *Sceaux*. In October, 1973, Christie's of London auctioned a porcelain inkstand with rococo scroll outline, 7 inches long, for $236. In New York, at about the same time, a pair of Sceaux jardinieres, made about 1770, 3¾ inches high, sold for $475.

The *Rouen* plant also ranks high. An outstanding Rouen piece— a covered ewer with chinoiserie decoration, 11½ inches high, made about 1750 to 1770—was sold in New York in October, 1973, for $6,000.

Also important French faience plants are *Nevers* and *Niderviller*. In April, 1973, a decorative Niderviller cylindrical pot and cover, painted with sprays of flowers, about 3 inches high, brought $135. In the same sale a very attractive figure of a girl wearing a striped and flowered skirt, a yellow bodice, and a hat, and holding a dog, on a grassy base, brought about $250.

One more plant is *Lunéville*. In the April, 1973, sale a fine Lunéville oval bowl with chinoiserie motif, about 14 inches long, brought about $1,600, while a larger bowl, about 19 inches long, but with no decoration except a crest, brought only $150.

In this entire group of French faience, the highly decorated, well-designed pieces, and those with colors, tend to bring the most money, as do the finer earlier pieces, and there is a great difference in price between the simpler and the finer, more elaborate pieces.

English pottery

There are two main categories of English pottery that are at the forefront in collector interest at the present time and both are avidly sought. One of them is *Staffordshire*. In this category there are three preferred designer-makers—Thomas Whieldon, Ralph Wood, and John Astbury.

In 1973, Christie's of London auctioned a pair of Staffordshire fighters, identified as Messrs. Cribb and Molyneux. They were 9 inches high and they brought $4,788. In the less expensive range, the same auction house conducted a sale in 1973 of fine English pottery in which a rare Staffordshire globular teapot and cover, enameled in colors and with a portrait of the king of Prussia, was sold. It was 7 inches high and brought $473. A teapot and cover decorated with scrolling and trellis panels went for $130.

The other main type of English pottery is that produced by the *Wedgwood* plant, which is actually a kind of subdivision of Staffordshire.

Collecting of Wedgwood is done by categories. One category is jasper ware, and this is in lilac and white, green and white, and blue and white. In general the more colors the more valuable is the piece. Another category is the black basalts, which are usually large, utilitarian pieces.

Josiah Wedgwood founded the factory in 1759. Agate (or variegated) wares were turned out by Wedgwood between 1759 and 1781. Pieces in this category resemble marble or porphyry, and are generally priced in the thousands of dollars. Then there are the lesser categories of Wedgwood known as *rosso antico*, cane ware, and fairyland luster. Very often collectors want an example of each Wedgwood series.

In the summer of 1973, Christie's of London sold a pair of Wedgwood plaques of blue and white jasper, one *The Marriage of Cupid and Psyche* and the other *The Sacrifice to Peace*. Each was 3¼ inches wide, and the pair brought $2,572.

Many sales in England and on the continent of Europe specialize in faience, or pottery (the English designation), or in porcelain. The sale held by Christie's on May 21, 1973, concentrated on English pottery, particularly Wedgwood. One lot was a rare *rosso antico* potpourri bowl with cover and pierced over-cover. It was enameled with a bird and Oriental-style flowers, and was 12 inches high. It sold for $919.

The very next item was a black basalt oil lamp with a boat-shaped body, $9\frac{1}{4}$ inches wide. It brought $525. A rare oblong-octagonal jasper plaque in four colors, with nymphs and *putti*, $2\frac{3}{4}$ inches wide, brought $919.

Lesser-priced items always appear in the English sales. A black basalt cream jug, $5\frac{1}{2}$ inches high, two more cream jugs 5 inches high, a bowl $7\frac{1}{4}$ inches in diameter, and another bowl 6 inches in diameter, together brought $92.

German faience

In the words of the director of Sotheby Parke Bernet's European porcelain department, "German faience has skyrocketed, especially Hausmaler." Hausmaler designates faience that is produced in a factory and sent to the home of a painter, who decorates it by hand. One Meissen Hausmaler coffee pot recently brought $100,000 at auction, and a Nuremberg Hausmaler jug realized $20,000. The finest Hausmaler wares, and the most sought after, are those decorated in bright colors.

The main German factories which produced faience during the eighteenth century were *Nuremberg, Frankfurt, Hanau, Fulda, Löwenfinck, Höchst*, and several in *Berlin*.

The identification of most German faience is by the city in which a particular plant was located. An exception is Löwenfinck, which is the name of the maker, Adam Friedrich von Löwenfinck. He apparently started work at Meissen, and then moved to Bayreuth, Ansbach, Fulda, and finally to Höchst, where in 1746 he opened his own faience factory.

The Frankfurt and Hanau plants turned out a vast amount of pottery very similar in style and decoration to the Delft ware of Holland. They also produced many pieces in the Chinese style.

The Fulda and Löwenfinck plants manufactured a good deal of pottery in the Chinese, and particularly *famille rose*, style and this is very much sought after today. The signed pieces, including Hausmaler pieces, are particularly valuable.

In the latter part of 1973 a very rare pair of Fulda figures of a boy and a girl, circa 1775 to 1780, $5\frac{1}{4}$ inches high, was sold at the Sotheby Parke Bernet galleries in New York for $3,750. In contrast, the very next lot in the sale was a rare Berlin potpourri vase and cover, floral decorated, 6 inches high, circa 1760. It sold for $525.

Dutch faience

Delft pottery was turned out in the seventeenth and eighteenth century in immense quantities. Of course the famous blue and white ware is produced today, also in immense quantities, and marketed all over the world.

A record price for majolica—$60,375—was paid for this rare Urbino dish in late 1973.

When this pottery was introduced it became popular throughout Europe and was used as the basis for designs by other European plants. Much of the Delft pottery copied the Chinese shapes and patterns more or less directly.

Much period Delft ware is still available and at not very high prices, but if there are colors in addition to blue the value mounts rapidly. Delft *doré* giltware sells for much more than the blue and white pieces. The chimney set, or garniture, of five pieces has been a more or less standard product for decades. Ten years ago it brought perhaps $250. Now it brings $1,000 or more, depending on the size and the quality. In April, 1973, a very fine chimney garniture of five polychromed vases, the center vase 24½ inches high, brought $4,032 at Christie's auction.

Figures—human and animal—are rare and valuable pieces of Delft ware.

Italian majolica (maiolica)

In the eighteenth century nearly every Italian town turned out majolica. In many ways Italian majolica is similar to French faience of the same period. Like French and German faience, Italian majolica is experiencing a substantial price rise.

Important Italian factories whose majolica is sold from time to time on the open market are *Pesaro, Milan,* and *Castelli.*

A Castelli rectangular plaque of Venus and Cupid, 10½ by 8¼

inches, with an ebonized frame, brought $394 at auction in London in December, 1973. In the same sale a Pesaro circular plate in various colors, decorated with bouquets and with a pink rim, 8½ inches in diameter, brought $118.

Although the title of the sale catalog was "Fine Italian Maiolica and Porcelain and Continental Pottery," the Italian items were scarce. However, a high price was paid for one very rare, very fine Italian piece—a dish, 17 inches in diameter, made in Urbino by Francesco Ravelli in 1534. The subject was Diana and Actaeon. The dish sold for $60,375.

The state of the market

In the United States there is very little demand for French faience as compared with the Italian and German versions. English pottery is the most sought after in this country. There is a wide range of prices for almost every type of porcelain and pottery.

Ceramics in general are the specialty of more or less expert collectors who place a premium on technical attributes, the main ones being early year of manufacture, fineness of design, elaborateness and excellence of decoration, bright colors, rarity, and excellence of condition.

The price rise in the collectors' items during the past decade has been great. A fine Meissen dish, circa 1740, with attractive Kakiemon decoration, sold at Sotheby's in London on March 10, 1970, for $1,008. The same piece sold again in June, 1973, for $2,000—about double the price in three years.

A Meissen Hausmaler (Meyer of Pressnitz) plate sold at Sotheby's in 1970 for $1,728. In June, 1973, it sold again, for $2,300. Had the piece actually been signed by the painter it would have been worth much more.

Another Meyer of Pressnitz piece, circa 1750, but chipped, sold for $1,100 in December, 1971. An almost identical plate, but in perfect condition, brought only $168 in May of 1956. Today, this perfect plate would bring at least $2,500. The chipped one would bring $1,500 today.

The wild boom in Chinese ceramics has resulted in many new price records being set. Pieces made during the Ming dynasty are among those most in demand. This blue and white Ming double-gourd vase would have sold for $1,000 in 1960. It is valued at $18,000 today.

17

Chinese Ceramics

A woman living in Chicago purchased a Chinese pottery figure of a horse and rider dating from the T'ang dynasty (A.D. 618-907) from a dealer in 1959. T'ang dynasty figures of horses and riders have never been very rare, but this was a particularly fine one of glazed pottery, 16½ inches high and 13½ inches long, and the woman paid almost $2,000 for it. The original price tag was still in existence at the time the figure was auctioned in New York in February, 1974, by Sotheby Parke Bernet.

The auction house made an estimate of what this figure would have brought had it been auctioned in 1965—about $2,500. Had it been offered for sale in 1970, it would have brought about $20,000. On February 7, 1974, the figure of the horse and rider sold for $92,500.

In the same sale there was an unglazed T'ang dynasty prancing horse, 17 inches high. It realized $17,000 at auction. The gallery estimated that had this horse been auctioned in 1965 it would have brought $800.

Also in that sale, a Han dynasty (206 B.C. to A.D. 220) wine jar was offered. It was 15½ inches high, glazed, and of an iridescent cucumber green color. The gallery estimated its auction price in 1965 at $500. In February, 1974, it brought $6,500.

Prices booming

Early Chinese ceramics are the subject of perhaps the wildest boom of any collectible category at the present time. One New York dealer, Leon Medina, in the late 1950s and early 1960s, regularly had T'ang horses for sale for about $1,000 apiece. Conservatively, these horses would bring $25,000 each at auction today.

At the beginning of the 1960s, when the Austrian government was negotiating for the purchase of a large house in Washington, D.C., for use as its embassy and did not want to purchase the entire contents of the house, a collector was invited to look over what remained in the estate for sale. Among the various things that the collector saw, and finally bought, was a T'ang horse about 12 inches long and 8 inches high. It had a broken foot, so the collector offered the bank administering the estate $10 for the horse. The bank accepted the offer. The foot was repaired and the collector now displays the horse in his living room, but each year—as its value rises —he moves it to a higher shelf away from possible breakage.

One of the great discoveries of the 1973-74 art and antique sales season took place at an auction house in Hong Kong when a Chinese lady brought in a saucer she wanted to sell, obviously not thinking that it had any great value. It turned out to be a rare piece dating from the Ming dynasty (1368-1644) and sold for $384,000.

The auction record for an entire sale of Chinese ceramics was set in the 1973-74 season in London. The total was over $6 million.

One explanation for the price boom was illustrated at the Grosvenor House Antiques Fair in London in June, 1973. On the day the fair was to open, about two dozen Japanese were outside the main door of the hall waiting for it to be unlocked. Some of them sat on the steps, since they had arrived well before the opening hour and had become tired. Within twenty minutes after the door was opened the Japanese had purchased about half of all the Chinese ceramics available from the dealers exhibiting at the fair.

The prosperity of the Japanese to a considerable extent fueled the rise in the market for Orientalia, including ceramics. One important motivating factor was the rate of inflation, which at times approached 20 percent per year and encouraged the owners of yen to trade their currency for objects that were not only an inflation hedge but were also desirable purely as collectibles. Oriental ceramics served the purpose beautifully—until Japan ran into economic difficulties and the activities of Japanese collectors decreased in the latter part of 1973.

In a major sale of Chinese ceramics all of the following types may be offered:

Early dynasty pottery figures and wares
T'ang and Liao wares
T'ang pottery figures
Sung wares, including Tz'ŭ Chou and Chün Yao
Honan wares and teabowls
Ting Yao, related wares, and Ching Pai
Sung, Yüan, and Ming celadons
Ming porcelains, including blue and white
Southeast Asia and export wares
Tileworks and other Ming wares
Ch'ing blue and white porcelains
Blanc-de-Chine
Various Ch'ing wares
Ch'ing yellow and other monochromes
Famille rose wares
Famille verte wares

The periods most in demand—at escalating prices—are Han, T'ang, Sung, and Ming.

Popular with investors

The entire field of Chinese ceramics became exceedingly popular with investors in 1969 and 1970. It was in those years that a turning point was reached. In the period from 1960 to 1969 there was only a 20 percent increase in price—less than 2 percent per year on the average—but in the two-year period from 1969 to 1971 there

The Ming saucer that sold for $384,000 at a Hong Kong auction during the 1973-74 season.

was a 200 percent increase in prices realized by selective areas.

The early wares have experienced the sharpest price increases, as have the major dynasties. Until the late 1950s it was difficult to sell any T'ang horse for more than $1,000, no matter how large or how fine. In 1969 a T'ang horse brought $32,000—four times the price paid at auction to that date for any T'ang ceramic. Yet in 1973 a T'ang horse brought four times this 1969 price. The horse sold in 1969 was 33 inches high, a very large piece. In early 1974 this same horse probably would have brought $100,000.

A T'ang period blue vase was sold at the Parke Bernet Galleries in New York to a Chicago dealer for $70 in 1947. The dealer sold the vase to a doctor for $500. The vase appeared at auction in New York again in 1973, and was sold to the Hartman Galleries (Rare Art) of New York for $47,500. The unique feature which has given this vase such great value is the blue glaze.

In November, 1973, the Hartman Galleries (Rare Art) bought a Ming blue and white porcelain bowl for $46,000. This bowl would have brought no more than $1,500 in 1958.

About ten years ago an Oriental pot was bought by a woman at auction in New York for a small sum of money—a "decoration" price. It had been converted into a lamp, with a hole drilled through the bottom for the electric cord. The buyer brought it to the Brooklyn Museum, where curator Lois Katz identified it as a rare red-underglaze Ming piece and wanted to buy it for the museum. Miss Katz asked the owner to show it to some dealers in New York to get a price quotation. The owner telephoned one dealer who, without seeing the piece, said that it might be worth $1,000.

The woman then went back to the museum with her pot and said she would be willing to take $1,000 for it. Miss Katz suggested the owner speak to another dealer as the piece might be worth more than $1,000. The second dealer, a famous and knowledgeable one, also gave an estimate by telephone—$2,000. The owner communicated this fact to the curator, who then went to the trustees of the Brooklyn Museum and said she would like to purchase the lamp for $2,000. The trustees turned her down. She then went to a friend, Chinese ceramic collector Paul Manheim, who agreed to buy the lamp and lend it to the museum for display.

Recently a member of a Japanese group of ceramics buyers visited the museum and saw the piece. The Japanese group members had been visiting museums looking for privately owned items which were on loan, in order to make offers of purchase to the owners. This one Japanese who located the piece at the Brooklyn Museum is said to have offered Mr. Manheim about $200,000 for the pot. The offer seemed to Mr. Manheim to be too good to refuse, but the London dealer, J. E. Eskenazi, heard of the offer and was reported

Classifications of Chinese Ceramics

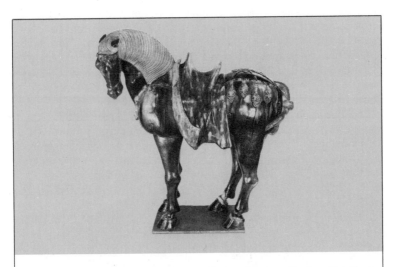

Chinese ceramics are classified according to the dynasties in which they were produced. These are the major dynasties:

Shang or Yin	c. 1523 to c. 1123 B.C.
Chou	c. 1123 to 255 B.C.
Ch'in	255 to 206 B.C.
Han	206 B.C. to A.D. 220
Three Kingdoms	A.D. 220 to 265
Northern and Southern Six Dynasties	265 to 589
Sui	589 to 618
T'ang	618 to 907
Five Dynasties	907 to 960
and Liao	907 to 1125
Northern Sung	960 to 1127
Southern Sung	1127 to 1280
Yüan (Mongol)	1260 to 1368
Ming	1368 to 1644
Ch'ing (Manchu)	1644 to 1912
Republic	1912 on

to have told Mr. Manheim, "If the Japanese dealer will pay you $200,000, I will pay $250,000." Mr. Eskenazi acquired the Ming piece and later reportedly offered to sell it for about $400,000.

One buyer was apparently determined to corner the finest ceramics that could be purchased in 1974, almost regardless of price. This buyer is London dealer Helen Glatz. A pair of birds that would have sold for $22,500 in London in 1973 was bought by Mrs. Glatz in 1974 for $158,000 at Sotheby's. Buying reportedly for Portuguese interests, she then paid $1,005,000 for a Ming bottle at Sotheby's—an auction record price for a work of art other than a painting.

In 1972, Anthony Derham of Christie's auction house in London was called upon to do an appraisal of a collection for insurance purposes. As he entered the house he noticed the umbrella stand, which was obviously Chinese. Upon closer examination, he determined that what was being used as an umbrella stand was a fourteenth-century wine jar of rare red-and-blue underglaze. It was 13½ inches high and 6¾ inches wide at the base. Unfortunately, the neck was cracked in various places—possibly by the umbrellas which had been placed in the jar—and the cover was missing. On June 5, 1972, this jar brought at auction 210,000 guineas— $573,300—a world record auction price at the time for any work of art other than a picture. This Ming jar is not unique. There is a similar jar in Peking and one at the Percival David Foundation of Chinese Art in London. If one of these others were sold (with its cover), it would probably bring close to $1 million.

Characteristics of various periods

Following are the characteristics and recent prices of Chinese ceramics dating from various dynasties:

Han dynasty. These are extremely early pieces. They are also very primitive, natural in color, and not highly decorated. They are for the most part items for dedicated collectors and museums, and do not have the decorative value which the later pieces have.

At the end of 1973 an important auction sale of Chinese ceramics was held in New York in which Han pieces, among others, were sold. A well-modeled pottery horse's head, 6¼ inches high, brought $2,750. A rare green-glazed pottery figure of a dog—not a particularly beautiful animal—12¼ inches high, brought $5,250. An iridescent green-glazed pottery granary jar, 9½ inches high, sold for $2,500, and a small green-glazed jar, 4½ inches high, brought $1,600.

T'ang dynasty. These pieces are not extremely rare and are generally more decorative than the primitive pieces of the Han dy-

The world record auction price for a work of art other than a painting—$1,005,000—was paid in April, 1974, for this Ming blue and white bottle.

nasty. In the 1973 sale just mentioned, a straw-glazed T'ang pottery tripod dish, 7¼ inches in diameter, brought $1,400. A splash-glazed pottery jar (amphora) with handles in the form of dragons—an attractive but primitive piece—13½ inches high, sold for $2,100. The next lot in the same sale was a three-color glazed pottery amphora with dragon handles, 11 inches high. It brought $2,400. A splash-glazed small terra-cotta bowl, 3½ inches in diameter, went for $1,400.

Rather attractive little figures of the T'ang dynasty can be purchased for reasonable amounts of money. A small unglazed red pottery figure of a woman, 9 inches high, sold in late 1973 for $800. A similar figure, 14¾ inches high, brought $950, and one 16 inches high brought $850. A fine glazed terra-cotta figure of a warrior, 16¼ inches high, was sold for $1,800. Two small red pottery horses, 5¾ inches long, brought $2,000 for the pair.

Sung dynasty. Important Sung dynasty pieces are extremely rare and sell at prices few people can afford. Simpler, but very decorative, pieces do come onto the market for reasonable sums.

In a late 1973 sale in New York a large (20¾ inches high) wine jar of ovoid shape with a short cylindrical neck, painted dark brown, with sprays of foliage, leaves, concentric rings, and character inscriptions, brought $1,500. An unusual painted figure of a man on horseback, 4⅝ inches high, sold for $950. A highly attractive marbled ware tripod pot, called a censer, just 2¾ inches high, with colors of bluish gray, cream, and brown beneath a transparent glaze, brought $525. A brown-glazed stoneware vase, 13 inches high, was purchased for $800, and a teabowl, 5 inches in diameter, of cone shape with a thick blackish gray glaze, brought $625.

A number of celadon pieces of the Sung dynasty appear on the market. One such bowl with finely shaped sides was offered in late 1973. The exterior was carved in the shape of petals, the glaze was sea green, and the diameter of the bowl was 4¾ inches. The price was $600.

Another celadon bowl appeared in the same sale, this one 8⅛ inches in diameter, conical in shape, the interior carved and molded with scrolling stems, blossoms, and leaves. The glaze was olive green and brown. The price realized was $1,000.

Ming dynasty. Ming pieces are generally rather ornate and decorated in a sophisticated manner. In 1973 an early Ming copper-red decorated bowl painted in underglaze red, with a peony spray in a center medallion encircled by a chrysanthemum scroll, 8⅛ inches wide, brought $212,500 at auction in London.

In the same year a blue and white dish, 6⅝ inches in diameter, the interior decorated with a pair of dragons, brought just $150. A large blue and white bowl, 13⅛ inches in diameter, painted with blossoms and leaves on the exterior and a floral medallion on the interior, sold for $300, and a fine stoneware vase, with green-gray glaze and molded decorations in the form of branches, 18½ inches high, brought $900. An attractive pair of turquoise-glazed vases, 8⅜ inches high, with hexagonal necks, and with molded dragons and molded flames on the sides, brought $500.

There are a number of attractive celadon pieces of the Ming dynasty. A vase of grayish green glaze, with tapering sides and carved with blossoms and leaves, 6¾ inches high, was auctioned for $575 in late 1973, and a beautifully shaped celadon bronze vase, with olive green glaze of even tone, 9½ inches high, brought $1,000.

Ch'ing dynasty—K'ang-hsi period (1662-1722). There are many pieces of this relatively late period of Chinese ceramics on the market at all times, and they are some of the most decorative ceramics that can be purchased. They are also relatively low in price.

One such item—a blue and white decorated beaker—was recently sold at auction. It was decorated with underglaze blue, copper red, and pale brownish celadon, with designs of shrubs, insects, rockwork, and branches of blossoming magnolia. The piece was 16½ inches high and brought $2,200. A blue and white temple jar and cover of the same period was sold at the same time. It was of baluster form, painted in underglaze blue and ornamented with two deer, cranes perched and in flight, and pine trees springing from rocks. It was 10½ inches high and sold for $1,600. A beautiful blue

Covered bowl of the K'ang-hsi period, circa 1690, 9 inches high, is valued at $3,500.

One of a pair of *famille rose* vases made in the nineteenth century that sold for $475 at auction in 1974.

and white dish, 14 inches in diameter, painted in underglaze blue and with arrangements of flowers and plants enclosing a medallion of chrysanthemums, peonies, and other flowers, was purchased for $1,100.

A number of particularly beautiful pieces were made in this period, and these were known as *famille verte* items. A *famille verte* dish, 10¾ inches wide, was sold recently for $425. It was decorated, in dark enamels and iron red, with a hummingbird hovering over a lily pond, and had a border of flowers. For $400 one could have purchased a fine and highly decorated *famille verte* teapot and cover, 5 inches high, of spherical design, decorated with a landscape of a river, mountains, and a flower-strewn ground of pale green.

The *famille verte* designation comes from the use of green, but iron red, yellow, and aubergine were also used. There are two subsections of *famille verte* known as *famille jaune* and *famille noire*, where yellow and black, respectively, were the predominant colors.

Ch'ing dynasty—Ch'ien Lung period (1736-1795). A major group of products of this period consists of *famille rose* pieces. *Famille rose* enamel was made from gold chloride and iron and has a distinctive appearance.

In late 1973 a beautiful, large *famille rose* bottle-form vase with a yellow ground was offered for sale. It was 13 inches high and was covered with *famille rose* enamels with lotus and chrysanthemum

Brilliantly enameled pair of *famille rose* hawks, 10 and 10½ inches high, from the Ch'ien Lung period, brought $86,000 in March, 1974.

scrollings and gilded bandings. The interior was of robin's egg blue. It brought $1,300.

An oviform vase with flaring neck, coated with a speckled green glaze, 11 inches in height, was sold in November, 1973, for $850. A very large (15 inches high) bottle-form vase with incised dragons, a flaming pearl, waves, and rockwork beneath a turquoise blue glaze, brought $1,100. A beautiful bowl, 4⅜ inches in diameter, painted in *famille rose* enamels and decorated with butterflies, fruit, and flower branches, brought $450.

The risks in collecting Chinese ceramics

The greatest risk in collecting Chinese ceramics lies in purchasing a piece which later proves to be not as represented. The inexpert buyer investing large sums should make his purchases from reputable dealers or large auction houses which unconditionally guarantee the period of the pieces they sell. Otherwise only small sums should be put into such ceramics so that if they have no investment value as antiques, they will be worth their cost as home decorations.

There are many Chinese ceramic fakes offered and, unlike most fakes, most of them were done centuries ago. A ninth-century piece might well have been copied in the twelfth century or in the eighteenth century, and a twelfth century piece might have been copied in the nineteenth century.

To become an expert collector of Chinese ceramics who can buy without any guarantee that the piece is genuine and of the period requires long experience. Such experience could begin with detailed examination of pieces in such fine collections as those of the Freer Art Gallery, Washington, D.C.; Cleveland Museum of Art; Brundage Asian Art Center, M. H. deYoung Memorial Museum, San Francisco; Metropolitan Museum of Art, New York; Museum of Fine Arts, Boston; Eugene Fuller Collection, Seattle Art Museum; and the City Art Museum of St. Louis.

The crackle on a piece should be examined under high magnification after one has learned the characteristics of period crackle. There is generally much more crackle on the glazed genuine T'ang pieces than on fakes.

For unglazed ware, the thermal luminescence test is probably the best way to ascertain whether a piece is genuine. This test is administered by the Philadelphia Museum of Art, the Museum of Fine Arts in Boston, and by Dr. Stuart J. Fleming at Oxford University, among others.

The condition of a Chinese ceramic piece is important, but not as important as in the case of European ceramics, since the European pieces were made later, and damages are less common and less excusable in later pieces. The fewer broken fingers on a figure piece, the more it is likely to be worth.

Rarity determines value

There is one general value determinant in Chinese ceramics—rarity. The rare red underglaze makes a piece virtually priceless if it is of the Ming period. In the case of the $92,500 T'ang horse mentioned earlier, the fact that the rider carried a dog in his arms—a rare feature—increased the value.

The less rare the piece, the more damage can affect its value. A very rare red underglaze Ming piece can have more damage with less adverse effect on price than a blue underglaze piece. The piece that was drilled and fitted with electricity for a lamp and then lent to the Brooklyn Museum was certainly damaged by the drilling. It had a rare red underglaze, however, and this made it worth $250,000 to a dealer. Had the underglaze been blue, the piece might well have brought only one-tenth of this price.

The Chinese ceramics that might well be concentrated on now by the investor are the less expensive but beautiful pieces, as these still seem to be something of a bargain.

A bronze by Pierre Jules Mène, *Le Cheval à la Barrière*, signed and dated 1846, was purchased at auction in late 1973 for $3,800. Mène is among the leading sculptors of animalier bronzes, and some of his works appear.to be underpriced at the present time.

CHAPTER 18

Animalier
Bronzes

Bronze statues of animals were produced in France in the nineteenth century, beginning in 1830, by sculptors who specialized in creating these animal bronzes. The bronzes, which range in size from a few inches to a foot or more, are works of art, even though several copies were made of each original statue. Since they are to an extent reproductions, these bronzes may not have the potential of rising sky-high in price.

Animalier bronzes are bronze castings of an original wax model or sand model made by the sculptor. In these works there are two elements of artistry: the making of the original model by the sculptor, and the casting of the metal statues from the original. This metal casting and the finishing of it result in the final product. Some of the animalier sculptors did their own casting, but others used foundries such as Barbedienne, the Susse Frères, and Ganon.

At a recent auction of animalier bronzes in Canterbury, England, one of the buyers—a dealer—asked if there was a foundry mark on a particular statue that was being put up for sale. All selling activity stopped until the name of the foundry was located on the bronze.

It turned out to be one of the very important names: Barbedienne. Without the founder's mark, it is highly unlikely that the piece would have achieved the price it did.

The castings of each animalier bronze were usually not numerous. One edition of a particular animal group by the sculptor Mène, for instance, might be limited to a total of ten copies. Another statue by Mène is known to have been used for forty metal copies. In all, about 200 different statues by Mène are known.

No one knows exactly how many bronzes from a particular wax or sand model actually exist or were even produced by the sculptor's foundry originally. A buyer thus cannot be certain when he purchases an animalier bronze whether he has something unique, or even something relatively unique.

An expert in this field, Jane Horswell, in her standard reference work, *Animalier Bronzes,* lists a number of sculptures by each important animalier sculptor, together with the probable number of copies of each statue in existence. The rarer the edition of any sculpture, generally the more valuable it is.

What to look for

These are the points, in order of importance, to look for when purchasing animalier bronzes:

1. *Originality.* Later casts are not at all in the class or price range of the bronzes cast originally, and they do not represent the same investment potential. At this stage of animalier collecting activity, they should be avoided. Perhaps in the future they too will have artistic and collector value. Later casts not done under the sculptor's supervision lack the fineness of detail and the quality of the patina of the original castings. The original casts were usually worked over a good deal by the artist to make them acceptable semi-original works of art.

There are of course outright fakes on the market and they are usually characterized by far less quality in the casting, and poorer detail and patina of the bronze.

A usual type of fake is a bronze cast from one of the bronzes of the original edition. These fakes are characterized by being just a little smaller than the originals (whose measurements can be determined by reference to Jane Horswell's book). The fakes are almost always of inferior quality.

2. *Signature.* All animalier bronzes should bear the imprint of the sculptor's signature. The artist did not sign each individual piece but he did place an imprint of his signature on the original sculpture from which the bronze statues were made.

3. *The artist.* The work of the great sculptors of animalier

bronzes can be purchased on the market at the present time. Lesser artists may have to be turned to if and when prices rise. The biggest name is Barye, followed by Mène. Probably Fratin and Moigniez follow next. The next sculptors in order of value are quite likely Frémiet and Rosa and Isidore Bonheur.

4. *Size.* As a general rule the larger sizes of bronzes bring proportionately more money today.

5. *Quality.* A fairly extended examination of offerings in the field of animalier bronzes indicates that quality ranks fifth as a determinant of value. In assessing the quality of a piece, the excellence of the sculpture as a work of art should come first, followed by finish, and then patina. If the statue "does not look like much," it will probably not be worth much. Beauty and quality of execution must be present for the piece to have value.

6. *Rarity.* Generally, all other things being equal, the rarer the piece the greater its value. It is expected that in the future rarity will be far more important than it is at the present time as a value determinant.

7. *Number of figures.* All other factors being equal, the greater the number of figures in a bronze the more it is worth.

8. *Elaborateness of the base and of the setting.* These elements add greatly to the artistic merit of any bronze and required much additional work on the part of the sculptor. Some bronzes have flowers, rocks, and grass on the base. In the future the base and setting may well be very much more important as a value determinant than at present.

Collectors believe that many pieces being offered today as original animalier bronzes are actually later copies. Sotheby's Belgravia gallery in London is extremely cautious in its attribution of animalier bronzes so as to protect the buyer. In a recent sale this gallery offered "A Rare Bronze Figure of a Camel" by Delabrière, signed and dated 1849, 11½ inches high. The statue brought $387. The very next lot was listed as "A Bronze Figure of a Labrador" *after* Delabrière, signed, 8 inches high. This lot brought $687— hardly an "after Delabrière" price. The next lot was also 8 inches high and listed as "after Delabrière"—and realized $675. The buyers apparently thought they were more knowledgeable than the gallery in the matter of attribution.

The subject matter of animalier bronzes is somewhat controversial. Many of them depict animal conflicts or suffering animals. Still, a statue of a dying stag does not necessarily sell at a discount simply because it is not a pleasant piece for the living room.

The creators of animalier bronzes

The leading sculptors of animalier bronzes are:

Antoine-Louis Barye (1795-1875) is the outstanding animalier sculptor in popularity and in price. Even as late as the 1920s possibly hundreds of thousands of his lions were turned out and sold in department stores and specialty stores. These lions were of plaster and painted in the characteristic Barye green. They have no collector value as far as animalier bronzes are concerned.

Barye was the great innovator and the other animalier sculptors were to a considerable extent his followers. In 1831, Barye exhibited at the prestigious French Salon a group of animals entitled *The Tiger Devouring a Gavial*. This group was an instantaneous success and was purchased immediately by the French Minister of the Interior for the Luxemburg Palace.

From that time on, Barye never lacked commissions for his work. In 1833 he again exhibited at the French Salon, this time his *Lion and Serpent*. The government purchased this work too. The Duke of Orleans and the Duke of Nemours, the two sons of Louis Philippe, also purchased Barye's works. Upon the close of this showing at the salon, Barye was awarded the Legion of Honor.

Barye began to manufacture for the general public in the 1840s. In 1847 he issued his first sales catalog in which were listed 107 different sculptures. From 1848 to 1850 he was curator of the Louvre. When he left this post he again began to sell to the public and in the 1850s he issued four more sales catalogs.

The United States and France have the finest collections of Barye's work in the world. The Walters Art Gallery in Baltimore and the Corcoran Gallery of Art in Washington are repositories for many of his greatest works.

Recently a Barye serpent and lion group, 10 inches long, was offered. This is one of Barye's better works, found in the collections of seven museums in the United States. The asking price was about $1,900. This group sometimes sells for up to twice this figure.

Barye's important *Turkish Horse (Cheval Turc)*, 15 inches high, can sell for up to $10,000, while his *Reclining Bear*, 3 inches high and not rare, brings up to $750. His *Little Fawn Recumbent*, 2¾ inches high, brings about $750. The little rabbit with raised ears, 2 inches high, and the seated hare, 4 inches high, might each be purchased for $250.

Pierre Jules Mène (1810-1879), like Barye, spent much time at the Paris zoo studying animal forms and movements. He exhibited at the French Salon and twice received the First Class Medal. In 1861 he received the Cross of the Legion of Honor. Twice he exhibited in the Great Exhibition in England. He became a tremendous artistic and commercial success. His sculptures are anatomically correct and filled with movement. In these respects he had no peer, not even Barye.

Large bronze group of a tiger killing an antelope, by the outstanding animalier sculptor, Antoine-Louis Barye, sold for $1,200 in 1973.

Recently a medium-sized Mène statue of a setter, 6½ inches in height, was offered for sale in London. The asking price was a little less than $500. A tiny Mène setter was offered for $200. The same firm offered a rare Mène horse and foal, 18 inches high, for $3,000, which is less than the general market price.

Some of the works of Mène, like those of Barye, seem to be underpriced. Two setters and a mallard on an elaborate base, 17½ inches long, was for sale recently for about $1,000. A rare Mène of two pointers might sell for $500 or even less.

Jules Moigniez (1835-1894) is without peer in the sculpture of birds. He did not produce the usual animalier subjects of one animal attacking or devouring another. From age twenty-four on, Moigniez exhibited at the Salon, and in 1861 he showed at the Great Exhibition in London.

One of the best recent offerings of the work of Moigniez was a pair of dogs, large sculptures, for $850 the pair. The bases were ovals of grass, rocks, and plants. The patina of the bronzes was excellent.

One London dealer recently offered for sale a statue of a fairly large heron for about $135.

At the present time a top-quality Moigniez can probably be purchased for $2,000, and little bronzes of dogs or cows can be acquired for about $125 each.

Emmanuel Frémiet (1824-1910) is perhaps best known for his Jeanne d'Arc on horseback in the Place de Rivoli in Paris. The French government presented a duplicate of this statue to the United States, where it can be seen in Meridian Hill Park in Washington.

It seems to be a characteristic of the animalier bronze sculptors that they met with instant public and artistic acclaim. Frémiet was no exception. Many of his works were purchased by the French government. He was made a Grand Officer of the Legion of Honor and an Associate of the Royal Academy in England. He first exhibited at the Salon when he was nineteen years old. His exhibitions over the years at the Salon were prodigious in volume. He also exhibited in the Exposition Universelle and in the Centenary Exhibition of French Art as well as in the Louvre. He met with equal success in countries other than France.

Recently a little heron was offered in London for sale for $170. Important Frémiets, however, bring high prices, and *Two Racehorses and Jockeys,* a rare piece, 18 inches high, can sell for $5,000.

At this time, $1,000 to $1,500 might purchase an excellent Frémiet, 10 or 11 inches high, while little models up to 4 inches in height might be acquired for $500 or less.

Christophe Fratin (1800-1864) first exhibited at the Salon in 1831 and thereafter continuously until 1862. Fratin's output of bronzes, while small, was of excellent quality. His large group, *Two Eagles*, is on display in Central Park in New York. After his exhibition in England in 1851 there was considerable critical opinion to the effect that he was the greatest of all of the animalier bronze sculptors.

A box with a deer on the top was recently offered in London. It was about 8 inches long and 6 inches high. The price was $360. A statue of a small cow was offered by the same dealer for $350, and a mare and foal of medium size for $562. Another dealer offered a medium-size statue of a bear for $837.

Isidore Bonheur (1827-1901) was the brother of painter Rosa Bonheur. Like his sister, Bonheur specialized in the depiction of horses, and especially the movement of horses.

In 1848, Bonheur made his debut at the Salon, where he exhibited *An African Horseman Attacking a Lion*. He won medals for his work in 1865 and in 1869. In 1889 he received the Gold Medal at the Exposition Universelle.

Recently there was offered in London a large and important Bonheur horse for about $1,250. A sculpture of two hunting dogs, perhaps 12 inches long, was for sale for $575, a low price considering the importance of the work.

Bonheur's important statues are relatively expensive. His *Mare and Foal*, 7 inches high, might well bring above $3,500. His large *Racehorse and Jockey*, 25 inches long, would sell for a similar price. On the other hand a cow or a group of cows might bring only $650 to $700, even though the figure or group would measure over 12 inches in length. Most of Bonheur's statues are in the $1,000 class.

For about $1,000, a very good Rosa Bonheur bronze might be purchased, although her works number fewer than a dozen in all and are quite rare on the market.

Auguste-Nicolas Cain was Mène's son-in-law. Between 1847 and 1888 he exhibited thirty-eight of his works in the Salon, and he was well supplied with government commissions to adorn public parks and buildings. Cain specialized in the "animal struggle" type of bronze that was popular at the time of the animaliers but that was rejected in certain circles as being too heartless for public display.

A short time ago a small Cain statue of a bear with a shell-shaped dish under each arm was offered for about $435 in London. For $500 a statue of a donkey 5 inches long could be purchased. For about the same price Cain's *Heron*, about 14 inches long, is sometimes available. A rooster, 6 inches long, can at times be purchased for $250.

The other animaliers

The "big names" should probably be concentrated on at the present time as they are still available at prices within the means of many collectors. If the upward trend of interest in animalier bronzes continues, however, other sculptors may have to be purchased as the important animaliers move out of reach. Some of these other sculptors are: Alphonse-Alexandre Arson, Alfred Barye, son of Antoine-Louis Barye, Paul Comolera, Paul-Edouard Delabrière, Alfred Dubucand, Georges Dardet, Paul-Joseph-Raymond Gayrard, John Willis Good, Pierre Lenordez, Arthur-Marie-Gabriel, LeComte du Passage, Ferdinand Potrot, LeComte G. de Ruille, Emmanuel de Santa Coloma, and Charles Valton.

These animaliers appear less frequently on the markets: Jean-François-Théodore Gechter, Jean-Léon Gerome, Emile-Joseph-Alexandre Goujet, Hippolyte Heizler, Louis-Théophile Hingre, Henri-Alfred-Marie Jacquemart, Dominique Laquis, Lambert Alexandre Leonard, Clovis-Edmond Masson, Georges Malissard, Victor Peter, Pierre Rouillard, John Macallan Swan, and Waagen.

Price trends

At the time the animalier bronzes first appeared in the early nineteenth century they, unlike almost all other art, were a complete success from the point of view of public acclaim and buyer interest. Animalier bronzes have never returned to anything like this early preeminance. In recent years they have been coming back into public favor almost unobtrusively. Prices rose steadily in the early 1970s. Then, in the summer of 1972, a sale took place in Paris which may forecast the market to come. In this sale the price of Barye bronzes about quadrupled.

From 1972 to the early part of 1974, prices of animalier bronzes doubled. Still, auction houses as a rule do not have separate sales of such bronzes, although recently there has been some grouping of them in catalogs and sales, and a Barye sale was held in New York.

Major auction houses are not particularly interested in animalier bronzes and bronze collections. Sotheby's Belgravia gallery and the smaller auction houses from time to time make good offerings of these works. In Canterbury, England, Worsfold's specializes in them, and in one recent sale forty-five such bronzes were offered.

Animalier bronzes are not usually offered by important art dealers of the United States and Europe, but are still occasionally found in antique and curio shops.

Except for contemporary, and particularly abstract, works, the art-buying public has not turned to sculpture to any appreciable degree, and animalier bronzes are a division of sculpture. This type of sculpture is not entirely original of course, and the question is not, "Is it an original?" but rather, "How many of this one are there?" This "copy" character of animalier bronzes may limit collector interest in them.

Animalier bronzes for the most part lack distinct color. They tend to be a dull natural bronze, although many of them have developed an interesting patina. Still, they do not sparkle and thus are unobtrusive as a part of the decor of the modern home. Also, the subject matter of animals killing one another does not increase their decorative possibilities.

Still, the price trend is definitely up and, considering the artistic acclaim these bronzes once had, it is not unreasonable to forecast a continuing rise in the market. Such bronzes can be purchased for modest sums of money, particularly while the collector is learning about them. They are certainly works of art, to a considerable extent original, and they have definite merit. It may well be that the European market will rise faster than the market in the United States with its fairly large supply and relatively few collectors, which creates a very favorable climate for collecting this form of art.

One of a pair of fine Kashan silk rugs purchased in 1973 for $11,000. As is characteristic of Persian rugs, the border is in the form of a frame and the design embodies natural subjects—animals, birds, trees, and flowers. Kashans of good quality are available for about $1,000.

Oriental Rugs and Carpets

In the lobby of Sotheby Parke Bernet, the auction house in New York, there is a large Oriental carpet, measuring 15 by 25 feet. It was made in Persia in about 1850.

This carpet was placed in the lobby in 1970 by its owner, Vojtech Blau, the rug dealer located in the same building as Sotheby Parke Bernet. Although thousands of people walk over the carpet every week, often tracking in rain, snow, and dirt, there is no detectable wear on it.

A short time ago the carpet was priced at $9,500. Today it is worth perhaps $15,000. A carpet such as this would have sold in 1968 for $5,500. In 1964, it would have sold for $3,500, and in 1960, its price probably would have been $1,500. The price thus may well have risen ten times in less than fifteen years, and this rise is not at all unusual for the better Oriental carpets.

The carpet in the lobby is a Bijar, made of a very tough wool. Sometimes camel's hair is used in Bijars. In the February 1, 1974, sale of Oriental rugs and carpets at Sotheby Parke Bernet, a Bijar runner, 3 feet wide and 15 feet long, with a red field woven with polygons in pale blue, ivory, and rose, and enclosed by a crab pattern border, brought $650. This was a more modest Bijar than the one in the lobby but still the same make that has lasted like iron under the feet of people visiting the galleries.

Types of Oriental rugs and carpets

The five major categories of antique Oriental rugs and carpets are *Persian, Caucasian, Turkestan, Anatolian,* and *Turkish.*

The fine, antique Persian rugs and carpets and the finest, antique silk rugs in general rose in price about 100 percent in 1973. Caucasian rugs and carpets had a big price rise a few years earlier than the Persians. A Kazak, a Caucasian rug, brought $6,000 at auction in 1971, a very high price for the time, and the rug measured only about 5 by 7 feet. The rise in Caucasian rugs began about the middle of 1971. By 1973 the price level of these rugs was very high, and the rate of increase slackened off.

In 1968, Vojtech Blau, the rug and carpet dealer, sold a similar Kazak rug, 5 feet by 7.6 feet, in pristine condition, for $1,500. Today it would bring between $6,000 and $7,000. Blau sold another Kazak, made in about 1800, for $2,500 in 1968. It would be worth about $10,000 today.

A Saryk—one of the many Turkestan rugs—sold for $2,500 in 1970. It was in excellent condition and measured 10.4 by 6.4 feet. Today it would bring $8,000 to $10,000.

An example of the price rise in Anatolians is an antique Bergama (or Bergamo) rug, 6.7 by 5.10 feet. This rug—made in the eighteenth century—sold in 1968 for $2,500. Today it would bring $15,000.

By far the largest percentage of all investment-quality rugs and carpets are Oriental. Following is a guide to the five basic types of these rugs and carpets:

Persian. The country today corresponding most nearly to ancient Persia is Iran. The great age of Oriental rugs in Persia was the sixteenth and seventeenth century. In that era designers, artisans, and patrons combined to create a new artistic excellence in carpet making. Of great importance was the fact that Shah Abbas the Great patronized rug making. At the end of the sixteenth century Shah Abbas moved his capital from Tabriz to Isfahan. Both these cities gained fame as sources for the finest Oriental rugs and carpets of that era.

The rugs and carpets of Persia are renowned for these characteristics:

• A fine balance between the center and the field.

Eighteenth century Bergama rug, 6.7 by 5.10 foot, was sold in 1968 for $2,500 and is valued today at $15,000.

- A border in the form of a frame—a broad band with a continuous motif.
  - Designs from nature—flowers, animals, birds, and trees.
  - A large medallion in the center.
  - The use of silk.

Some of the best-known Persian carpets are Tabriz, Kashan, Meshed, Kerman, Isphahan (Isfahan), Karadagh, Sarouk, Hamadan, Sarabend, Feraghan, Gorevan, Heriz, Sehna, Bijar, and Shiraz.

In February, 1974, a Tabriz silk prayer rug, 5.2 by 4.2 feet, made in the nineteenth century, of excellent design and in fine condition, brought $7,250. In the same sale a Kashan embossed silk rug, 7.4 by 4.7 feet and about sixty years old, sold for $7,750. On the other hand, in the same sale a much more modest Tabriz silk rug, 5.4 by 4.1 feet and not "antique," brought only $500, and a good Kashan rug, 4.7 by 7 feet, brought $1,000.

Caucasian. The origin of these rugs is mainly what is now Armenia in the Soviet Union. The main characteristics are:

- The use of geometric patterns rather than curves.
  - A field often divided into diagonal bands with small patterns.
  - Sometimes large rosettes along the border.
  - Wool is the main material.
  - The weave is generally coarse—under 100 knots per square inch.
  - The pile is short.
  - Blue, terra cotta, red, ivory, yellow, and green are among the colors used.
  - They are extremely durable.

Most Caucasian rugs are the products of nomadic tribes. Some of the main types are Daghestan, Kabistan, Shirvan, Chichi, Baku, Kazak, and Karabagh.

Early in 1974, an antique Kazak rug, 6 by 6.9 feet, brought $2,600. A fair Kazak, not antique, 3.5 by 6.2 feet, sold for $425, and a Kazak runner, also not antique, 3.4 by 11 feet, sold for $700.

Turkestan. Now a part of the Soviet Union, Turkestan is located north of Iran and Afghanistan and east of the Caspian Sea. Characteristics of Turkestan rugs and carpets are:

- Red, in various shades, as the usual dominant color.
  - The knotting of the rugs is very close.
  - The pile is short.
  - Sheep's wool and goats' hair are used.
  - Some show a geometric design.

Antique Heriz carpet, 15.8 by 12.3 feet, purchased for about $5,500, increased in value in a few years to more than $15,000 in 1974.

Most Turkestan rugs were made by nomadic tribes. In the eastern part of Turkestan (Samarkand), there is clear Chinese influence on the design. Some of the representative rugs of Turkestan are Tekke-Turkoman, Beshir-Turkoman, Afghan, Baluchistan, and Samarkand.

In early 1974 a Tekke-Turkoman carpet, 6.7 by 9.2 feet, sold for $500. A Beshir-Turkoman, 12.2 by 5.4 feet, realized $750.

Anatolian. Anatolia is generally synonymous with Asia Minor—the peninsula forming the western extremity of Asia. It is bounded by the Black Sea, the Aegean Sea, and the Mediterranean Sea, and encompasses most of Asiatic Turkey.

The main characteristics of Anatolian rugs are:

• Geometric design in early products.
• Persian curves and medallion used from the sixteenth century.

Some types of Anatolian rugs are Hereke, especially silk prayer rugs with the mirab or dome-shape, prayer-niche motif, Ghiordes woolen prayer rugs, Bergama, Oushak, and Kilim.

Outstanding in the February, 1974, rug sale was an antique Hereke silk and metal-thread prayer rug with the dome, or mirab, design in the center. The rug was 3.9 by 2.7 feet, and the design and weave were extremely fine. It realized $16,000. A similar rug, 5.2 by 3.10 feet, made in about 1800, has a present value of from $12,000 to $15,000. It was sold in 1968 for $2,500.

Not all Anatolian rugs are this high in price, and in the early 1974 sale a Kilim rug, 8.7 by 4.9 feet, brought only $500.

Turkish. The category "Turkish" generally denotes later carpets. The term is also used in the sale room to describe a rug whose city of origin is not known.

Value elements

The rugs in greatest demand are the so-called antiques, and these are at least 100 years old. Semi-antiques are also in great demand, and these are about 50 to 100 years old. However, it is quite difficult to date rugs exactly.

The rugs and carpets of investment quality are always handmade. They are usually knotted and not the flat weave. The knotted material is principally sheep's wool, silk, and cotton. The wool is the main material used for the pile and to a lesser extent for the warp and weft. In the finest rugs, silk is employed for pile, warp, and weft. Cotton is often used for warp and weft and is sometimes used for the pile, but wool is preferred for pile.

The pile is the essence of the composition of Oriental carpets.

The value of this Ghiordes prayer rug, 5.2 by 3.10 feet, circa 1800, increased from $2,500 in 1968 to between $12,000 and $15,000 in 1974.

Rugs made for the Persian court can have 800 or more knots to the square inch. Most Persian carpets in which wool was used for the pile have 90 to 180 knots per square inch.

Beginning with the premise that an Oriental rug or carpet of value should be antique or semi-antique and that it should be of fine construction and excellent design, then the next value element is condition. However, condition is a relative term, and one cannot expect a rug made in 1800 to be in the condition of one made in 1974. Rug experts use a special word when speaking of condition. It is "respect." If a ten-year-old rug is stained and has moth holes, the dealer or expert will say that he has no "respect" for it. On the other hand, the same condition in a fifteenth- or sixteenth-century rug may call forth from the dealer or expert a good deal of "respect." Condition is related to age, but the better the condition, all other things being equal, the higher the value of the rug or carpet.

The fine rugs for investment have a low pile, and the finest ones are "flat." Still, the pile should be high in relation to what it was originally. The pile in all rugs diminishes with use, and one must know about how high the pile should be in a good antique Kazak, for example, or that an Anatolian Kilim has no pile, and is flat-woven and thin. One should also know that the very thick pile was developed for the American market early in this century.

After condition, the next most important element of value is rarity. The scarcity of a particular type of rug or carpet is important. So is rarity of design, and sometimes a type of rug in plentiful supply will have great value because it has a design used only in a limited number of rugs. Also important is that the rug and the design must be beautiful. Value depends to a considerable extent on how much of a "work of art" the rug is.

Demand is a value element of great importance. If it is a rare and fine carpet but is not in demand, it will not be of much commercial value. This is the situation at the present time with regard to Aubusson carpets from France. Unless they are very early and in "like new" condition, Aubussons are simply not in demand and bring virtually nothing on the auction market. Of course, one element which is basic to demand is fashion. As recently as ten years ago the Aubusson carpet was highly respected and highly valued.

In the last quarter of the nineteenth century, Oriental carpets and rugs were the hallmark of the well-to-do. Most of the houses of the very rich contained Oriental carpets. The John D. Rockefeller home in New York City was almost entirely furnished in the fashionable "Turkish taste" of that era. Many homes had a so-called smoking corner with furniture designed in the Far Eastern manner and with Oriental rugs on the floor. The desire for things Oriental in Europe and America had become a near-craze.

The fashion for fine rugs continued in Europe and America in the early part of this century, but died out in the era of the Great Depression. Functionalism was the new artistic concept. Oriental carpets were out of fashion to all but connoisseurs and collectors. Few decorators seemed to want such "floor ornaments."

During the last two decades, interest in Oriental rugs and carpets has revived, and they are almost basic to the furnishing of a fine home. The Caucasian geometrical patterns fit in well with even the most modern interior, and the flowering Persian motifs go well with traditional furniture and fine English and American antiques. The trend to fine rugs and carpets for decoration and as an investment, with the exception of Aubussons, seems likely to continue.

Buying rugs and carpets

There are two main sources of rugs and carpets—auctions and dealers. The smaller auction houses in New York have had almost a monopoly on the auctioning of Oriental rugs. For decades, they have conducted periodic auctions in which only rugs and carpets were offered, and many of these were of investment quality. A good number of the items were put up for auction by dealers and there were usually firm reserves.

Since 1972, Sotheby Parke Bernet has held auctions devoted exclusively to rugs, which come from estates for the most part rather than from dealers. At the present time about 95 percent of these auction offerings are privately owned rugs and carpets.

Dealers dominate the buying at all rug auctions. At the Sotheby Parke Bernet galleries they do about 30 percent of the purchasing, and tend to buy the most expensive and finest rugs. At other auctions the dealer group is present in force, examining every carpet and rug coming up for sale. A serious collector can watch how dealers inspect rugs and adopt their methods. He can also discuss particular rugs with the dealers, and benefit from their knowledge.

Relatively few private buyers attend the major rug auctions regularly. There are perhaps thirty to fifty families who buy rugs and carpets regularly at the leading New York auction house, and they buy both for home decoration and for investment.

At the present time auction houses appear to sell at prices which average about one-half of dealer prices. The dealer usually marks up his rugs and carpets 100 percent, as is standard procedure for many works of art, antiques, and other collectibles. The dealer price is, however, subject to some negotiation, so the best buys are not necessarily limited to auctions.

The dealer generally buys the best in order to sell his customers the best. However, determining what is the best, as well as what is poor merchandise, is a highly technical matter.

Suggestions for the investor

A would-be investor in rugs and carpets should:

1. Spend at least one month studying all available books on the subject of carpets and rugs. *The Book of Rugs Oriental and European* by Ignaz Schlosser, Bonanza Books, New York, is a good starting point. It can be used as a directory, so that if you are offered a Kilim runner, for example, you can refer to this book to learn about the materials used for this type of rug, its origin, and its special features. In addition, the book contains a map showing the cities of origin of many Oriental rugs.

2. Talk with rug dealers and with rug specialists in the auction houses. Examine rugs with auction officials and with dealers to learn what constitutes value and how to judge condition.

3. Buy recent priced catalogs of the auction houses to get an idea of price levels and trends. Such catalogs could well include those of the Plaza Art Galleries in New York, which has probably sold as many carpets over the years as any auction house in the United States. The illustrated rug catalogs of the Sotheby Parke Bernet galleries might also be purchased. They cost very little and show exactly what was sold and at what price.

4. Buy the better rugs. It is not necessary to buy the best, which are often priced extremely high, but buy very good rugs, as these are most likely to appreciate in value and can be resold to dealers or at auction with the least chance of rejection.

5. Buy antique or semi-antique rugs and carpets. Newer rugs and carpets have appreciated in value, but antiques and semi-antiques appear to be more certain investments.

6. Seek out rugs with fine material, workmanship, and design, as these are important to price appreciation over the years. The signs of fine quality and design can be learned by visiting dealers and by studying authoritative books containing color illustrations.

7. Buy rugs in excellent condition—with little wear and little or no repairs or recoloring.

To protect your investment in fine rugs and carpets, you should:

Place carpets (which by definition are 6 feet by 9 feet or larger) on the floor away from sunlight and high heat, away from metal casters and very heavy pieces of furniture, and away from the front door so that dirt is not constantly tracked in on them. If there is no space on the floor for them, carpets can be rolled, but not folded for long periods as folds tend to cause cracks.

Rugs (which by definition are under 6 feet by 9 feet) can be "stored" on the wall, provided warp threads can stand the strain.

PART FIVE

Investing in Hobbies

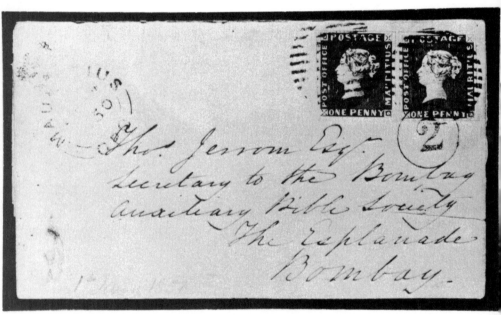

A philatelic world record price of $380,000 was paid in 1968 for this Mauritius cover. Even modestly priced stamps have appreciated substantially in recent years. Investors are finding that stamps provide an excellent hedge against inflation and weak currency.

CHAPTER 20

Stamps

Acting on the instructions of "a prominent New Yorker," the Guaranty Trust Company of New York City purchased stamps on several occasions in 1943 and 1944 for the account of this gentleman. The stamps were purchased from the store of J.W. Scott in New York and were placed in the client's safe-deposit box as an investment. There they remained until 1973, when the now Morgan Guaranty Trust Company sent the stamps to the international stamp auction house of H.R. Harmer in New York, with instructions to dispose of them at auction as the owner had died.

On February 6 and 7, 1973, the foreign stamps in the "philatelic portfolio" were sold, and on February 22 and 23, the United States stamps were sold. The British Commonwealth stamps had cost about $13,000 when purchased in 1943 and 1944. They realized $30,000—two and a half times their cost. The foreign stamps brought $58,000. They had cost about $20,000, so their realization was three to one. The stamps of the United States returned $60,000. Since they had cost about $9,000, their return-to-cost ratio was almost six and three-quarters to one.

In the British Commonwealth group of stamps, Australia rose to a ratio of nine to one. Canada rose from $218 to $2,209, making a selling price to cost ratio of just over ten to one. Newfoundland did poorly by comparison, rising from $608 to $1,074, a one and one-half to one ratio.

While the investment made by the bank for this particular client was strong in three main divisions of the stamp market—British Commonwealth, American, and foreign—it was weak in the older stamps which are known as classics. The "investment portfolio" did contain a few classics, however, and their costs, selling prices, and cost-price ratios are listed on page 267. Some of the costs in relation to prices in the foreign group of these auctioned stamps are shown on page 268.

The overall performance of this stamp investment portfolio was:

Original cost: $42,000
Selling price: $150,000
Net of $120,000 on gross realization of $150,000
Profit: $78,000

Stamp prices have increased substantially since 1972. The table on page 270 shows the price growth for representative stamps in each of the three categories: United States, British Commonwealth, and foreign. In each case the grade is a "very fine copy." When the word "mint" is used, it means a stamp with complete original gum which may have a light hinge at the back. The hinge is a small piece of tape which permits the stamp to be affixed in an album without moistening the glue on the stamp. A never-hinged stamp is usually worth at least 10 percent more, and sometimes the issues of a few countries, such as the Vatican and Israel, are worth 50 to 75 percent more if they have never been hinged.

America ranks high in degree of price appreciation, as it does in most collectibles. Europe ranks even higher in price appreciation, and Asian stamp prices in 1971 were five times their 1958 base.

An example of the appreciation of American stamps is the 1918 airpost twenty-four-cent stamp on which the airplane is inverted. One of these stamps was auctioned by H.R. Harmer in 1964 for $15,500, was resold by them in 1969 for $31,000, and again sold by them in May, 1974, for $47,000—a record price for an American stamp.

Not very many serious collectors

It would probably be difficult to find someone who did not collect at least a few stamps during his life—particularly during his early years. In most cases, this early tendency to collect stamps dies out

How Classic Stamps Have Risen in Value

Country	1943-44 Cost	1973 Selling Price	Markup
Austria			
(1858-59, 3 kr., type 1, used)	$ 5	$ 30	6 to 1
Denmark			
(1851, 2 rs., 1st printing, unused)	42.50	900	23½ to 1
Dutch Indies			
(1864, 10-cent Lake, original gum)	14	50	3½ to 1
Germany			
Bavaria (1849, 1 kr., two used)	72.50	860	12 to 1
Bavaria (1850-58, 18 kr., used)	8.25	65	8 to 1
Hannover (1859-61, ½ g., rose gumé, o.g.)	19	150	8 to 1
Oldenburg (1852-55, 1/3 sgr., o.g.)	34.50	170	5 to 1
Saxony (1850, 3 pf., used)	225	3,400	15 to 1
Württemburg (1873, 70 kr., red violet, unused)	70	170	2½ to 1
(70 kr., violet, thinned)	55	260	5 to 1
Norway			
(1855, 4 sk., 3 copies, used)	9	86.50	9½ to 1
Spain			
(1850, 10 r., used)	40	135	3½ to 1

How Foreign Stamps Have Appreciated

Country	1943-44 Cost	1973 Selling Price	Markup
Japan			
(1908 and 1924)	$ 97	$2,225	23 to 1
Italy			
(mostly rare airpost)	227	4,212	19 to 1
Monaco	670	5,504	8 to 1
German States	876	6,374	7 to 1
San Marino			
(1928 on)	294	1,760	6 to 1
Spain			
(semipostals and airpost)	211	1,297	6 to 1
France			
(mostly sets with airpost)	746	2,738	3¾ to 1
Austria			
(mostly sets)	449	1,218	3 to 1
Belgium			
(mostly sets)	983	2,463	2½ to 1
Egypt	988	1,420	1½ to 1
Uruguay	250	307	1½ to 1
Venezuela	42	22	½ to 1

as the person becomes older. Still, there are approximately six million active and semi-active stamp collectors in the United States today. The vast majority of this number would have to be classed in the semi-active category.

Serious stamp collectors are few, considering the number who collect stamps in their youth and the reputation of stamp collecting as the number one collection hobby in the country, if not in the world. There are probably about 25,000 to 50,000 serious stamp collectors in the United States. These are the collectors who regularly buy stamps offered by the major dealers and auction houses.

The business of auctioning postage stamps is prodigious. There are three main auction houses specializing in stamps in New York City: H.R. Harmer, Robert A. Siegel Auction Galleries, and Harmer, Rooke and Company. The H.R. Harmer firm, with its London affiliate, sells at auction each year about $6 million worth of stamps. In New York, this firm holds twenty-five auctions each year and each of these auctions has a duration of two or three days, with some lasting as long as four days, for a total of sixty to sixty-five sessions a year. These large stamp auction houses sell on commission only. Unlike many of the smaller houses in this field, they do not first buy and then auction off what they have bought.

Adding together all of the auctions held by all of the stamp auction houses in New York City, we arrive at a total of about three stamp auctions held every working day during ten months of the year. Only in July and August is almost no auction business done. In addition to the auction houses, there are about one hundred stamp dealers in New York City and several thousand dealers throughout the country.

Over half of the stamps offered at auction come from estates. Most of the rest of the stamps for sale at auction come from older collectors who would like to liquidate their collections toward the end of their lives or from collectors who have achieved "completeness" in a particular country and want to move on to different philatelic fields. Very few stamps come from dealers. At art and antique auctions, very often reserves are set by the owners. These reserves are the minimum prices at which they will sell. Such reserves are almost unknown in stamp auctions, and when the auctioneer's gavel falls, the stamp (or the lot, as it is called) is sold. Perhaps only 1 percent of the stamps offered at auction have reserves.

Collectors often attend the more important stamp sales, but many have stamp dealers who buy as their agents. The collectors and agents (dealers) acting for collectors total about 60 percent of the buyers at auctions. The remaining 40 percent are dealers buying for their inventory.

The Increase in Stamp Prices, 1972-73

	Jan. 1972	End of 1973	Percent Increase
United States			
1847 5¢, used			
(first general issue in U.S.)	$100	$ 140	40
1893 Columbian $5, mint	800	1,200	50
1926 White Plains			
2¢ sheet of 25, mint	80	130	62½
Presidential $5, mint	20	40	100
Airpost 1930			
Zeppelin set, mint	450	650	44½
British Commonwealth			
Great Britain, 1929			
U.P.U. 1 pound, mint	105	150	43
Canada, 1897			
Jubilee $2, mint	210	325	55
Newfoundland, 1933			
Gen. Balbo $4.50, mint	150	120	−20
Foreign			
Austria, 1936			
Dollfuss 10 s., mint	155	220	42
France, 1937			
Paris Exhibition sheet, mint	26	38	46
Japan, 1934			
Philatelic Exhibition sheet, mint	160	230	44
Vatican, 1934			
Provisional set, mint	850	1,200	41

Average Increase in Two Years 46½%

Stamps are sometimes mailed to customers for viewing before a sale, and many bids are sent by mail to the stamp auctions. Stamp bids are also sent by Telex and are telephoned. The catalogs of the major auction houses are not only prepared with extreme care, but feature descriptions which use the terminology of *Scott's Standard Postage Stamp Catalogue* and sometimes other catalogs such as that of Stanley Gibbons (London). The values quoted in these catalogs are also printed in the auction catalogs for the guidance of stamp buyers.

Stamp auctions move at a tremendous rate of speed. The Sotheby Parke Bernet art and antique auctions sell about sixty lots an hour. In the smaller auctions, items move at a rate of perhaps eighty to one hundred lots an hour. In the stamp auctions, about three lots are sold each minute. This is close to 200 lots per hour, and in a three-day sale, over 2,000 lots may be sold.

Examples of stamp investments

The sale of three highly significant collections indicates both the investment significance of stamps in prosperity and depression and the price trend over the years.

The first of these is the Arthur Hind collection, which was sold at the very bottom of the depression of the 1930s. Arthur Hind, a businessman, began collecting stamps in 1891 at the age of thirty-five while residing near Utica, New York. In 1903 he began a series of world travels and apparently on each trip purchased entire and notable collections of stamps. He continued to purchase stamps until 1929, with particular emphasis on those of the United States and of the Confederate States.

Upon the death of Mr. Hind, his executors undertook to dispose of the stamps. The probate court listed, valued, and grouped all of the Hind assets. In total dollar value, the stamps ranked below four other categories of assets.

A portion of the stamps was sold in the United States at auction —from November 20 to 24, 1933, a poor time economically, to say the least. They realized $250,000 and did not make the probate appraisal.

The rest of the stamp collection was sold by the executors at the probate price to a syndicate formed by Mr. Hind's nephew, who had agreed to sell the stamps through H. R. Harmer, and that organization then proceeded to auction the stamps in London. They brought from 30 to 40 percent over the probate price, and realized a total of $750,000.

The liquidation of Mr. Hind's entire estate resulted in a new ranking: the stamps were the number one asset of the estate. It would be hard to find any other collectible which could have made

How Stamps From Different Areas Have Climbed in Price

1958-1971

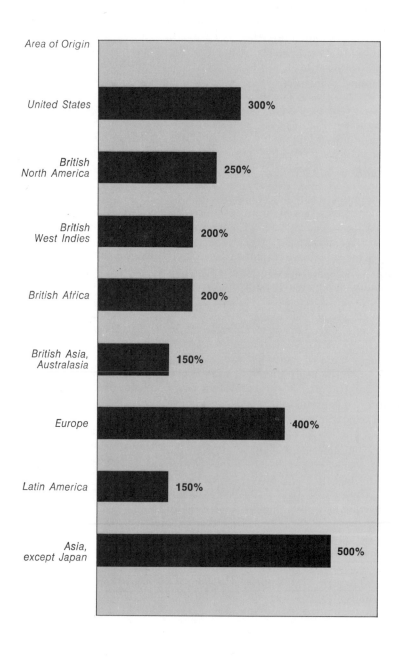

Area of Origin

United States — 300%

British North America — 250%

British West Indies — 200%

British Africa — 200%

British Asia, Australasia — 150%

Europe — 400%

Latin America — 150%

Asia, except Japan — 500%

such an outstanding price showing in the trough of the depression.

A highly significant stamp sale took place in a series of sixteen auctions in the 1950s, when the Alfred H. Caspary collection was sold. These sales were spaced widely apart and held from November, 1955, to October, 1958. The total realized was an almost unbelievable $2,895,146. Stamps reached a higher price level in this sale than had existed in the past, and thus achieved a new importance as investments.

From October, 1968, to December, 1970, part of the Louise Boyd Dale collection of stamps was disposed of in ten sales by H.R. Harmer of New York. The total realization of these sales was $2,897,657.

Under the terms of Mrs. Dale's will, much of the collection was bequeathed to a foundation. This latter group of stamps was worth approximately 50 percent of the value of the portion sold, making the total collection enormously valuable.

In the Dale sale of October 21, 1968, an envelope with two stamps affixed to it achieved a philatelic world record price. The stamps were the Mauritius "Post Office" issue of 1847. Both were one-penny stamps. The envelope was addressed to the Secretary of the Bombay Auxiliary Bible Society, The Esplanade, Bombay. The stamped envelope, containing a letter, was purchased by the Raymond H. Weill Company of New Orleans for $380,000.

Sales volume

Sales of stamps throughout the world have increased sharply, particularly in the last twenty years. In the period beginning in 1950 and ending at the present time, stamp sales volume more than tripled, with only a slight downward drift in the recession year (and stock market retreat) of 1970.

Stamps can be divided into three historical categories. "Moderns" were issued between 1910 and the present. "Middles" date from about the 1890s to 1910. "Classics" include those produced from the advent of the postage stamp in 1840 to the 1890s. In the price drop of 1970, the classics and middles did not do badly. Those that fared the worst were the stamps in which speculation ran riot in 1968. The Italian moderns dropped to one-third of their 1968 peak. So did many other European moderns.

American stamps were the great exception to the drop in stamp prices in 1970. They did not decrease in price then, and today they are at their peak.

A quality stamp today is an even greater prize than it was in 1969 and 1970, brings in more buyers, and achieves a generally higher price. Mediocre stamps are less in demand today, and their prices, while not off, are not rising as fast.

Objections to stamp collecting

Collecting stamps is easily done. It need not be costly, and it can be rewarding from the viewpoints of both artistic satisfaction and monetary gain. There are, however, several reasons for the failure of stamp collecting to have spread further:

1. *The belief that it is too late to begin collecting stamps.* There seems to be a widespread belief that all the good stamps are now in albums which are characterized by their completeness and that there are no more stamps available for the new collector.

One answer is that entire collections of stamps come regularly onto the market, and these collections can be purchased for as little as $25 and as much as $10,000, or more, in the case of great collections. One recent H.R. Harmer auction sale in New York concentrated on albums and entire collections. These are cataloged as "Collections and Various."

Thus it is entirely possible to get into stamp collecting by acquiring an entire collection at one time.

2. *The reaction to collecting "one stamp at a time."* If a person purchases one stamp, he may feel he has nothing. In fact, he may feel he has nothing until he has filled at least one album. The answer is to purchase an entire album or a collection at the start, or else collect such well-known stamps that the ownership of them will give satisfaction and lead to the collection of more stamps.

3. *The feeling that stamp collecting is too technical to be understood.* The major stamp auction houses authenticate stamps and will return the buyer's money if the stamp turns out to be not as represented. The buyer is allowed four weeks or more to return the stamp for a refund. In the United States, the Philatelic Foundation passes on the authenticity of stamps, and for a fee will issue a certificate. So does the American Philatelic Society. In England, the Royal Philatelic Society and the British Philatelic Association do the same thing, and there are such authenticating bodies in most European countries. Fakes are a real and continuing problem in the stamp business, and such authentication is a vital aid to collectors, particularly to beginners.

4. *The lack of appreciation of the artistic element in stamp collecting.* Artistic values in any field of collecting must be learned, and it is necessary to study the design and engraving of stamps in order to appreciate their artistic merit.

5. *The lack of ornamental value.* Stamp collecting does not add to the beauty of the home, but the acquisition of beautiful and perfect stamps is satisfying to the collector, as is the probability of the stamps' price appreciation.

6. *The lack of snob value.* The rare Penny Black stamp is not

likely to impress guests as much as a painting on the wall, and a
sheet of inverted airmail stamps will not do nearly as much for a
collector socially as will ownership of a small Renoir. Thus the
hobby does not appeal to those who feel that whatever they collect
must be impressive.

Advantages of investing in stamps

Stamps are an excellent hedge against both inflation and weak-
ness in currency. They have recently risen more than enough to
offset both the rate of inflation and the decline in value of the weak
currencies of the world.

Stamps are also easy and inconspicuous to ship. To cite one example of how important this can be: The Allende government in Chile
moved very quickly to expropriate private property. The large
American companies were not the only ones to have their property
taken; Chilean corporations and individuals suffered the same fate.
There is, however, a good deal of evidence that at least one type of
asset was not confiscated: stamp collections. These, for the most
part, "went underground." Stamps from Chile found their way to
the markets of the world for conversion into dollars, pounds sterling, and other currencies that represented a transfer of at least
some of the seller's assets out of Chile.

While it is likely that Americans need never fear having their
assets confiscated, the performance of stamps in both good and bad
times should not be overlooked by anyone seeking to invest in a
collectible.

This 1918 stamp with an inverted airplane was auctioned in 1964 for $15,500,
resold in 1969 for $31,000, and again sold in 1974 for a record $47,000.

Part of the treasure brought up from *Le Chameau,* which sank off Nova Scotia in 1725. The gold coins, called louis d'or, were sold at auction in 1971 for an average price of $400 each. The Highest Order of Saint Louis, also shown, was purchased at that time for $3,000.

CHAPTER 21

Coins

Prices of gold coins have skyrocketed since the low point of 1970 and early 1971. In the words of David Tripp, head of the coin department of the Sotheby Parke Bernet auction house in New York, "Gold is magic."

One reason for the rise in the value of gold coins is, of course, the rise in the price of gold. In the November, 1973, Sotheby Parke Bernet auction an "average date" $20 gold piece (double eagle) brought about $175. Two months later dealers were paying $225 for the same coin, and dealer buying prices tend to be under auction prices.

Foreign gold coins have performed in a manner very similar to American gold coins, chiefly because of the rapid rise in the price of gold. American gold coins are purchased primarily by American buyers while foreign gold coins are mostly purchased by foreign buyers. These foreign gold coins are usually sold in Switzerland—a convenient place for sellers and buyers to meet because of its central location. In addition, the Swiss government and economy are very stable, unlike those of some other European countries. Thus assets kept in Switzerland are considered to be comparatively safe.

Since 1971 foreign gold coins have risen in price about 100 to 150 percent. The Mexican centenario weighs just about an ounce, and can be used to measure the effect of the rise in gold prices on at least this one foreign coin.

Some investment services list the monthly buying and selling prices of the Mexican centenario in pesos. A peso is worth about eight American cents and rarely varies in price in relation to the dollar. The centenario contains 1.205679 ounces of gold. At the end of 1972 the bank's selling price of a centenario was 1,090.50 pesos—$87.24. In December, 1973, the price was 1,945 pesos—$155. This price can be used to determine the price per ounce of gold in the centenario, which rose in the year from $72.40 to $129.10 and closely paralleled the price of gold on the international market.

The coin premium of the centenario is less than that of most foreign coins. The premium of a coin is determined by subtracting the world market price of gold per ounce from the quoted price per ounce of the coin.

Silver content is not as important to the value of silver coins as gold content is to the value of gold coins. Between 1971 and late 1973 the average price for silver dollars rose from about $4 to $5— a rise of about 25 percent in two years. In the decade from 1963 to 1973 the price of American silver coins rose about 100 percent. The "average" silver dollar rose from $2.25 to about $5.

Foreign silver coins have not been a high riser in the past two years, especially as compared with gold coins of all kinds. Possibly the only category of gold coins, or, for that matter, of any coins, not showing a rise in price has been Islamic coins. These are made of a debased gold and are not of much interest to collectors.

Coin categories

From the viewpoint of collectors, coin categories are:

1. *American gold coins.* This is the most popular category with collectors in America at the present time. It was the most popular category before gold started its upward price movement. Now the interest in this category is phenomenal.

2. *American silver coins.* In 1971 this category of coins was in the midst of a price disaster. Now there is a great turnaround under way.

3. *Foreign gold coins.* Each nation with a money economy strikes coins in gold, silver, and bronze. Gold coins date from the tenth century to the present time.

4. *Foreign silver and bronze coins.*

5. *Ancient coins.* This category is often divided into ancient

Greek coins and ancient Roman coins. Here the gold or silver content is not so important as in the case of modern coins, which are very closely tied to the value of their metals. In ancient coins, rarity is of far greater importance than metal content.

Until 1972 there was very little American interest in ancient Greek and Roman coins. If one such coin sold for, say, $150 in 1971, it would now sell for about $500 to $600. The degree of price rise in a little over two years was about 200 percent.

During 1969 and 1970 a doctor built a collection of Roman gold coins. He put about $36,000 into his collection. In June, 1973, Sotheby's in London sold the collection. It realized about $120,000, almost two and a half times its cost. It might be pointed out that the coins the doctor purchased were exceptionally good and beautiful pieces, the kind other collectors would want.

6. *Hammered coins.* These coins with hammered edges were minted in Europe from the eighth to the fifteenth century. They are beginning to climb in price but are not often available on the American market.

7. *Treasures.* These coins have been excavated in various parts of the world and have been brought up from sunken ships. The *Chameau* treasure created a sensation when it was auctioned on December 11, 1971. This was before excavation and dredging methods increased the number of treasures on the market and coins in this category became less valuable.

Le Chameau went down off the coast of Nova Scotia at Cape Breton in 1725. The ship contained a military pay chest for the support of the French regiments in Canada. Many attempts were made in the nineteenth century and in the early twentieth century to bring up the treasure, but the near-freezing water and the coastal reef were obstacles too great for the times. The treasure

Silver dollar dated 1799 sold for $650 in 1974.

was finally brought up in 1966 by Dutch archaeologist Alex Storm.

About 99 percent of the treasure consisted of silver and gold coins—all in fine condition. The gold coins, known as louis d'or, are dated 1723, 1724, and 1725, and represent all of the French mints of the period. There were 493 gold coins and these averaged about $400 each at auction in 1971.

Items in two categories allied to those listed above are often grouped for sale with coins:

1. *Peace medals.* These have in recent years achieved great collector interest and high prices. There are perhaps 500 of these items available, so the supply is extremely small in relation to demand.

2. *Commemorative medals.* These have been in the public eye in recent years. They have gone up in value at times, but they have gone down as well.

Value determinants

There are three main determinants of value in coins. The first is scarcity or rarity. One of the coin catalogs gives an example of the importance of rarity by citing two Indian-head pennies, both in fine condition. One is dated 1865 and the other 1877. The 1877 coin is worth $90; the 1865 coin, although twelve years older, is worth only $1.75. The reason is that there were 35 million of the 1865 coins minted and fewer than one million of the 1877 coins.

The record price for a coin—$200,000—was realized at auction in New York in May, 1974, when Stack's sold a very high relief proof of the Saint-Gaudens double eagle $20 gold piece dated 1907 with Roman numerals. Fewer than twenty coins of this type are known to exist.

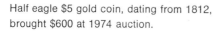

Half eagle $5 gold coin, dating from 1812, brought $600 at 1974 auction.

American quarter dollar was purchased in 1974 for $1,600.

The next value determinant is condition. This is how coins are graded:

Proof. This coin is struck from scientifically polished dies and blocks. There are no imperfections and, since the coin has never been circulated, there is no wear. These coins are sold to collectors at more than face value. A proof set consists of a penny, nickel, dime, quarter, and half-dollar all of the same year.

Uncirculated. This coin is new, has never been circulated, and shows no wear or damage. Such coins are purchasable at banks as they are received from the government.

Extra or extremely fine. These coins show no wear or loss of original luster as they have been circulated only briefly. Details of design and lettering are all in uncirculated condition. Coins in your pocket which bear this year's or last year's date are probably of this grade.

Very fine. There are few signs of wear on this grade of coin, and all details of design and lettering are sharp.

Fine. These coins have obviously been circulated. Design and lettering are still sharp but the high points show signs of wear.

Very good and good. These two grades are to some extent misnomers as the coins thus graded are obviously worn. Most of the lettering and the design are in good condition, but some of the details have disappeared.

Fair and poor. One might have difficulty in discerning exactly what design and lettering are on these coins.

In connection with condition, the would-be collector should be warned never to clean a coin. Cleaning not only lessens value, it can destroy value. Any dealer who sees that a coin has been cleaned

English coin issued in 1553-54 sold in 1973 for $3,600.

with anything stronger than a little soap and water will generally refuse to purchase it.

The third value element is demand. Without demand, rarity has little significance. To take just one example:

Four-dollar gold pieces were struck in only two years—1879 and 1880. These coins were experimental, and only proof prices are quoted. There were ten of these so-called Stellas made in 1879 with the model wearing coiled hair. These bring $17,500 each. In that same year 415 coins were made with the model wearing flowing hair, and these bring about $7,000 each. Ten more of the coins with the coiled hairstyle were made in 1880 and also bring $17,500. However, in 1880 an additional fifteen coins were made in which the model wears flowing hair. These sell for $10,000 each. The differences in price are not great enough to be primarily due to the number of coins of each type issued.

Market values

The grading of coins permits the establishment of market values. Some catalogs offer three grades—extra fine, fine, and very good—together with prices. Other catalogs, such as Norman Stack's *U.S. Coins of Value,* offer two grades with prices.

Before the tremendous slide of the dollar and the rise of the German mark, the Swiss franc, and the Japanese yen, gold coins were moving up rather strongly, but not at the present steep rate.

The "very good" grade of 1849 gold dollar was worth $15 in 1967. A "fine" one was worth $20, and an "extra fine" one was worth $25. Two years later these coins were worth, respectively, $20, $22.50, and $32.50.

These same grades of the 1874 three-dollar gold piece were worth

Cromwell coin dated 1656 brought $2,000 in 1973.

$60, $90, and $140, respectively, in 1967. In 1969 they were worth $65, $110, and $165. The fine double eagle of 1850 was worth $47 in 1967, and the extra fine, $80. Two years later these two grades of the double eagle were worth $65 and $82.

In the recession of 1970 coin prices in some categories dropped materially. Silver coins were particularly hard hit. The U.S. government had on several occasions released old silver coins and speculators had gone wild, causing a boom in prices, which then plummeted. The prices of gold coins, on the other hand, did not even waiver, and the overall decline in the value of coins was only 5 to 7 percent.

In late 1971 these might well have been some of the realized prices on the market:

1849 gold dollar: $37.50, $50, and $65.
1839 quarter eagle: $100, $140, and $175.
1874 three-dollar gold piece: $175, $225, and $290.
1850 double eagle: $125 and $160.

Prices of these coins in mid-1974 were:

1849 gold dollar: $90, $100, and $115.
1839 quarter eagle: $120, $160, and $250.
1874 three-dollar gold piece: $200, $300, and $400.
1850 double eagle: $300, $350, and $400.

Reasons for investing in coins

There are a number of reasons for the popularity of coins as an investment:

• High value and small bulk. A limited amount of space is required for display or storage of coins as compared with many other collectibles. Funds can easily be "stored" in coins and, if necessary, they can be moved quickly from a country with economic or political problems to a safer one.

• Easily determinable market value. There are many coin directories and price lists, all brought up to date frequently. The best-known directory for American coins is R. S. Yeoman's *Bluebook of United States Coins/Handbook of United States Coins, With Premium List*, Western Publishing Company, Racine, Wisconsin.

• A highly developed auction market, which provides fairly rapid liquidity.

• A well-developed dealer market. Purchases can be made from dealers at or near quoted prices, and sales can be made to dealers for sums reasonably close to quoted prices.

- The opportunity for almost any kind of specialization—either a wide specialization or an extremely narrow one, according to the collector's preference.
- A closely knit, highly expert group of collectors, in addition to a great number of occasional buyers.
- A well-defined system of gradation which simplifies value determination.
- An enormously rising market in recent years, particularly in gold coins.

In addition to the world currency crisis which developed in 1971, there are at least five reasons for the rise in coin prices:

- The substantial increase each year in the number of coin collectors.
- The limit in the number of coins available, particularly as compared with the increasing number of collectors.
- The fact that coins are offered for sale by dealers and collectors, all of whom expect to make a profit. In certain collectibles, such as antiques, estates provide much of what comes onto the market, and there is not the same requirement for a profit from these sources. Coin collectors are fully aware that theirs is an investment, and they rightfully expect a return on their money.
- The full realization on the part of coin collectors that in part at least they expect coins to be an inflation hedge. To provide this hedge, coins must rise in value at a greater rate than inflation.
- An organized market with a price for almost everything, so that buying and selling are easily done. Without this developed market mechanism, which tends to appeal to professional investors such as stockbrokers, it is unlikely that coins would have become the professional investment they are today.

Why coin values decrease at times

Coins can move downward in price and occasionally do, and it is important for would-be collectors to recognize this fact. Coins decrease in price for these reasons:

- Speculative buying by dealers and professional collectors. When the dealers and large collectors sell, the small buyers tend to "dump" their investments and scramble for cover, just as small speculators do in the stock market. When the large buyer simply stops buying and thus slows the upward movement of the coin market, the small buyer tends to sell and thus starts a downward price movement.
- Estates which come onto the market more or less fortuitously,

and dealers who sell in order to realize cash for at least a part of their investment. Such market actions tend to depress prices temporarily.

• Occasional actions by the government, as, for instance, the release of silver coins in large volume by the Federal Reserve System. This action had a deadening effect on the market for United States silver coins.

• A drop in the value of the basic metal. When the silver market dropped precipitously so did the market for silver coins. Recently, metal markets have been moving up, led by the gold market, but it is correct to anticipate periodic drops in the metal markets of the future, and these drops will no doubt decrease the values of coins.

• Speculative upward market thrusts. Hysteria seems to develop in regard to many collectibles and prices become overinflated. When this happens the groundwork is laid for a price collapse. Investment value, collector interest, and artistic merit all take a back seat to the "psychology of 1929."

• Recession and a drop in the stock market. In almost every field of collecting, business conditions and the level of the stock market have had at least some effect on prices. Coins are no exception. Unlike many other collectibles, however, the recession of 1970 did not greatly depress the coin market.

Coin sellers and buyers

In the city of New York there are only five or six important coin dealers. In the area which includes New York, New Jersey, Pennsylvania, and Connecticut there are about forty significant coin dealers, but there are hundreds of dealers who handle coins along with other merchandise.

As for the auctioning of coins, Sotheby Parke Bernet in New York holds six or seven coin auctions a year, Sotheby's in London holds a coin auction about once a month, and Christie's in London holds approximately three such auctions a year. Catalogs are issued, together with price estimates, and a list of prices received is issued after an auction has taken place. Any of these catalogs provides a good deal of information on just what is available in the coin market and at what price. By comparing catalogs of different dates, one can become aware of trends.

In Paris, although the great auction house, the Hotel Drouot, conducts coin sales, dealers handle much of the coin business because the tax situation militates against auction sales in this field.

There are probably over 500 coin auctions held in the United States each year, and the magazine *Coin World* lists the upcoming auctions. In any year there are also over 200 coin shows or coin and stamp shows held in the United States at which sales are made.

In addition, coin dealers offer their wares at a good percentage of the many antique exhibitions and sales held each year. *Coin World,* incidentally, prepares a monthly price index of coins which are valued at up to $1 and are not gold. A selection of twenty representative coins is valued each month by a panel of experts. The price movements are combined into an index of percentage price rise or price decline in the month.

Coin portfolios

In the United States at least one organization specializes in the management of coin portfolios, the same type of management that has been common practice with regard to securities for many years. Most of the coin portfolios managed by Hoglund and Company of Westport, Connecticut, are individually owned. Some are jointly owned by several people. The value of each portfolio when it was started was $20,000 on the average. No portfolio of under $10,000 has been handled by the firm. One portfolio was recently valued at $250,000.

The firm goes heavily into American gold coins. In fact, Hoglund and Company was at one time known as "The Home of the Stella," the highly valued and extremely rare American four-dollar piece. This one firm had in its portfolios as many as ten Stellas. It has also invested heavily in silver dollars.

The compensation to the firm is payable only on final sale of the portfolio or any part of the portfolio, when a percentage of the sales price is taken. To date, this percentage has amounted to a very small part of the owners' profits because of the rapidly rising market.

A major advantage to investors has apparently been in the firm's successful buying. It has concentrated on purchases from estates when they come onto the market rather than purchasing from dealers or at auction. Reported increases in the overall value of the coin portfolios have been 12 percent in 1971, 42 percent in 1972, and an almost incredible increase of 105 percent in 1973.

There are variations and refinements in coin collecting and coin buying, at least as far as the professional investor is concerned. One of these developments, similar in many ways to an old practice in the stock market, is margin buying, in which the investor puts up only a fraction of the cost of his "portfolio." Coin America of Phoenix, Arizona, is a coin investment firm handling margin accounts. Although the firm is only two years old, it has developed a monthly sales volume of over $1 million, and in some hectic months volume is well over this figure.

Coin portfolios may attract more investors than other collectibles. Coins are money, and the switch from bank accounts and stocks and bonds to gold and silver coins does not require as great a reorientation on the part of the investor as investments in art and antiques do.

In addition, gold represents something that is stable while the currencies of almost every country in the world are being devalued or floated downward. Gold and gold coins actually offer more than stability, as they are rising in value more than currencies are declining in value. Gold coins—even the later so-called bullion coins which have more gold value than collector value—are in many cases rising faster than gold and are exceeding the rate of inflation by a good margin. In fact, the rate of increase of gold coins today exceeds the rate of inflation and currency declines *combined*.

For these reasons, coins—particularly gold coins—are becoming more of an investment and less of a collectible, and the professional investor is fully accepting coins in his overall investment portfolio.

In 1973 coin sales volume in the United States may well have passed the half-billion-dollar mark, and in the same year the number of coin buyers in this country probably increased by more than 10 percent. As in anything else, the more buyers the greater the demand and generally the higher the price.

This page is from one of the most luxurious copies of Chaucer's *Canterbury Tales,* an illuminated manuscript on vellum, circa 1440-50, which sold in June, 1974, for $216,000. Although some rare books bring very high prices, there are others available for moderate sums.

CHAPTER 22

Rare Books

A rare book is a fine book that is hard to find. It is also usually expensive. A book can of course be scarce, but if no one wants the scarce book, it is not a rare book.

In the highly sophisticated world of old, fine, and rare book collecting there are several recognized categories of rarity. The first is absolute rarity, which results from the fact that few copies of the particular book were printed originally.

There is also relative rarity. A book possesses relative rarity if there are few surviving copies, regardless of how many copies were printed when the book was first published. Sometimes sales catalogs describe a book as "so rare as to be virtually unprocurable." This can indicate either absolute rarity or relative rarity.

There is still another kind of rarity called temporary rarity. This condition exists when demand increases and supply lags. When this occurs, prices rise and the higher prices call forth copies from book dealers and from the shelves of collectors.

One more kind of rarity is localized rarity. As an example, a copy of the first edition of *Madame Bovary*, published in Paris in 1857, is much easier to find in France than in England or the United States.

The first edition is probably the principal category of rare book. However, not all first editions are of equal importance or value. The most valuable of these books might be called "the first of the first." Often copies of the first edition of a book are not all the same. Anyone who has written a book, and particularly anyone who has followed his book through the printing process, knows that when the book first appears it is likely to contain errors and peculiarities, no matter how careful the writer and editor were or how many times the text was read and checked. Quite often there are glaring errors that are first seen by the writer or editor only after the book is printed and bound. A date may be incorrect or there may be misspellings, or some other mistake will suddenly be all too obvious.

Sometimes these "firsts of the first" are recalled and corrected copies are substituted for them. There are, however, some that are never recalled, and these have a greater value to collectors than subsequent more perfect ones.

One notch lower than the first editions are the limited editions, which are published in limited numbers for a particular group of buyers. Limited editions are often printed on premium-grade paper and finely bound. They too are collectible books.

Another area of book collecting is presentation copies. These are signed by the author, and are most valuable if, in addition to being signed, they are dedicated in the author's handwriting. An example of such a desirable rare book would be a copy of a book by Keats dedicated to Shelley.

Still another category of rare and valuable books consists of association copies. These are books from the library of a prominent individual. A book from George Washington's library is an important and valuable association copy.

A book also gains in value if a prominent collector such as Morgan, Widener, Huntington, or Folger has owned it.

Age can give a book value, aside from the above categories. Any kind of book dating from the fifteenth century has value simply because of its age.

Categories most in demand

The main types of rare books sold today are: early printed books (before the year 1600) and incunabula (before 1500), natural history, color-plate books, science and medicine, Americana, later literature, fine bindings (almost regardless of the book itself), voyages and travel, music, and art.

The sales catalogs of rare book sellers and auction houses contain a wide variety of subject matter in the rare book field. As an example, on March 18, 1974, Sotheby's in London conducted a sale of "Printed Books Including an Extensive Collection of Books on Conjuring and Magic."

To a considerable extent what qualifies a book as collectible, fine, or rare is a matter of degree. The leading dealer in old, fine, and rare books, Bernard Quaritch of London, lists *The Life of Florence Nightingale* by Sarah A. Tooley, third edition, with eighteen plates and six text illustrations, cloth, spine faded, for a little over $7. This he does not consider a fine or rare book. Seventeenth-century sermons may be worth only a dollar apiece. If the bindings are poor, they may bring virtually nothing at auction. At the other end of the scale, a New York book dealer, whose volume of business may be the largest in the world, bought a copy of the Gutenberg Bible dating from the middle of the fifteenth century for a reported $1,500,000.

Value factors

The factors that create value in a book are almost limitless. They include whether the book is a first edition, or a limited edition, or a presentation copy, the quality of the binding, the quality of the printing, the historical significance of the book, whether the book is attractive overall, whether it is a dedication copy, whether it dates from the fifteenth century, and whether it belonged to a famous person. Lucien Goldschmidt, the New York rare book seller, recalls having bought some books that had once belonged to Albert Einstein. "They were shoddy books from Einstein's library that had been donated to a charity bazaar. The texts themselves were not collectible; yet I paid somewhere between $700 and $800 for the lot," says Mr. Goldschmidt.

A book can have value as a collectible because it sheds insight on the social scene of a particular era. Thus a book about the life of a tailor in the seventeenth century that describes buying fabric, fitting customers, and hiring assistants at certain wage rates may be a rare book.

A book dealer in New York has a copy of Raoul LeFèvre's *History of Troy*, dated 1490, published in Lyons, France. The Library of Congress and the Pierpont Morgan Library also have copies of this book. The dealer-owned copy is the third known to exist in this country. What is it worth? The answer may well be, "What someone is willing to pay for it."

Auction catalogs are helpful in determining the selling prices of rare books. However, these catalogs are rather sketchy and rarely contain illustrations of a book or any part of a book. On the other hand, the priced catalogs of the major rare book sellers are in many ways equal in quality to the rare books the dealers sell. Lucien

Goldschmidt of New York periodically issues large catalogs on fine paper with excellent illustrations. A recent one of these is Catalog No. 41, *Books About the Fine Arts*. Catalog No. 40 concerns *Illustrated Books From the Renaissance to the Present,* and illustrations from a number of the books are included, along with prices. Seven Gables and John Fleming, both of New York, issue catalogs for their specialty, English and American books, whereas Goldschmidt specializes in books from continental Europe.

It is possible to walk into the Bernard Quaritch bookshop in London and acquire an armful of catalogs: *Science and Medicine, Natural History Books, European Maritime, Martial and Historical Books, The Near and Far East, Paleography, Press Books, The Fine Arts,* and even *Japanese Illustrated Books,* among others. This firm, incidentally, seems to cater to all pocketbooks. Although they list some books for about $7 each, they have probably handled half of the total number of Gutenberg Bibles ever sold.

Rare book collectors

A high proportion of the collectors of rare books are intellectuals, who presumably collect simply for the love of books. Another very substantial category of buyers consists of institutions. Bernard Quaritch's chief customers are not private collectors but libraries, primarily libraries in the United States.

The mainstay of the rare book market for both American and English dealers is the buying done by university libraries, general and specialized libraries, and foundations. Some dealers in rare books specialize in sales to the smaller American colleges. While book auctions seem to be dominated by dealers, these dealers are often buying on commission for institutions or are buying for themselves with a view to a quick sale to an institution.

This characteristic of the rare book market is highly important to the individual collector because these institutional buyers remove the books from the market forever. Thus the supply diminishes while the institutions which are endowed or have continuing sources of income are always buying to some extent and are not as affected by economic conditions as individual collectors. Then too the tax laws in the United States very much favor the donation of books to colleges, museums, and charitable institutions. It is often easier and more profitable to donate books which have appreciated in price to institutions than to sell them, particularly for upper-income collectors.

However, many books are still sold directly by owners to book dealers, and at least one major American dealer states that he buys many more books privately than he does at auction. Sometimes a collector changes his residence and parts with some of his books in preference to moving them. Sometimes a collector moves to smaller quarters which lack room for his entire library. Sometimes upon a collector's death his entire estate comes onto the market. All these events present buying opportunities to the book dealer.

Price history

There are fads in rare book collecting as there are fads in art collecting, antique collecting, and in collecting almost anything. Until 1920 no one collected much concerning the history of science. Then two major collectors turned to this field. Today history of science books are a major collectible.

Natural history is probably the area of greatest collector interest and fastest rising values in the entire rare book field today. Until about 1966, Christie's auction house in London held no specialized sales of natural history books—zoology, ornithology, and botany. In 1973, Christie's held an "all natural history book sale." It turned out to be the largest single-session sale of printed books in history, realizing $742,161.

In this record sale Daniel Giraud Elliot's *Monograph of the Felidae*, 1883, brought $4,560. In 1967 it had brought $1,290. Also in 1967, Christie's sold three books by Thomas Martyn, the draftsman of shells and insects, all printed in the late eighteenth century, for $2,655. In 1973 the same copies reappeared at the same auction house and brought the equivalent of $7,000.

There has been a steep rise in rare book prices since 1968. Books dealing with the subject of music may have started to rise in price even earlier, and illustrated books began the steepest part of their rise in about 1971. If we take as an example a book with illustrations by surrealist painter Max Ernst, we might estimate a price for this book in the spring of 1974 at $1,000 to $1,500. In 1973 this book might well have brought $1,200. In 1972 it might have reached $600 to $700, and in 1971 about $300 or $400. Thus in three years its value may well have risen four times.

The category of American and English literature has been a less spectacular price riser in the past two or three years. Its heyday was in the 1920s when book prices competed with stock prices in steepness of rise. American books were at the forefront of the rise at that time, and the highest prices were realized in the Jerome Kern sale of books and autographs held in the winter of 1928-29. Composer Kern had assembled his collection in the fifteen-year period prior to the sale and had emphasized British authors, particularly of the eighteenth and nineteenth century. It was the most successful sale of rare books in history. The average price per lot of books sold was a very high $1,166.

Prices of rare books collapsed along with the stock market in

1929. They did not recover until well after World War II. In the
early 1950s the rare book market began to revive and in the early
1960s prices accelerated. There was no slump in rare book prices
during the recession of 1969-70, although impressionist paintings
showed a 25 percent drop and Georgian silver dropped 40 percent,
along with many other categories of collectibles.

Rare books had risen less spectacularly than other collectibles
before 1968. In that year the Guillaume Paradin Bible, dated 1558,
with 231 woodcuts of the Old Testament and 96 of the New Testament, would have brought about $100. In the January, 1974, sale
held at Sotheby Parke Bernet in New York a copy of this Bible
brought $1,100.

Also offered in that sale was Mark Twain's *Adventures of Tom
Sawyer,* Hartford, Connecticut, 1876, first edition, first issue. It
realized $750. In 1968 it might have sold for $150—20 percent as
much as it brought in 1974.

The rarity factors

Eight rarity factors in large measure determine the supply side
of the supply-demand equation, which in turn determines the price
of a book:

- The number originally printed.
- The existence of limited editions.
- The reputation of the book. The better the reputation the more
the chance of copies having survived.
- The breadth of the original distribution of the book, and the
publisher's reputation—his reputation having secured the original
distribution and caused buyers of the book to esteem it and keep it
in their libraries.
- The size of the first printing in relation to subsequent sales.
Certain books were completely sold when they originally appeared;
others were not and many copies are still available.
- The rarity of "collectors' state" books, not just run-of-the-mill
books.
- The relationship of a particular book to a stage of an author's
literary career. Very often an author's first book will not be his big
seller nor will a new author be granted a big first printing. These
early books may well turn out to be an author's most valuable books
on the market today.
- The reputation of the book with booksellers and auction houses
as to its rarity. Whether correctly or not, if a book is described as
"so rare as to be virtually unprocurable," this designation tends to
raise its value, even though subsequently many more copies of the
particular edition of the book come onto the market.

Rare natural history books are in demand. This illustration is from John Gould's monograph on hummingbirds, which sold for $25,000 in 1973.

An illustration from a rare book by Joseph Jakob Plenck that was purchased for $38,000 at an auction in 1973.

The condition factor

A book's condition can be classified as pristine, fine, very good, good, fair, poor, or as is.

The importance of condition to the value of a rare book is immense. In the October 30, 1973, rare book sale held at the Sotheby Parke Bernet galleries in New York one lot was a first edition, first issue, of Walt Whitman's *Leaves of Grass*. It was described in the sales catalog as being in "fine condition." It sold for $5,000.

The very next lot was the same book—first edition, first issue. It was in the same original green cloth, but in this copy the outer hinge was split halfway down and across the spine, and the top and bottom of the spine were worn. Gabriel Austin, head of Sotheby Parke Bernet's book department, described the book as having been "fooled around with." It brought $1,600.

In the January 29, 1974, sale held by the same gallery one lot was Mark Twain's *Adventures of Tom Sawyer*, the already mentioned book that brought $750. The book was described as "rubbed, the spine slightly defective at the head and foot." Had the book been in better condition, it might have brought $900 to $1,000. If it had been in fine condition, it might have sold for $1,500, and if in pristine condition, it might have brought $3,000 to $4,000.

What all book collectors would probably like to have is a copy of the first printed book, the Gutenberg Bible, which, incidentally, is a magnificently made book, particularly since it was a "first try." Collectors would like to have this book in the exact condition in which Gutenberg produced it 500-odd years ago.

Since pristine books—even those produced in the last century—are virtually nonexistent, collectors try to acquire books in as nearly original condition as possible. Condition is of course related to age, and poor condition which is not excusable in a fairly recent book may be quite acceptable in a sixteenth-century book.

There are three requirements a rare book should meet with respect to condition: that it be complete, that it be clean and sound, and that it be "undisturbed."

There was an early English book about architect Andrea Palladio for sale recently in Canterbury, England. Four pages of the book were missing, which probably reduced its value by 90 percent. It therefore could be bought for about $25.

It is a fairly common practice to take two books which each have missing pages and combine them into one complete book. It is also possible to clean a book by washing the pages, and a book can be made sound by rebinding. Such books have not been left "undisturbed" and this reduces their value considerably.

Repairs of a book which is dirty, dog-eared, or battered are permissible without lowering the value of the book, if repairs are done

298   INVESTMENTS YOU CAN LIVE WITH AND ENJOY

expertly and with a minimum amount of major alteration. Purist collectors, however, like to have an exact description of what repairs were made and when, although such a requirement is not generally complied with by book owners.

The earlier a book the less the importance of repairs to value, but, as rare book authority John Carter points out, "A doctored *Eothen* (1844), *Vanity Fair* (1848), or *Portrait of a Lady* (3 vols., 1881) is practically worthless." The theory is that the later the book the more original and the less disturbed it should be.

If the binding is original and in good condition, it adds greatly to the value of the book. The next level down is to have a binding which, although not the book's original one, was made in the same era. The next level is a binding which is close enough in style to the original binding to be equivalent to the original.

Finally, in books made prior to about 1810 boards or wrappers were generally all that was provided, and it was up to the buyer to have suitable bindings made. If these original boards or wrappers are present but there is no cover, the book still has value as far as the binding is concerned.

Investment outlook

Rare books may be a good investment for these reasons:

1. They have not been greatly publicized as many other collectibles have. Prices have thus not boomed as they have in other areas.

2. Rare books do not lend themselves to quick promotional run-ups the way more spectacular collectibles do.

3. Books are not among the conspicuous elements of decor promoted by interior decorators and decorator magazines in recent times.

4. Rare books do not obviously advertise either the culture of the collector or the size of his bank account as do fine carpets, ornamental glassware, and some other collectibles. Thus there are not the superficial inflationary elements in book collecting that exist in other fields.

5. Collectors of rare books have not generally tried to beat inflation and currency depreciation by investing in books. Buying rapidly for quick appreciation therefore has not run up book prices the way it has prices of other collectibles.

6. While prices of rare books have been rising well in the past five years, they have not boomed as much in the past year or two as have many other collectibles, and it is therefore likely that book prices have not yet peaked.

7. Rare books are disappearing into institutions faster than other collectibles are. This institutional buying does not dominate

any other field of collecting as it does rare books. Buying by libraries, foundations, universities, and colleges permanently removes rare books from the market each year. Demand must then be satisfied with what remains, and this remaining supply is much smaller than that of most other collectibles.

8. There is a fairly good system of grading books according to their condition, and auction and dealer catalogs are reasonably accurate in describing condition, which makes it possible to purchase rare books from description only. This method of purchase would be quite unsuitable for either antiques or paintings, which should always be carefully examined before purchase.

9. In very few fields of collectibles do dealers prepare highly descriptive periodic catalogs complete with prices, as book dealers do. The market can thus be judged easily from dealer catalogs available at no cost to the would-be collector.

10. There is a rare book to fit the pocketbook of almost everyone. At the October 30, 1973, New York auction of rare books, if a collector could not afford to buy Lot 114, Walt Whitman's *Leaves of Grass*, first edition, first issue, in fine condition, for $5,000, he might have been able to purchase Lot 119, a group of John Greenleaf Whittier's first editions, "most uniformly bound in half calf"— over thirty of them in all—for $550 the lot.

At least one collector of antiquities—a collector who has antique furniture, old master paintings, Georgian silver, glassware and porcelain, among other things—insists that, of all collectibles, rare books are by far the best investment. In recent years, his major source of income—for maintaining his elaborate Queen Anne home, his Bentley, and his Ferrari—seems to have been the profit on the rare books he has sold. Whenever he has been in need of funds he has simply offered one or more of his books for sale. The sales transaction has been rapid, with little quibbling over price, and apparently highly satisfactory from the point of view of profit.

Few autographs bring high prices. Among the exceptions is a group of nine letters written by famed composer Handel, including the above letter dated July 19, 1744. The group brought $84,000 at auction in 1973. Autographs of musical greats are among those rising most in value.

CHAPTER 23

Autographs

In many ways, autographs offer an ideal collectible for investment, not just for the well-to-do collector but for the would-be collector with almost no purchasing budget.

Early in 1974 a lot consisting of several autographs was offered at auction. The first item in the lot was a letter signed by Lee De Forest. It reads, "When I invented the radio tube, 43 years ago, I foretold some of the blessings that the Radio Broadcast would bring. . . . But what I foresaw was not one-thousandth part of what Radio has achieved. . . ."

In the same lot were autographs by Thomas A. Edison and Generals Courtney Hodges, Joseph Stilwell, Lucius Clay, J. M. Wainwright, John J. Pershing, George C. Marshall, and Douglas MacArthur. Also included were autographs by Fiorello LaGuardia, Charles Evans Hughes, Bernard Baruch, and Clare Boothe Luce. Of the clergy there were autographs by Cardinal Spellman, Cardinal Hays, and Rabbi Stephen Wise. Autographs of Italian patriots Garibaldi and Mazzini were in the lot, as were those of Irish patriots Daniel O'Connell and Eamon De Valera. There were also examples of the handwriting of Raymond Poincaré and Madame de Maintenon, as well as a William Gladstone frank. Some postage stamps, assembled to be mounted with the autographs, were also included. In all there were 220 separate pieces in this one lot. The entire lot sold at the Charles Hamilton Autographs auction in New York for $300—about $1.50 for each item—indicating that even the collector with a modest budget can invest in this collectible.

Most autographs appear to be great bargains. For about $200 a letter signed by Napoleon can be purchased; for $600 one can buy a letter signed by Abraham Lincoln; and for $500 one signed by John Hancock. Sometimes successful collecting begins with the reaction on the part of the would-be collector, "How can anything of that significance sell for so little money?"

While it is true that autographs as such do not add much to home decor, there is some decorative value to framed signed photographs of famous persons, or photographs, engravings, or stamps accompanied by signed letters or documents. The B. Altman and Company department store in New York City mounts and frames autographs so that they can be hung decoratively, but this does raise the price.

It is possible to assemble a well-rounded collection of interesting autographs for relatively little money. This cannot be achieved in many other fields of collecting. Even in the less expensive schools of art and the less expensive antiques, considerable money and time are required to build a collection.

Autograph collectors

The field of autograph collecting seems to attract people who are highly cultured and well read. A leading New York dealer, Mary A. Benjamin, has further observed that collectors feel a rapport with the persons whose autographs they collect. Usually a collector will seek out the autographs of those he most admires. Collecting therefore becomes a very personal matter. Self-made successful businessmen often want Napoleon's signature, lawyers want Lincoln's letters, writers choose literary figures, and so on.

One of the attractions in collecting autographs is that, in a sense, it brings historically significant persons into the collector's home.

Another good reason for beginning a collection of autographs is that there are relatively few autograph collectors as yet. Probably not over 5,000 persons collect autographs in the United States, although the number has increased greatly in the past two decades. Most of the collectors are very knowledgeable about quality and value, and want interesting and important items for their collections, but they have not yet created an unrealistic boom as has been the case with other collectibles at times.

If one qualifies what a collector is, it may be that there are really only 500 true collectors in the entire field, those who are not limited financially in what they choose to collect.

Demand determines price

Demand is the most important factor in determining autograph values today. However, as the collecting of autographs becomes more popular, supply may very well replace demand as the factor determining price level. Autographs available for sale are, for the most part, absolutely limited, and the interaction of an increasing demand and a fixed supply must result in rising prices.

There are very many prime autographs in dealers' stocks at this time. It is still possible to purchase letters signed by George Washington, Abraham Lincoln, and Napoleon—completely written in the hand of the signer. Unlike many other collectibles, in autographs one can still obtain the best items, with very few exceptions, for less than astronomical sums.

Another fact of importance in determining whether autographs are a good candidate for investment is that a high degree of price rise is possible because they are now generally so low in price. Many significant autographs are still obtainable for $10 apiece. These do not have to be great performers in the market to double in price— to $20. Fewer and fewer people can purchase a collectible as the price rises to great heights. Yet the collector who can afford an autograph for $10 can probably also pay $20, or even $30, and there are many people who can afford to pay double the present price— $1,500—for a letter signed by Abraham Lincoln.

Many of the prices of autographs are so low that a mistake is not extremely costly to the collector. If he buys a letter signed by Napoleon for $200, he cannot lose more than $200 if it turns out to be a forgery. The investment risk is not great in the field of autographs.

Until fairly recently the buyer at auction did not receive a guarantee that the item he purchased actually was as described in the catalog. This lack of assurance held true for paintings, antiques, autographs, and many other collectibles. Sotheby Parke Bernet now offers a five-year guarantee on the authenticity of the autographs it auctions. The Charles Hamilton auction guarantee went into effect earlier and was a great innovation. This lifetime guarantee states: "All autographs listed in this catalog are unconditionally guaranteed to be genuine."

Another provision in the Hamilton sales catalog is of importance to the collector: "If any material defect is found by a purchaser who was unable to examine the lot or lots prior to the sale, the item in question may be returned within three days of receipt."

Reputable dealers also offer guarantees. Mary A. Benjamin offers her lifetime guarantee on what she sells and on what she buys at auction on commission (10 percent) for her clients.

Preferred categories

Autographs which attract collectors usually are those of the great and renowned. In this overall category there are definite subcategories. These are some of the subcategories that are rising the most in value at the present time:

- Composers and musicians
- Presidents of the United States
- Revolutionary War personages and signers of the Declaration of Independence
- American and British authors
- Famous artists
- Theatrical performers
- Scientists
- Nazis
- Astronauts
- Civil War participants—Confederate and Union
- Napoleon and his family and marshals

The least valuable autograph is the simple signature—the signed name of the personage on a card or cut from a letter or document. This value is perhaps the aspect of the entire field most misunderstood by the noncollector or novice.

Mere signatures, with exceptions of course, have relatively little value to the connoisseur. The most desirable autographs are usually those items written entirely by the personage who signed the letter or document.

Knowledgeable collectors look for interesting, significant letters or important signed documents. As institutions are major buyers of autographs, material of historical importance is always in demand. These institutions—libraries, historical societies, university archives, and so forth—are always on the lookout for material for their collections. When they buy, the material is virtually taken off the market permanently, and the supply is lessened.

Classifications

Following are the abbreviations used in classifying the various types of autographs:

A.L.S. means Autograph Letter Signed—the signer wrote the entire letter in longhand himself.

April 11, 1881.

*I will see Mr. Bal-
lett at 10³⁰, tomor-
row morning*

J. A. G.

This note written by President James A. Garfield is valued today at $350. Autographs of Presidents of the United States are popular with collectors.

A.N.S. means Autograph Note Signed—a note written and signed by the person.

A.D.S. means Autograph Document Signed—the document was written in longhand and signed by the person who wrote it.

A.Ms.S. means Autograph Manuscript Signed.

A.Q.S. means Autograph Quotation Signed.

L.S. means Letter Signed—the letter might have been written in longhand by a secretary, or typewritten, but it was signed by the person whose signature it bears.

N.S. means Note Signed—the note might have been written or typed by another person but was signed by the person whose signature appears on it.

D.S. means Document Signed—the document might have been printed, or partially printed, or prepared by a secretary, but the signature is handwritten and genuine.

Ms.S. means Manuscript Signed.

S. means Signature—nothing else is included.

A signed autograph letter of a President written when in office is worth vastly more than an A.L.S. done when out of office. A Herbert Hoover A.L.S. as President is probably worth $1,500. Harry Truman's A.L.S. as President is worth perhaps $750 to $1,000. William Henry Harrison was in office for just one month; his A.L.S. as President might bring over $20,000. Several years ago, Mary A. Benjamin sold a Harrison A.N.S. for $15,000.

As an example of how autograph values can change, a collector of the autographs of Dwight D. Eisenhower made these observations: An L.S. (signed letter) by Eisenhower brought $60 when

Eisenhower was alive. When he died the price rose to $80. By 1974 the price had fallen to $30. At the $30 price, a "floor" developed— a floor placed by the pure investor, not the collector or dealer.

In early 1974 at least some collectors believed that if President Richard M. Nixon resigned, the value of his autographs would sky-rocket for a short while because a President who resigned would be unique in American history. Nixon signatures sold for about $7.50 in early 1974. His signed letters (L.S.) went for about $55, but his handwritten signed letters (A.L.S.) realized more than $1,500.

Where autographs are sold

The selling organization for autographs is not extensive. There are in this country about five auction houses for autographs and about thirty dealers. The two major New York autograph auctions each have an annual volume of about $600,000, and the total annual volume in the United States is about $10 million.

In 1973, Sotheby Parke Bernet held sixteen auctions which in-cluded autographs. Charles Hamilton scheduled ten sales in 1974. Each of the Hamilton auctions offers 300 to 400 lots, and lots are sold at a rate of about 100 per hour. Some lower-priced items are grouped in one lot so that the auction does not last an interminable time.

The main sources of autographs are collectors and people who have had autographs in the family for a number of years and have for one reason or another decided to convert them into cash.

The auction houses sell most autographs on consignment for the owners. The Charles Hamilton auction also sells some items it has purchased previously from sellers.

Expert collectors

About 90 percent of those who buy autographs at auction are quite expert in the field, which makes this collectible somewhat unique. These very knowledgeable buyers include regular collectors, dealers, investors, and representatives of institutions—libraries, foundations, museums, universities, and colleges.

A good deal of bidding and buying is done by mail or by tele-phone, and often in the Hamilton auctions 90 to 95 percent of the lots will be covered by bids by the time the sale begins. How-ever, the actual purchases are usually about equally divided be-tween mail bids and salesroom bids. Most major dealers attend the sales or send representatives.

For ten days prior to each Hamilton auction, all of the material is displayed at the Hamilton galleries in midtown Manhattan. The actual sale is held in a suite at the Waldorf Astoria Hotel. Unlike

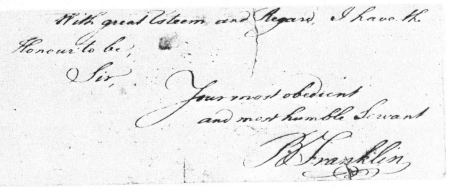

Autographs of American Revolution personages are rising in price as the bicentennial celebration nears. This Benjamin Franklin letter is valued at $300.

the usual auction procedure, no merchandise is present when the auction is in progress.

Estimates are placed on each lot by the Hamilton galleries and by Sotheby Parke Bernet. The buyers, being for the most part old hands, do not take these estimates very seriously and apparently prefer to do their own estimating. Still these estimates are helpful to the novice collector and also to the dealers in that they indicate what the auction house feels the condition and content are worth. Prices sometimes fall within the estimates, but more often than not they exceed—at times considerably exceed—the estimates.

Every three weeks autograph dealer Kenneth Rendell of Newton, Massachusetts, issues a sales catalog, as do leading dealers throughout the world. Rendell's catalogs number about seventy-five pages each and include the price of each item. This practice of frequent dealer catalogs also is almost unique in the entire field of collectibles. Dealers and collectors read these catalogs immediately upon receiving them and quickly make their purchases by telegram, telephone, or letter so as not to miss the best values.

The performance of the autograph market

Autographs boomed along with many other things in the 1920s, and in the spring of 1929 composer Jerome Kern sold his rare book and autograph collection for about $1 million. This sum he invested in the stock market with disastrous results.

Most autographs went down in price during the Great Depression along with the prices of many other collectibles and in general lost at least 75 percent of their 1929 value. Some autographs went down to 5 percent of their 1929 peaks.

It was not until the early 1950s that autograph prices began to move upward significantly. Between then and the present time, autographs have moved up in price by about 10 percent per year.

Certain autographs and certain categories of autographs have, however, deviated from this approximate overall percentage figure. Gabriel Austin of the Sotheby Parke Bernet galleries estimates that autographs of famous composers have increased in price 100 times in the past two decades. In March, 1973, Sotheby Parke Bernet offered for sale an autograph manuscript of Beethoven's Rondo a Capriccio consisting of eight pages with sixteen staves to the page. The gallery estimated that this lot would sell for $20,000 to $25,000. It brought $57,500.

In May of the same year a letter by George Washington—twenty-two and a half pages in length—sold in the same New York gallery for $27,500. Later in 1973, the Hanzel Gallery in Chicago sold a Washington letter for an even larger sum—$37,000. At this auction a record of $800,000 was established for a sale of rare books and autographs.

A fairly good indication of the market can be obtained by noting the prices at various times for George Washington's autographs. Charles Hamilton bought a George Washington letter from a Paris dealer for $500 in the late 1950s. The price of $500 was high for the time. Ordinary letters by George Washington were selling closer to $100 in that era.

Hamilton offered the letter for sale privately a short time after he had purchased it, and received $1,000 for it. Five years later the owner gave the letter to a school and had it appraised at the time. The appraisal figure was $5,000. Ten years later the school decided to sell the letter in order to raise cash. It brought $25,000 at auction. Today the value of the letter would be about $40,000.

Value determinants

The factors which determine the present and future values of autographs are:

1. *Quality*. This does not simply mean good condition but rather an autograph which is highly thought of by collectors, in demand, *and* in good condition.

Charles Hamilton advises, "Buy the best—everything rare and fine and important—the gilt-edge autographs." Mary A. Benjamin also lists quality at the top. Gabriel Austin of Sotheby Parke Bernet says, "Pay 20 percent more for something good rather than 20 percent less for an autograph that has something wrong with it. If you have to apologize, don't buy it. You will be apologizing for the rest of your life."

Quality does not mean, "Always buy a George Washington A.L.S. in mint condition." It does mean, "Buy an autograph that you like, but one that is also a good overall collectible."

The Present Values of Famous Names

The following names are a selection of autographs valued according to three classifications—*S.* (Signature only), *L.S.* (Letter Signed), and *A.L.S.* (Autograph Letter Signed):

	S.	*L.S.*	*A.L.S.*
John Adams	$350	$ 900	$1,600
Napoleon Bonaparte	110	225	7,500
Winston Churchill	50	250	400
Albert Einstein	25	125	450
Sigmund Freud	100	500	1,000
John Hancock	175	350	650
William Henry Harrison	40	100	300
Adolph Hitler	100	300	2,000
Herbert Hoover	7.50	45	800
Jacqueline Kennedy	20	150	500
John Kennedy	150	400	2,000
Abraham Lincoln	300	650	1,750
Mary T. Lincoln	125	500	1,000
Harry Truman	7.50	75	350
George Washington	600	2,000	3,250

Note: These are approximate prices and probably no item will sell for the exact amount given above.

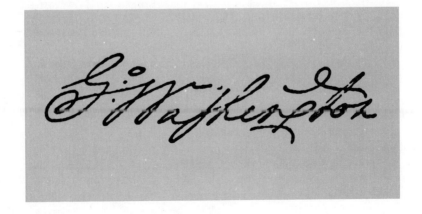

2. *Demand*. This is a highly important value-determining element in autograph collecting. There are many autographs by George Washington, Abraham Lincoln, and Napoleon that come regularly onto the market. Prices of these autographs are high because demand is great. However, overall demand is small for autographs at the present time, compared with the demand for many other collectibles, and an auction with relatively few bidders will result in low prices. As demand grows, prices are very likely to rise, as they have done in the past.

3. *Rarity*. Rarity ranks next in importance, unlike in many other fields of collecting. If demand is high for a particular type of autograph and the supply is limited, the price will be high. The highest priced of all of the signers of the Declaration of Independence is Button Gwinnett. His autographs are much in demand and only about seventy-five of them are known to exist. A letter signed by Button Gwinnett might well bring $35,000 on the present market. His signature alone would bring at least $2,000 at auction today, according to Charles Hamilton.

4. *Condition*. There should be few, if any, spots, stains, or torn places. The signature should be intact, and preferably all parts of a letter, including the wax seal (if used) and the envelope with canceled stamps or frank, should be with the letter.

5. *Content*. This is of tremendous importance in determining value. Is the text historically significant? Is it interesting? These are value-increasing factors. If the letter is merely in the "invitation to dine" category, it is of less value than a letter of the same date by the same person in which matters of concern are discussed. However, "thank you" notes which say little but were signed by a President when in office are avidly collected to complete a series of the Presidents. A similar series of the signers of the Declaration of Independence is also popular among collectors.

6. *Size and clarity of the signature and of the writing in a letter*. The signature should be clear—not faded or smudged—and should be genuine, not a facsimile. Often signatures are written by secretaries or, more recently, by the autopen. The length of the text, its placement on the pages, and other aspects of the format might be of some importance. How these technical points may apply to the autographs of a particular writer can be learned by studying auction and dealer catalogs and by visiting auctions, dealers, and public collections.

7. *Fashion*. At the present time, the category of musicians and composers is in great demand. Interest in the signers of the Declaration of Independence and Revolutionary War heroes has increased because of the 1976 bicentennial celebration. Artists are fashionable, as are astronauts and Nazis. American and British

48 Doughty Street
Monday morning

Dear Sir.

I am very much obliged to
you for your elegant little present
which I have received with great
pleasure.

Let me beg you to accept
my best thanks, and to believe
me,

Dear Sir

Very truly yours

Charles Dickens

Although autographs of British authors are popular, this letter signed by Charles Dickens is valued at just $100.

authors are also popular. Religious figures are less in vogue, and the Civil War might be considered "undervalued." World War I heroes and statesmen are in less demand now than previously, and World War II personages never have been in much demand.

Guide to buying

The novice collector of autographs should:

• *Specialize to a certain extent,* in order to become knowledgeable in a few particularly attractive areas.

• *Avoid spending much money too early in the game,* as mistakes may discourage you. Later, when you are an expert, it may prove wise to pay higher prices for quality autographs. The best autographs do not cost a great deal more than the average ones, but they tend to retain their value even in poor times. Top quality tends to find a buyer—if anything can. Then too, fine items bring great psychic rewards to the collector, who can feel proud to own and display his collection.

• *Buy from reliable dealers and auction houses.* There are many fake autographs on the market. There are also many poor-quality autographs that arrive at small auction houses with furniture consignments. Investing in these "finds" should be postponed until the novice collector gathers greater knowledge.

• *Inspect before you buy, if possible.* However, a reputable auction house will make refunds to those who did not have time to inspect items before purchase and later find that the items are not as represented.

• *Watch fad buying.* Fads tend to carry everyone along on a wave of enthusiasm, with expectations of enormous profits just around the corner. Yet fads go out as fast as they come in and they are very risky. It is far better to build solidly in an area in which values are still low or rising moderately year by year, or to acquire items considered to be long-term gilt-edge investments.

• *Buy for a solid investment* but do not expect a bonanza. Overall, autographs appear to be a solid investment in the present market. During the recession of 1970 several types of collectibles fell in price substantially. Autographs were for the most part unaffected by the recession, probably because the field has not yet entered the high-price category of collectibles.

PART SIX

Investing in Superluxuries

The finer pieces of nineteenth-century jewelry can be good investments as well as attractive ornaments. This suite of gold and pink topazes in filigree gold with a fitted case, circa 1830, was purchased for $1,500 at auction in 1973.

24

Precious
Gems
and
Jewelry

To a considerable extent precious gems are regarded as investments. Of course a fine diamond, ruby, or emerald is a beautiful thing, as is a finely made piece of jewelry, but the value of modern pieces does not depend on artistry. In antique jewelry the artistry which created the piece is an important element in value. In fact if some of the finest and most valuable pieces of antique jewelry were broken up and sold, the gold and gemstones they contain would be of very little value.

While jewelry has been made since the pre-Christian era, antique jewelry can be conveniently divided into four categories: Greco-Roman, at about the beginning of the Christian era; Renaissance, sometimes divided into Early Renaissance and High Renaissance; eighteenth century; and nineteenth century, including Victorian.

Greco-Roman

In general Greco-Roman jewelry is fairly simple with few elaborate designs, and on the present market it seems inexpensive in view of its age and quality.

On December 1, 1969, an antique jewelry sale was held in New York in which the first lot offered was a Greco-Roman agate cameo made around the turn of the Christian era. The piece was in the form of a large oval with a diameter of just under 2 inches. It realized $375. As cameos have risen greatly in price, today this same piece would realize three to four times this sum.

In the same 1969 sale was a Roman agate intaglio of the third century A.D. It measured 1-3/16 inches in diameter and had been displayed in the Minneapolis Institute of Arts. It sold for $100, and today would bring four times this sum.

An excellent, museum-exhibited, female portrait bust in profile, a Roman agate cameo of the third or fourth century A.D. brought $2,500 in the 1969 sale. It contained emeralds, had an elaborate open gold border, and was 2¼ inches high. Today this piece too would bring from three to four times the 1969 price. Although the market has risen since 1969, Greek and Roman pieces of jewelry are still not expensive, on the average, and cameos in particular are undervalued.

Renaissance

The jewelry of the Renaissance was not marked and therefore it is difficult to date and to determine the country of origin of many pieces.

Recently two loans were made with pieces of Renaissance jewelry as the collateral for the loans. The loan on the first piece was $350,000 and on the second piece $130,000. The loans were defaulted, and when the leading New York auction house estimated the probable auction price of each piece, the estimates turned out to be $12,000 for the first piece and $20,000 to $30,000 for the second piece. In 1967 a photograph of the first piece had been published in a leading art magazine, which stated that the piece was made in 1540. Still, the recent examination found it to be too perfect; the pose of the figure seemed typically Victorian and too romanticized.

Renaissance jewelry is usually ornate and intricately carved and pierced. Pendants were very common, and enamel, gold, diamonds, and pearls were often used. Many pieces had a religious theme.

One of the most successful auctions ever held was the Sydney J. Lamon sale of "Continental Silver, Renaissance Jewelry, Gold Boxes and Objects of Vertu," on November 28, 1973, at Christie's in London. At this sale a German enameled and jeweled gold pendant in the form of a bust of a warrior, set with diamonds and pearls, 4⅜ inches high, brought $11,025. A somewhat similar Spanish pendant made about the same time—1600—and 2⅜ inches high, brought $7,350.

An even smaller piece of jewelry, made in Italy about 1550, 1¾

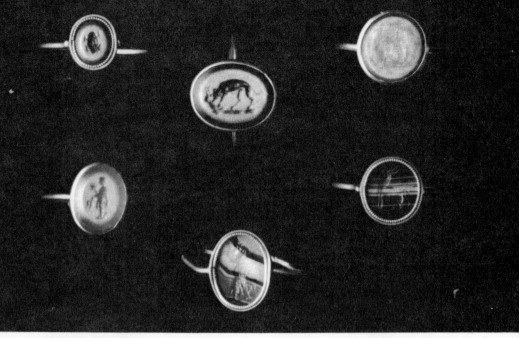

Despite its age and quality, Greco-Roman jewelry is not expensive. These intaglios of the second/third century A.D. sold for $1,000 in late 1973.

inches high, went for $13,650. The piece was made of gold and enamel, and the figure was of John the Evangelist. A German gold and enameled chain, 17¾ inches long, made in the sixteenth century, with imitation jewels in each link of the chain, realized about $25,000.

In all of these pieces the stones and the gold were of very little value. The value of each piece depended strictly on collector interest combined with rarity.

On December 10, 1973, Sotheby's in London sold some simpler Renaissance pieces for prices more within the range of most buyers. A German gold signet ring made in the second half of the sixteenth century brought about $550. A fourteenth-century Italian gold signet ring sold for $450. A very fine Italian agate cameo pendant, 2¼ inches high, of the late sixteenth century, was purchased for about $2,500, and a sixteenth-century English gold and enamel reliquary pendant brought about double this figure.

The jewelry of the seventeenth century is about as scarce as that of the Renaissance and much of it is the same in style. As in the case of Renaissance jewelry, the "breakdown value" is not great since the stones are not of modern cut and many of them are of poor quality by today's standards. The value depends on rarity, specialized collector interest, and artistry.

In the December 10, 1973, sale at Sotheby's, a Spanish gold and baroque pearl pendant of the seventeenth century, 2¾ inches high

Jewelry with a religious theme is often reasonably priced. These pieces were bought in 1973: top—gold cross set with blue crystals, made in Spain circa 1700, $850; left—gold pendant with wax Nativity scene, early eighteenth century, $1,500; right—gold framed infant Saint John painted on glass, early eighteenth century, $1,600; bottom—pendant with enameled Christ Child, circa 1600, in gold and pearl frame, circa 1800, $700.

and carved in the form of a griffin, brought about $1,100. An Italian seventeenth-century gold, enamel, and rock crystal pendant with a miniature of Mary Magdalene, 2¾ inches high, sold for $600, and a very fine French gold and enamel locket, 2¼ inches high, circa 1640-50, was purchased for $720.

One of the leading dealers in antique silver and jewelry is N. Bloom and Son of New Bond Street in London. From time to time they issue catalogs containing color illustrations of their jewelry and silver. While their early 1974 catalog contained descriptions of well over 100 items, there was only one seventeenth-century piece, a cameo of a man's head mounted as a brooch in an eighteenth-century frame of gold and pearls. The price was about $850. It might be noted that later framing and alterations of early jewelry are not at all uncommon, and this later work does not seriously diminish the value of such pieces.

Eighteenth century

Enamel was deemphasized in the eighteenth century. The stones themselves were featured, rather than the jewel as an overall work of art and craftsmanship. Prior to the eighteenth century the designers of jewels also made the jewelry pieces. In the eighteenth century the two functions were separated.

In England and France the diamond became the preferred stone. Jewels took on a new balance of design very similar to today's jewelry.

In the second half of the eighteenth century jewelry craftsmanship was superb. Pearls were more esteemed than ever before, and the posy of flowers design was very popular.

Although eighteenth-century jewelry is not a rarity on today's market, it is quite high in price. A well-made and attractive pin or pendant sells for about $2,000, and the finest pieces, which rarely come onto the market, are extremely expensive.

In October, 1973, a late-eighteenth-century cameo of good quality was sold at auction. It was a framed gold intaglio in the form of a camel, 3 inches high, and was signed by the maker—Pichler. It realized $3,900. In 1969 it would probably have brought $1,000. With this jewel there was a bill of sale dated 1926—for fifty pounds, about $250.

The eighteenth-century style of jewelry continued to be made until about 1820, and in this respect antique jewelry parallels antique furniture in style change. The year 1820 is the rough cutoff date in antique furniture, the earlier period being much preferred.

The early 1974 catalog of the London antique jewelry dealer, N. Bloom and Son, listed a Swiss painted enamel and pearl brooch, circa 1820, with figures of a man and woman, for $880. Also offered was an attractive Regency baluster-shaped gold fob seal. The piece contained a family crest and motto. The date was 1820 and the price was $97. Another fob seal of about the same date in three-color gold with a citrine base and the forms of a snake and a mandolin was for sale for $230.

Nineteenth century

Most of the jewelry offered for sale in the United States and in England that dates from the nineteenth century is called Victorian, although it must be pointed out that Victoria reigned from 1837 to 1901. The so-called Victorian style was native to England but influenced the craftsmen and factories of other countries.

Victorian jewelry is available all over the United States, and in London alone one could easily acquire a truckload of it today. Until about 1969 it could be bought at low prices in the United States and at even lower prices in England. It was generally considered by jewelry collectors to be second-rate, and only the finest pieces were collected or worn, and if worn, then only as a novelty. In the past few years collectors have been taking a second look at nineteenth-century jewelry and its price has risen.

The industrial revolution which had its strong beginnings in England from 1795 to 1815 brought forth a great demand for jewelry which could be produced at more reasonable cost through mass-production methods. Colored stones, particularly amethysts and topazes, were favored, and gold was the preferred metal for settings. Miniature mosaics were fashionable for a time.

Before the middle of the nineteenth century a Tudor-Gothic style came into vogue in England. This style was developed in Paris by François Désiré Froment Meurice, who later turned to the style which in some ways was dominant during the latter part of the century—Art Nouveau. Meurice's style was taken up by A.W. Pugin. Jewelry in the classical style was created by John Brogden of England and by two eminent Italian jewelry makers, Castellani and Giuliano. Other prominent designer-makers were Falize, Foutenay, Hancock, Morel, Robert Phillips, and G. Cayley. If one of these names can be attached to a piece of jewelry, its value is increased.

Near the middle of the nineteenth century diamonds and pearls began to predominate in jewelry. Mass production caused a decline in the quality of jewelry design and manufacture, but there were still a few artist-artisans creating fine pieces. By 1895, René Lalique had innovated in the field of Art Nouveau. Meurice, Falize, and Giuliano also worked in the Art Nouveau style. Carl Fabergé produced jewelry with top-grade craftsmanship in St. Petersburg, Russia. Fabergé pieces—almost never reasonable in price—are as avidly sought after as any jewelry ever made.

There could hardly be a better investment in nineteenth-century jewelry than pieces made by Castellani and Giuliano. Their jewelry was original and handmade, and their "antique" style was dominant until the last part of the nineteenth century when Art Nouveau came in. The work of these two craftsmen is in many ways like jewelry of the seventeenth century and earlier. Classical designs were used and artistry was emphasized rather than simply a display of brilliant stones.

Although Castellani and Giuliano were both Italians and competitors, Giuliano worked in London. What is of some significance in his jewelry is that he "signed" most of his pieces. In early 1974 a London sales catalog listed a green sapphire, pearl, and enamel pendant in the sixteenth-century style by Carlo Giuliano for $1,850.

Among the best buys in nineteenth-century jewelry are pieces by the leading designer-makers which have enamel work in perfect condition, particularly those in the "rococo revival" style. Important pieces are the surest candidates for value appreciation, and they do not represent too great an investment per piece. Secular pieces should be stressed as the market seems to shy away from jewelry with a religious theme. Seal rings are still inexpensive, but they are rising in value. Tiffany jewelry of the nineteenth century also seems to be very much wanted simply because it was made for Tiffany and Company and sold by them.

In early 1974 pieces of very good Victorian jewelry were for sale. These are some examples:

- Opal, ruby, and gold brooch-pendant with flower and leaf motifs—$825.
- Angel-skin coral and gold brooch-pendant—$410.
- Fine pair of earrings, gold and rose diamond in lily-of-the-valley design—$960.
- Locket and earrings with diamonds between numerous half pearls—$1,260.
- Excellent pendant of twisted gold rope, black and white enamel, oval cabochon sapphire, and pearls—$1,050.

Victorian rings of very good quality can be purchased in the United States for under $1,000. In London at retail an early Victorian rose diamond and garnet ring mounted in gold can be bought for about $190. The investment risk in purchasing this piece is not great, nor is it great for a ring of garnets and diamonds set in gold, offered at $145.

The center for Victorian and other nineteenth-century jewelry is London, and probably the lower prices asked there might pay for a trip to that city if the main objective of the visit is to buy nineteenth-century jewelry. Still such jewelry appears in the shops of many American dealers and in American auctions. In the smaller auctions, Victorian jewelry sometimes sells at under market prices. It must be emphasized, however, that many of these pieces are not a good investment as they are made of poor stones with an out-of-date cut. Still, Victorian jewelry of the finer individually designed, craftsman-made variety represents a very good investment.

Modern

Only the jewelry of the twentieth century can be strictly classified as modern, although the modern period is sometimes extended to cover the past 100 years.

The value of modern jewelry is determined mainly by the value of the gemstones and the scrap value of the metals. From a market point of view, the actual pieces of modern jewelry are considerably less important than the gems they contain—diamonds, rubies, emeralds, and sapphires, for the most part. In valuable jewelry, the value of the stones is of vastly greater importance than the setting or the gold, platinum, or silver in the setting.

At present, auction sales catalogs do not contain the weights of platinum, gold, or silver but only the weights of diamonds and sometimes of pearls and other precious stones. As metal markets rise, perhaps metal weights will be included in catalogs. It might be noted at this point that the quality of the diamonds is omitted from the descriptions in almost every auction catalog.

Diamonds

The mining of diamonds and their marketing are rigidly controlled by the syndicate regulating the flow out of South Africa, so that the price is very stable and rises a limited amount each year. Diamonds and jewelry containing diamonds come to auction houses almost exclusively from estates. This supply is of course uncontrolled and its volume is unpredictable.

To a great extent diamonds are a standard product whose values are determined by grade of gemstone. A great deal of experience is necessary to determine grade, which depends on color and degree of perfection. The investor in diamond jewelry might ask what difference grade makes if it cannot easily be determined, provided the diamond and the piece of jewelry containing it are attractive. The answer is that resale value—the price a dealer will pay, or the price an auction house will receive, for the piece—is determined strictly by grade. Investment value depends on grade.

Often the top grade of diamonds is called *fine white flawless*, and for years this was the accepted term for the best diamonds. Fine white is the best color on the commercial market. Flawless means free of imperfections. One method of grading starts with *fine white* at the top and goes down through *white, commercial white, yellow,* and *cape,* with a few other grades included at times. From *flawless* the classifications descend through *VVS* (very very slight imperfection) to *VS* (very slight imperfection), and so on down. This old means of classification is just one of many used at the present time.

Diamond grading and classification are not entirely fixed, and in the words of the director of the Gemological Institute of America, "What is 'fine white' to one man is another man's 'cape.' " The institute uses a system running from *D* for the best and whitest stone to *Z* for the worst color—yellow.

Some grading systems run from *AAA* to *AA* to *A* and then down to *B, C, D,* and so on. One color grading system uses *0* for the best (clear and colorless) and *10* for the poorest. Another system refers to origin, classifying the *Jager* mine and the *River* mine and their areas as being the best.

"Blue white" is not a grade and this is one of the first lessons a diamond investor learns. Approximately one in twenty diamonds will show a bluish color in sunlight if the ultraviolet rays cause the diamond to fluoresce. Sometimes artificial radiation is used to make a stone green or blue, but it cannot be used to make a stone clearer or colorless. If a diamond shows a yellow color under the jeweler's loop or magnifier in daylight, the stone has a minus against it. The closer the stone is to being colorless and flawless, the higher its grade.

The novice collector, after some schooling by a diamond specialist or a jeweler dealing in diamonds, can do some rudimentary grading and can gradually become more expert. Nevertheless, before actually investing in a diamond, it is advisable to pay a diamond specialist his fee for an expert analysis of grade and an appraisal of value.

Modern jewelry should contain modern-cut diamonds for it to be valuable. Old mine-cut diamonds have little commercial value as they have to be recut for resetting and they are frequently of poor grade. As a general rule, modern diamonds and settings are better than those that immediately preceded the modern period, and a piece of jewelry made in 1974 generally has more value than, say, a 1940 piece from a market point of view—other things being equal, of course—because of changes in fashion and taste.

Diamonds have standard weights and are measured in carats, a carat being one-fifth of a gram. The dealer's scales can be used to check the weight; calipers can be used only to estimate weight.

Anyone considering diamonds and diamond jewelry as an investment might well confine himself to the better-grade stones, perhaps

white and *VVS* (very very slight imperfection). He might begin by
looking for top-grade stones, whether they are called *fine white
flawless* or some equivalent term. He might then move down a grade
if he cannot find or afford the best, but in any event he should avoid
the many large and very flawed stones of poor color that are always
on the market.

Top-grade diamonds have been increasing in price in recent years
and the larger ones are becoming rare. It is still possible to find top-
grade stones of from one to five carats, but very difficult to find top-
grade ones of ten carats or more. The African mines do not seem to
be producing as many large diamonds as they did in earlier years,
and private owners have become reluctant to part with these stones
as they are increasingly considered to be a good investment.

On October 23, 1969, a diamond of 69.42 carats was sold at auction. It was known, and still is known, as The Cartier Diamond. It
realized $1,050,000 when it was bought by Cartier at auction. It
then became the property of Mrs. Richard Burton (Elizabeth Taylor) and at the time was regarded by some diamond collectors as
more of a splurge than an investment. Two years prior to this
auction date it had sold for approximately $500,000. Dennis J.
Scioli, vice president of Sotheby Parke Bernet in New York and
head of the jewelry department of that auction house, estimates
that if this diamond had been sold in early 1974 it would have
brought from 30 to 50 percent over the $1,050,000 it realized in
1969.

Smaller stones—those weighing from one to five carats—have
risen in price as the large ones have and in three years have shown
an appreciation of 50 to 75 percent. People have always invested in
diamonds, but now new buyers in the market are pushing up prices.

It is by no means certain that an investor can buy a diamond now
and make a profit regardless of when in the future he may sell it.
The diamond market does not move upward that fast. The natural
resale market is the auction market, and one should not buy at retail
and expect a short-term profit on resale at auction. Such a procedure
might result in a 25 percent loss, principally because the auction
market as a rule is lower than the retail market.

The person who wishes to make a strict investment, and not simply purchase an attractive ornament, might well concentrate on
acquiring those pieces dominated by the stones and not by the setting, since the stones determine resale value.

It might require four or five years to get back an investment in a
fine and intricately made piece of jewelry. The gem market would
have to rise enough to offset the original cost of the setting. It is a
corollary that large stones are more valuable than small stones as
they are more important than the setting and represent a larger

This antique diamond tiara was purchased for $17,000 in 1958. In December, 1973, it was sold at auction for $60,000.

percentage of the cost of the piece. It might also follow that loose diamonds are an even better investment since nothing must be paid for any setting that may prove of little value on resale.

Colored gemstones

The main colored gems from the viewpoint of value, and probably ornamentation too, are rubies, emeralds, and sapphires. These are the stones which have been preferred for many years by Europeans for adornment and investment. In the past fifteen years, however, Americans have been turning to colored stones and in consequence prices have been rising, probably even more than diamond prices.

The finest rubies and sapphires usually come from Kashmir and Burma, but these two areas are now producing fewer stones of investment quality. Originally, emeralds came from India, but most modern emeralds come from Colombia. The old Indian emeralds had a deep, rich color. While the Colombian emeralds perhaps have a poorer color they tend to be less flawed.

In 1968 the Audrey Kennedy estate offered for sale at auction in New York a nearly perfect and very large emerald weighing thirty-four carats. It was valued for estate purpose at $75,000, which seemed a fair valuation. The price realized at auction was $265,000 and the buyer was Enid Haupt. The same stone was offered at auction in New York in 1972 as a part of Mrs. Haupt's collection. It brought $385,000.

As recently as 1971 a ten-carat sapphire might have been auctioned for $10,000. The same stone might well bring $25,000 today. A one-carat stone might have increased in value by 50 percent in this same period.

Fine rubies are the rarest of all of the gemstones, and rubies of fine quality weighing from seven or eight carats upward, particularly those of pigeon-blood red, almost never appear on the auction market. Collectors search avidly for such rarities and the stones are virtually priceless. Even top-grade rubies weighing two or three carats are rare, but they can be found. Very nearly every ruby contains imperfections, and these flaws are accepted by experts. Sotheby Parke Bernet in the past decade has sold only a few top-grade large rubies. In November, 1973, a ruby of fine quality weighing about seven carats brought $150,000 at auction.

Pearls

In the first two decades of the present century the Oriental, or natural, pearl was the greatest treasure. One determinant of value was that anyone could recognize a pearl for what it was—a very costly ornament.

In 1929 the cultured pearl made its appearance on the market.

The important attribute of the cultured pearl was that the casual observer could not distinguish it from the Oriental (natural) pearl. The wearer of the Oriental pearl immediately lost a good deal of her distinction.

Both the Oriental pearl and the cultured pearl are made by the oyster. The former is made by the oyster entirely unaided. The oyster makes the cultured pearl by depositing the same substance on a little ball or nucleus inserted by hand into the oyster's shell, and unless one can see below the surface of the pearl, it is not possible to tell whether or not there is an artificial nucleus. The Gemological Institute, for a reasonable price, will take an X-ray picture of a pearl which will indicate whether it is Oriental or cultured.

When synthetic pearls were put on the market not very long ago, they were such good imitations of real pearls that Oriental pearl prices dropped even further. Then too, cultured pearls were imported in great quantities and the rarity of the pearl came to an end.

A pearl is a perishable adornment. It reacts unfavorably to the body chemistry if worn too much. It is sensitive to perfume and to hair spray, and if worn a great deal it tends to lose its roundness and to become barrel-shaped.

In the early part of this century, Cartier acquired its present Fifth Avenue building from Mrs. John E. Rovensky in exchange for two magnificent strings of pearls. The pearls had been carefully collected and matched by Cartier over a period of several years before the trade was made with Mrs. Rovensky, and each string was valued at $1 million. In 1957 the Rovensky collection, including the pearls, came onto the market after the death of its owner. One of the strings of pearls contained fifty-five pearls and weighed 851 grains. It brought $90,000. The other string contained seventy-three pearls and weighed 861 grains. It brought $61,000. If these pearls were auctioned today, they might bring only one-half of their 1957 prices.

A fine string of white or cream-colored Oriental pearls may well bring only $5,000 to $10,000 at the present time. An ordinary string of Oriental pearls may bring $1,000 today. A magnificent set of pearls that cost $100,000 before the 1929 crash may well sell for only $10,000 to $15,000 today.

In the 1920s a very fine pearl necklace was purchased for $500,000. In 1974 the owner felt he might consider selling it and brought it to an auction house experienced in pearl sales to determine the advisability of putting it up for sale. The auction house's estimate of the selling price was one-tenth of the $500,000 purchase price. The owner decided to keep his pearls, and many owners of pearls purchased decades ago at high prices have arrived at similar decisions.

Great rarities and museum pieces are quite another matter. On

May 17, 1973, Sotheby's in Zurich, Switzerland, sold a necklace of twenty-five large bronze-black pearls—a highly unusual color to find in even one pearl. The total weight was 1,243 grains, and the price realized was $99,875. In the same sale a pair of black pearl earrings weighing 111.88 grains brought $10,613. A ring containing one black pearl, weighing 81.60 grains and mounted with a few diamonds, sold for $16,230. These pieces were all great rarities, sought after by collectors and museums.

Recent prices

In February, 1974, an auction sale of jewelry—not the finest jewelry by any means, but some good pieces—was held in New York. These were some of the investment-quality pieces and their selling prices:

• Diamond and emerald bracelet, platinum mount with 3 marquise diamonds weighing 3 carats, 24 marquise diamonds weighing 4 carats, 126 round diamonds, 30 baguette diamonds, 24 French-cut diamonds totaling 12.25 carats, and 6 square-cut emeralds—$6,250 (about $300 per carat with, of course, no value attributed to the emeralds because no weights were given for these stones).

• Oval diamond brooch with 48 old mine-cut diamonds weighing 4.75 carats and a center mine-cut diamond of 1.25 carats—$1,100 (under $200 a carat, a fair price for out-of-date stones).

• Diamond and platinum bracelet with 1 pear-shaped diamond of 1.25 carats, 6 marquise diamonds totaling 2 carats, 4 round diamonds of 3.65 carats, and 125 diamonds of 6 carats—$3,000 ($230 a carat).

• Diamond and carved ruby bracelet, platinum openwork setting with 247 diamonds weighing 34 carats and 17 rubies carved as leaves—$5,750 ($170 a carat, with no value imputed to the rubies).

• Diamond and platinum bracelet with 71 French-cut diamonds and 238 round diamonds weighing 18 carats—$3,300 (under $200 a carat).

• Six pear-shaped diamonds without setting weighing 4.97 carats—$1,800 ($360 a carat).

Market factors

These are the significant market factors in modern jewelry:

• Diamonds are rising in value steadily but not spectacularly and not in a speculative fever.

• Sapphires, rubies, and emeralds are rising faster than diamonds.

• Pearls are at the bottom of a price decline that has gone on for at least forty-five years, and at present there is no upward movement, except for great rarities in matched and unusually colored necklaces and a few individual pearls.

• The resale or investment value of a piece of modern jewelry depends primarily on the value of the stones, with only scrap value imputed to the setting, no matter how elaborate or how costly to make.

• There is some temporary buying, such as Japanese buying, that has pushed up present prices, and such demand cannot always be counted on to hold up or raise the market in the future.

• The falling dollar increased European buying in the United States. The increase in the value of the dollar may very well reduce this demand.

• Auction prices are usually lower than retail, as the many dealers who buy at auction must mark up prices for resale.

• Private buyers were not increasing in the major jewelry auction market of New York in early 1974, and there may even be a decrease in private buyers until economic uncertainties are resolved.

• There is a tendency of investors who are not in the stock market to buy gemstones, but those who remained in the dropping stock market are not now inclined to get out and buy jewelry.

• The buyers of the higher-quality gemstones and jewelry are Europeans rather than Americans.

• The transportability of gemstones and jewelry is important to many investors, as such items can be easily carried from one country to another.

The would-be investor should remember that the gemstones determine the value of modern jewelry. Loose stones are therefore a good investment as no value is imputed to the setting, which is worth little either in resale value or in scrap value upon breakup of the piece. In today's market, diamonds and rubies might be concentrated on, particularly the larger and finer ones.

There has been a growing movement among larger investors to purchase shares in a bag of diamonds which is kept in a safe-deposit vault, generally outside of the United States. Such share ownership of diamonds can be safer than investing in one of the hard currencies of the world.

French wines lined up according to bottle sizes. From left, imperiale, jero-
boam, double magnum, magnum, and ordinary-size bottle. With the exception
of the Château Lafite-Rothschild 1949 in the center, these wines date from
the 1920s and are rarely obtainable.

CHAPTER 25

Wines

In the early summer of 1969 an American art and antique collector checked in at a hotel in Canterbury, England. He used this town in Kent, near the coast, as a base for his collecting as there are many antique dealers in the area and it also is well situated for taking a plane, a boat, or a hovercraft to the continent in order to do further collecting.

Across from his hotel there was a little wine shop, B.C. Blyth and Company. The wine shop appeared to have been there since the time the building was constructed, which was apparently during the fifteenth century.

Each time the collector strolled by he looked at the wines on display in the window and then often went into the shop to chat with the proprietor, A.M. Tee. From this knowledgeable wine merchant the American gradually learned a good deal concerning prices of fine vintage wines and market trends.

Eventually the visitor decided to purchase some vintage wines as an investment. Over the next three years on his visits to Canterbury he purchased what appeared to him to be a substantial amount of wine. He did not remove the wine from the shop. He simply stored it there and hopefully waited for it to rise in value.

Among his purchases were a dozen double bottles (magnums) of Romanée-Conti Burgundy, vintage year 1964, for $27 a double bottle, which amounts to $13.50 for the ordinary-size bottle, and a case of Château Latour 1959 for about $7.50 a bottle. He also bought the rare 1949 vintage Château Latour for $11.25 a bottle, and for the same price per bottle he purchased Château Latour 1952 and Château Mouton-Rothschild 1952.

As late as the summer of 1972 he purchased a case of Château Margaux 1952 and a case of Château Latour 1952 for $353 for the two cases—about $14.70 a bottle. He also acquired some Mouton-Rothschild 1955 for the same price.

To his collection of wines in Canterbury the American added a case of Lafite-Rothschild 1959 which he bought at Christie's wine auction in London for $13.50 a bottle.

In the spring of 1973 he sold his wines at Christie's wine auction. Among other prices realized, the Romanée-Conti magnums, which had cost $27 each, brought over $80 each. The Lafite-Rothschild 1959 realized $63 a bottle. It had cost $13.50 only a year earlier.

The collector totaled up what the wine had cost him. It came to $987.54. After his commission to Christie's and a few other expenses, he received a net of $2,992.21. His profit was thus $2,004.67 on his investment of $987.54 held for an average of about two and a half years.

What are investment wines?

There are three types of wine that are, at the present time, investments. Two of the wines come from France and the third comes from Portugal. The French wines are Bordeaux and Burgundy, both red, dry (sugar-free) wines. The Portuguese wine is red and sweet. All are what is known as vintage wines. The vintage year is on the bottle and to a considerable extent determines the market price and the investment value of the wine. A few American red, dry wines are investments also, but these are very scarce and are not readily available for purchase.

White wines, with the possible exception of a few French sauternes and barsacs, notably the Château d'Yquem—the best sweet white wine in the world—have a limited life. The drier the white wine the shorter its life. The same is true, but to a lesser degree, of the French Beaujolais wines which have a little less body and are slightly lighter in color than Bordeaux and Burgundies, although Beaujolais is technically also a Burgundy wine.

Champagnes have a life of about ten years. At the end of that period they should be drunk. If they are kept in a cellar at a carefully maintained temperature, they will last longer, and the best champagnes do become collectors' items, but collecting champagnes is only for the expert.

If investment-quality red wines are kept in a storage place, generally a cellar, in which the temperature is in the fifties or low sixties, they have an indefinite life. The life of any Bordeaux or Burgundy under these conditions should be at least thirty years, and perhaps very much longer.

Some of the greatest wines to come onto the market in recent years were in the collection of the French psychiatrist, Dr. Albert Barolet of Beaune, France. When Dr. Barolet died in 1969 he left a cellar of about 1.3 million bottles. Much of the wine was in casks. Improper storage and handling of these wines resulted in a loss of about one million bottles.

Investment-quality French wines are those produced from about 1945 to date. Wines produced before 1945 are extremely scarce, and wines of the vintage year 1945 are also rarely found in the United States and are all but priceless. Some good 1952 and 1953 wines are occasionally offered in this country, but more is available of the great vintage year 1955. The superb wines of 1959 and 1961 are still available at auction in London but are virtually unobtainable on the American market. In 1972 even the finest wines of these two excellent years could be purchased quite easily in case lots. Now only later vintages—1962, 1964, 1966, 1967, 1969, and 1970—can be readily acquired. Later vintages have yet to prove their quality, although both 1971 and 1972 may turn out to be very good vintage years.

These are the best years for the wine investor, in order of importance, beginning with the finest and most valuable: 1945, 1961, 1959, 1953, 1955, 1952, 1962, 1966, 1964, 1970, 1969, and 1967. The year 1945 is universally accepted as a great vintage year, with wines which do not show any deleterious effects of time. It is probably the most valuable of all of the postwar years. The year 1961 may well be the "new year of the century." Almost all wines produced by all châteaux and domaines in 1961 were fine, and they have many years of drinkable life remaining.

The year 1959 was formerly called "the year of the century." It may have produced better wines for drinking right now, but the longevity of the 1959 wines is not as great as that of the 1961 wines. The years 1953 and 1955 produced excellent wines, as did 1952.

The wines of the 1960s are still plentiful and worth far less at present than the earlier wines. The year 1962 produced some excellent Burgundies and Bordeaux, and the 1966 vintage is tremendously sought after today. The year 1964 is rated behind 1966 except, perhaps, in Burgundy. In 1970 great Bordeaux were produced and in 1969 great Burgundies. In both of these years the growers sold the wines at tremendous prices, but the prices may go even higher. The year 1967 is gaining recognition as an acceptable vintage year, particularly in Burgundies.

These are the generally unacceptable vintage years from a drinking and investment point of view, beginning with the worst and ending with the "best of a bad lot": 1965, 1968, 1963, 1958, 1956, 1954, and 1960. The years 1956 and 1954 rarely appear on the market. The year 1960 is on this list not because the wines of that year were poor—the Lafite-Rothschild of 1960 is excellent—but because the peak of quality has been reached and the wine may now begin to go downhill.

In port wines the year of the century was definitely 1927. These wines have hit their peak and are on a plateau. They are likely to continue to rise in value because they are rare, because they are being consumed, and because of the reputation of the year 1927 in port wines.

Port wine comes from Portugal and is generally bottled in Oporto. In Bordeaux wines, "mis en bouteille au château"—château bottling—is all-important. In port wines, it is not. The shipper does the bottling of port wine, and the shipper's name—Taylor, Dow, and others—is what matters. Much port wine is also bottled in London.

In Bordeaux and Burgundies the years 1965, 1968, and 1963 are important, indicating poor vintage and thus low value years. In port wines one does not have to worry about poor vintage years as there were no vintage bottlings at all in poor years.

Vintage port is a mildly sweet wine. It is generally not considered to be mature or very valuable until it is ten to fifteen years old, and it remains in top drinking condition from age fifteen to age thirty-five.

After the year 1927 the next most desirable and valuable vintage year in port is 1935. The next significant year is 1945, also the great year in French red wines. Next in importance are the years 1947 and 1948, and then the year 1955.

The fine investment years in port wines that are available for purchase now in quantity and at fairly reasonable prices are 1960 and 1963. The final "best year" is 1966. From these excellent port years we move down to the years 1950 and 1967.

Wines have become a very real investment in the United States, but mainly French wines. In England, investment wine has traditionally been vintage port, which is almost unknown over here. One collector found a bottle of 1963 port on the shelf of a wine merchant in Yonkers, New York. Perhaps the wine merchant thought 1963 meant the same thing in vintage port that it does in Bordeaux and

Burgundies—"poor vintage year." In any event the price was $3.25, and the collector snapped it up and asked for all the cases of the wine that might be in the dealer's cellar.

How to buy French wines

There is a game that is played by a number of people. It is played generally during the business lunch hour and on Saturdays. The men go on a window-shopping tour of wine dealers. There they note prices of various vintage wines—usually mentally, but sometimes on a pad. They generally do not buy anything, but rather estimate how much they might make in price appreciation if they did buy.

Actually, buying by the bottle is a poor investment; cases must be bought. Cases containing twelve bottles each are the method of buying and selling at auction and the usual way dealers buy. The original wooden case, unopened, is preferable to a cardboard box from the viewpoint of value.

Only vintage wines of good years should be bought. As to where to purchase wines, good buys are still possible from dealers—either big important dealers or out-of-the-way dealers. The first will have vintage wines at market prices. The second may have a few cases of vintage wines at old prices—bargains. These cases may have been around for a long time and the dealer may have neglected to increase the price as the market in wines rose.

The main places to purchase wines for investment are Christie's and Sotheby's in London. Christie's is by far the larger auction. Both of these auction houses issue catalogs prior to each sale and price lists after each sale, so the market can be determined rapidly by the wine investor or would-be investor.

As recently as 1971, prices at the London wine auctions were far under retail prices in America. Now the London auction prices have caught up with American retail price levels. In fact, wines have risen so high in price that demand may diminish at the retail level. Lafite-Rothschild 1961 is a really excellent wine, but not many people will purchase it at $150 a bottle.

Bordeaux wines to invest in

Of all the French red, dry wines, the château-bottled Bordeaux are the best investment. They are universally liked, collected, and drunk, particularly by the English, who call them "clarets." Highly important to the collector and investor is the fact that the wine is sturdy, much sturdier than the other great dry wine of France—Burgundy—and it is longer lived. The vintage year 1961 is available for purchase and is to a degree a magic number in wines, connoting a first-rate year with an extremely long life and with an excellent auction price history.

These are the leading top-grade Bordeaux investment wines, to-gether with late-1973 auction prices in London for the vintage year 1961:

	Per Case
Lafite-Rothschild:	$775
Mouton-Rothschild:	750
Latour:	625
Margaux:	460
Haut Brion:	488
Cheval Blanc:	438
Ausone:	288
Pétrus:	1,000

The first five listed are the most famous of all the Bordeaux châ-teaux and the most traded wines. The next two are the finest châteaux in Saint Emilion. The last is the great château in Pomerol and in the opinion of some wine experts the finest Bordeaux of them all.

Vintage year is of the essence in determining value. These are some representative auction prices as of late 1973 for the leader, Lafite-Rothschild:

Vintage Year	Per Case
1945	$925
1947	625
1952	375
1953	625
1955	525
1959	650
1961	775
1962	312
1964	300
1966	375

The value of each vintage year of the other châteaux might be determined by noting how the value of each year of Lafite-Rothschild varies as compared with the value of 1961. The vintage years between 1945 and 1966 which are not listed above might be disregarded by a novice collector as they are not the preferred years. The 1963 vintage, for instance, is of little interest to collectors, investors, or drinkers. The late-1973 auction price for Château Latour 1963 and for Château Margaux were $90 and $75, respectively—$7.50 and $6.25 per bottle, at twelve bottles to the case.

The great wines are by no means the only Bordeaux wines for

investment. Even wines which sell for $3 a bottle can be investment wines. Nor are the great wines always the highest risers in price. Château Lynch-Bages of 1962 vintage is probably the equal of any 1962 Bordeaux in quality, and it has risen in price from $3 a bottle in 1970 to over $20 a bottle today.

The *Encyclopedia of Wines and Spirits* by Alexis Lichine and many other wine publications give listings of châteaux and domaines by grade. Values can be determined by studying Christie's wine sales catalogs, which cost about twenty-five or thirty cents each and can be obtained by writing to Christie's Wine Auction, 8 King Street, St. James's, London. The catalogs issued by Sotheby's, of 34 New Bond Street, London, are also of interest, although they cost more than Christie's and are not as easy to read. Christie's is by far the larger wine auction and is under the direction of one of the world's greatest wine experts, J. Michael Broadbent.

Burgundy wines as an investment

Which wine is better, Bordeaux or Burgundy? The answer depends entirely upon personal taste. Bordeaux is traditionally preferred in England. It has a little more body, is generally longer lived, and is selling at higher overall prices in today's market. Perhaps the taste of Burgundy, particularly the great Burgundies, is a little more elegant. These are the leaders:

Romanée-Conti	Chambertin and Chambertin-Clos de Bèze
La Tâche	Musigny
Richebourg	Romanée-Saint-Vivant
Grands-Echézeaux	La Romanée
Echézeaux	

Romanée-Conti is unquestionably the greatest Burgundy. It is produced in a vineyard just four and one-third acres in size. Each year 650 cases of wine are produced—8,000 bottles—and no more. For centuries Romanée-Conti was the wine prepared for the dukes of Burgundy to present to the king. The same family that owns Romanée-Conti owns all or parts of the other domaines in the first group listed.

The four domaines listed in the second column are excellent and their wines can sometimes be obtained for a good deal less money than the Romanée-Conti group. Romanée-Conti owns a part of Romanée-Saint-Vivant but in this case their bottles are not the characteristic Romanée-Conti bottle used for the wines named in the first group.

Some 1961 Burgundies are still in stock, and often seem to be available at reasonable prices as compared with 1961 Bordeaux, which never seem to be reasonable in price. The vintage year 1962 is very good in Burgundies, as are 1964, 1966, and 1969, the greatest recent Burgundy year. Ranking just below 1969 is 1970, but these recent vintage years are very high in price and have been very expensive since they first appeared on the market. The year 1967 is developing well. In 1972 the vintage year 1967 could be purchased fairly cheaply. Now, however, it is rising in price quite rapidly.

These are some of the prices as of 1973 for the vintage year 1969 for wines produced by Romanée-Conti:

	Per Case
Romanée-Conti	$1,000
La Tâche	415
Richebourg	384
Grands-Echézeaux	258
Echézeaux	208
Romanée-Saint-Vivant	377

The other great Burgundies are in line in price with the above Burgundies of lesser quality than Romanée-Conti. In late 1973 a mixed case of Musigny, half 1959 and half 1961, sold for $312—$26 a bottle.

These are some sample London auction prices for good Burgundies as of 1973:

	Per Case
Richebourg 1961, Paul Bouchard	$80.00
Chambolle-Musigny 1955	92.50
Chambertin 1957, Bouchard Aîné	52.50
Chambertin 1961, Paul Deloux	55.00
Clos de Vougeot 1959	75.00
Clos de Vougeot 1961	82.50
Chambolle-Musigny 1961	62.50

In 1973 the great Romanée-Conti 1961 sold for $744 a case at auction in London—$62 a bottle. The other vineyards of Burgundy would sell for less than this figure in about the proportion of the 1969 prices listed above. In the United States, a bottle of Romanée-Conti 1961 would sell at retail for over $100, as would the great vintage of 1959.

Price trends in vintage port

Until 1970, vintage port wines rose very little in price. In fact in the last half of the 1960s prices decreased. Many vintage years were

Vintage Ports and Their Prices

These are some 1973 prices per case for vintage port by years, from the most desired brand on down to the "least of the greats." In addition to those listed, acceptable shippers are Fonseca, Sandeman, Warre, Rebello Valenta, and Quinta do Noval.

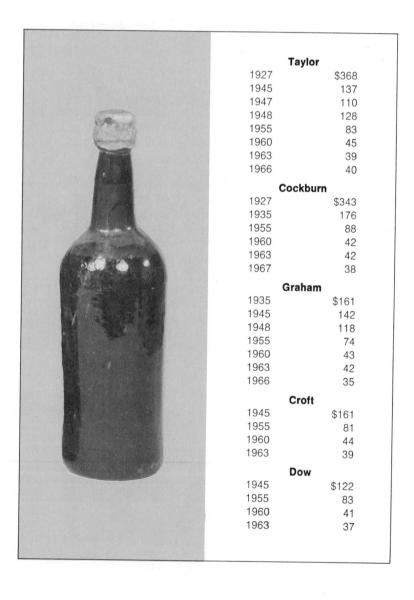

Taylor

1927	$368
1945	137
1947	110
1948	128
1955	83
1960	45
1963	39
1966	40

Cockburn

1927	$343
1935	176
1955	88
1960	42
1963	42
1967	38

Graham

1935	$161
1945	142
1948	118
1955	74
1960	43
1963	42
1966	35

Croft

1945	$161
1955	81
1960	44
1963	39

Dow

1945	$122
1955	83
1960	41
1963	37

announced and a large quantity of wine became available in Portugal. Carrying costs forced the wine onto the market earlier than it otherwise would have been marketed, with a resultant price drop.

Port has been a traditional British drink and a traditional British investment. The American market that boomed French wines has hardly heard of vintage port, nor have many European buyers of French wines. As prices of French wines rose, people turned to other wines, and one of these was vintage port, although Americans are still minor factors in the market.

In the first nine months of 1973, vintage port prices rose about as much as they might have risen in five years under normal conditions. The expensive older ports are still around, and in October, 1973, a dealer in England sold several bottles of Dow's 1927 vintage (the best year of the century) for about $22 a bottle, or $264 a case.

The increased interest in investing in vintage port in this nine-month period particularly affected prices of the less expensive ports of the later years. The 1963s that were selling for $37.50 to $42.50 per case approximately tripled in this period. Still, vintage ports do not seem to be overpriced, and the price trend is definitely up.

The place to buy port is at the London wine auctions. A few far-sighted wine merchants, such as Alfio Moriconi of the Calvert Wine and Cheese Shop in Washington, D.C., have laid in vintage ports in the past year or two at costs well under those of 1973. Such cases might be sought out and purchased at reasonable prices.

Price movements in Bordeaux wines

There was no significant upward push in Bordeaux wine prices until about 1969. A person who wished to purchase the finest Bordeaux wine for investment at that time could buy Lafite-Rothschild 1961 at retail for $19 a bottle.

Between 1971 and 1972 the price of Bordeaux wines rose about 80 percent. In the next year they rose about 22 percent over 1972 prices. Early 1973 probably represented the price peak at auction for Bordeaux wines. One investor was fortunate enough to sell his Lafite-Rothschild 1959 for $775 the case, which had cost him $205 a year earlier.

In some ways Christie's auction sale of October 18, 1973, one of the season's openers, was the most significant wine sale held anywhere during the past few years. This was not only a big sale—359 lots were sold—but a large proportion of the lots consisted of the very finest and highest-priced Bordeaux of recent vintage. All of the great post-World War II vintage years, 1945 to the middle 1960s, from the great châteaux were represented.

This sale to some degree represented buyer reaction to the high prices of vintage French wines. The offerings were absorbed by the

market, but there was something of a price dip. The previous high
for Lafite-Rothschild 1959 had been $775 per case, in February,
1973. In this October sale one lot of Lafite 1959 brought $525
and another brought $650. A reduction of $250 from the peak was
significant.

Of course the rapid rise of the market might have indicated the
necessity for a "consolidation," and it can be appreciated that there
was such a need when one studies the rise at retail of Lafite 1959
between 1969 and 1974. In 1969, Lafite 1959 was selling for $25 a
bottle at retail. In late 1973 the price of $160 was asked by at least
one big retailer in New York. He seemed very annoyed at the time
that he had made a mistake in the price and had sold a bottle of this
wine to a customer for $150.

Many people refused to pay $160 for a bottle of wine. Even at
$20 a bottle, customers to a considerable extent refused to buy, and
the smaller retailers gave up buying the finer wines. Still, the boom
seems by no means to be over. Although the wine moves slowly, it
is being gradually consumed or put away as an investment and does
not again appear on the market. The demand, smaller though it may
be, must be met out of the diminished dealer stocks. As more wine
is auctioned off, there is less left for dealers to purchase. Much of
the buying is by American dealers, and once the wine moves from
London to the stocks of American dealers, there is little likelihood
that it will ever return to London for auctioning.

Price movements in Burgundies

Between 1971 and 1972, Burgundy wines increased in price by
about 190 percent, as against an 80 percent increase in price for
Bordeaux. Romanée-Conti had already topped out at a retail price
of $100 a bottle or a little more as early as 1971. The rest of the
Burgundies caught up, and all of them, Romanée-Conti included,
rose significantly at auction until there was little disparity between
the London auction price and the American retail price by 1972.

Fine Burgundies, with the exception of Romanée-Conti, were
still available for purchase in retail stores in America as late as
mid-1973. Gristede Brothers' wine shops offered Chambertin 1961
and Chambertin-Clos de Bèze for a little over $6 a bottle. At this
price one collector put in an order with the Gristede in Greenwich,
Connecticut, for all the cases of these wines which could be located
in any and all of the Gristede stores as well as in their warehouse.

Burgundies are not the investments that Bordeaux are, but it is
difficult not to consider one purchase as both a fine beverage and an
investment. The New York firm of Leland Wine and Liquor had
in stock some excellent Pommard, vintage year 1964. It had been
imported into the United States many years ago when prices were

much lower than they are today. The firm offered this wine at $1.99 a bottle.

One wine collector placed an order for all of this Burgundy that could be secured. No fewer than seventeen cases were produced by Leland and bought by the collector. Then the dealer scouted around and found several more loose bottles. These he sold for 99 cents each. The collector served this wine at a dinner party and received many compliments on it. He then followed the 99-cent wine with a Romanée-Conti which he had purchased for $20 a bottle four years earlier when prices were vastly lower than at the present time. The guests generally agreed that the Romanée-Conti was better than the 99-cent Pommard. How much better was it? Perhaps 50 percent better, but not twenty times better.

Guidelines for investing in vintage wines

If you intend to invest in vintage wines:

1. Buy by the case, never by the bottle. There is no market anywhere for one bottle of wine.

2. Examine the wine against a strong light and reject it if there are particles floating in it, if the color is not ruby red, if the cork is leaking, or if there is considerable sediment in the bottom of the bottle. A little sediment is normal in an old wine.

3. Taste suspect wine to learn whether it has gone bad.

4. Be sure the dealer will refund your money if the wine is bad. Reputable dealers make such refunds.

5. Make sure the wine has come from a cool cellar. Often the wine dealer will ask the customer to inspect his cellar.

6. Store your wine purchases in a cool place, preferably a cellar where the temperature is always under sixty degrees Fahrenheit. Bottles should be stored on their sides.

7. Remember that to transport wine to the United States from London may cost a dollar a bottle, that pilferage on the dock does take place, and that there is often breakage.

8. Wine can be stored for a minimum cost in London, and the auction house will arrange transportation to and from the warehouse which will store the wine at the right temperature. St. Olaf's bonded warehouse in London stores wines reliably at minimum cost.

Vintage port wines are probably the best investment at the present time—before American investors turn to this wine. The later vintage years are still very much underpriced. Burgundies are both an excellent wine and a reasonably good investment with prices still not too high, but rising. The great Bordeaux wines are very high in price and lesser châteaux might be concentrated on.

The purchase price of this 1904 14-horsepower Gladiator was $30,000 in 1973. Prices of many antique and classic cars are rising rapidly, but there are still some available for less than $6,000, including the 1902 Olds, the 1907 Brush, and the 1901 Cadillac.

26

Antique
and
Classic
Automobiles

For a collector of classic and antique automobiles the major errors in judgment rarely occur in buying the wrong car, or paying too much, or spending too much on restoration. Rather the major errors occur in underestimating the rising market. Errors in judgment of this type were certainly made by one collector. His story also indicates what has happened to classic and antique car prices in recent times.

Just before the outbreak of World War II this collector bought a 1932 Auburn coupe with rumble seat and fabric top for $195. It had 4,500 miles on it. Two years later he traded it in on a Mercedes-Benz. His allowance was $200 on the Auburn. Today the Auburn would be worth about $7,500.

The car he bought was a 1928 Mercedes S model convertible with four-seater body by Erdmann and Rossi. He paid $150 plus his Auburn to get this car and put almost $100 into a new paint job and a new fabric top. After about a year he traded it in on a Phantom I Rolls-Royce Riviera town car. His allowance on the Mercedes was $350. The Mercedes would be worth about $15,000 today.

The Rolls-Royce was purchased with the Mercedes trade-in plus $200 in cash—$550 in all. The Rolls-Royce today would be worth at least $10,000.

He later sold the Rolls-Royce for $750. He then purchased for cash a 1927 Mercedes-Benz SS two-door touring car for $550. This car would be worth a minimum of $25,000 at the present time.

The Mercedes SS plus $1,000 was the purchase price of a 540K Mercedes coupe, costing about $1,500 in all.

Now he began to secure more cash from his transactions in automobiles. For his 540K Mercedes he received $350 and a 1941 custom Cadillac sedan with sliding sunroof, so that his net investment in the Cadillac was $1,150. The 540K Mercedes today would be worth about $25,000.

He sold the Cadillac for $3,000 cash shortly after purchasing it. This Fleetwood five-passenger sedan today would be worth a little more than he received for it, about $4,000 to $4,500.

His next purchase was a Mercedes 500K convertible cabriolet with Corsica body made in England. He paid $1,550 for this car. A year later he sold it to a dealer for $2,400. Today this car would be worth $25,000.

During the war this collector purchased a seven-passenger 1930 Lincoln touring car for $32, and sold it shortly thereafter for $50. Today its value would be close to $20,000.

In the 1950s the collector reluctantly took in trade on one of his sports cars a 1931 Marmon sixteen-cylinder sedan, allowing almost $500 for it. The price he received for the sports car was so high, however, that he felt the "oversized" Marmon was not worth the trouble of storing. He gave the car away. In the condition it was at the time it would be worth about $15,000 now.

Still later he made a fine purchase: a 1933 Stutz DV32 sedan for $175. After looking over the car carefully, he embarked on an extensive restoration job, but eventually gave up the project and made a gift of the car to a friend, a Stutz buff. The Stutz today would sell for about $10,000.

Despite these major errors of judgment, the collector made his little investments in cars pay, and such transactions supplied him with his initial fund of capital that has grown in size over the years.

To indicate how the prices of prewar automobiles have risen in recent years, we might make a comparison of the prices some of this collector's cars would have brought in 1971 and 1973. In two years this sample group of cars rose in value, assuming they were in fine condition, from $98,500 to $155,000—a little over 50 percent, or 25 percent per year. If the cars were in poorer condition, the increase in price would have been approximately the same but the figures would have been lower.

	1971 Price	1973 Price
1935 Auburn 851 speedster	$17,500	$ 25,000
1938 Cadillac sedan	4,500	7,000
1930 Lincoln seven-passenger touring	17,500	19,000
1931 Marmon 16 sedan	12,000	15,000
1938 Mercedes-Benz 540K coupe	9,000	25,000
1933 Stutz DV32 sedan	6,500	10,500
1936 Mercedes-Benz 500K convertible	14,000	25,000
1927 Mercedes-Benz SS touring	17,500	29,000
Total	$98,500	$155,500

This group of cars cost the collector $5,302. They have increased in value about thirty times in twenty years on the average. As an investment, this is not a bad performance. If an investment earns 1 percent per month, compounded monthly (12 percent per year) the money doubles in six years and quadruples in twelve years. In a twenty-year period at this 12 percent rate, an investment increases about seven times. Also by way of comparison, in twenty years the art market increased about eighteen times.

This rate of price increase in the prewar sample of cars is almost identical to the increase in price from 1971 to 1973 of a sample of postwar classics, also owned by this collector.

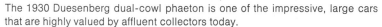

The 1930 Duesenberg dual-cowl phaeton is one of the impressive, large cars that are highly valued by affluent collectors today.

The classification of antique and prewar classic cars is somewhat arbitrary. One accepted classification is that cars built in the years 1925 to 1942 are classic cars and those built prior to 1925 are antique cars. However, the *Old Car Value Guide* has an overlapping category from 1925 through 1929 in which certain cars are listed as antiques and others as classics. In some ways it might be just as well to combine all these cars into pre-World War II classic and antique cars.

Value determinants

At the present time the car that has the most value and has experienced the greatest price rise is the impressive, big car. In general it is not the little car that is highly valued, no matter how rare or how perfect it is. The standouts on the present market are such cars as the Mercer Raceabout, the Stutz Bearcat, the Duesenberg J and SJ, the rare Rolls-Royces, the Mercedes-Benz 770K of the Nazi era, and the Cadillac V16.

The situation was not always so. At the outbreak of World War II, two Duesenbergs were for sale in New York. The first was a double-cowl, four-door convertible which drove very well and appeared to be in good condition. The price was $600. The second was an SJ two-passenger convertible in mint condition. Its price was $750.

During World War II a completely restored, mint-condition Mercer Raceabout was for sale for $7,000. In junkyard condition, this car would cost far more than $7,000 today.

Also during the war two Cadillac V16 coupes were for sale at the same dealer in New York for $250 each. In 1944 a Mercedes-Benz 770K four-door convertible was for sale for $750, although it was not quite as beautiful as the one belonging to Hitler which was sold in 1973 for $153,000. During the war years a Bugatti Royale was offered for $750. It is valued now at about $150,000.

There is a good deal of support for the belief that those who control the purse strings "buy with nostalgia." In other words, they purchase those things which represented the ultimate in quality, prestige, and elegance when they were younger and could not afford them. Those in the fifty-to-sixty age group who are affluent today purchase the high-quality, high-priced prestige cars of the 1920s and 1930s. There are, of course, collectors who want the greatest rarities and will pay for them, but even though these cars may date back to Edwardian times, they are still usually large, very impressive vehicles, such as early Rolls-Royces.

An important value determinant in the car market is rarity. There were very few Mercedes-Benz 770Ks and Bugatti Royales made. These cars have the two important qualities of being ex-

The 1913 Mercer Raceabout, in fine condition, has risen in price from $25,000 to $45,000 during the past 20 years.

tremely rare and being magnificent, large vehicles. Hence the huge prices at the present time for both of these models.

Not so long ago a 1913 Mercer Raceabout was purchased from a junkyard for $25. The car was restored to perfect condition. On the present market this car would be worth well over $40,000. The *Old Car Value Guide* gives the average value of an unrestored 1913 Mercer Raceabout as $16,000—about $25,000 less than the value of one in fine condition. Thus we have condition as being a determinant of value.

Some old cars have no value as subjects for restoration. If a car is for sale for $500 with rusted body and in need of a cylinder rebore which together will cost $3,000, and at the same time a car of the same model, not in need of body work and a rebore, sells for $1,000, it is obvious that the first car has no value at all to the collector. In fact to him it has a negative value since to repair the first car so that it approximates the condition of the second car would require more expenditure than the cost of the second car.

A car in "show condition" brings a super-premium price. If a car restored to so-called 90 percent condition brings $5,000 and an average car $3,000, then a car in show condition might well bring $7,000 or even more. Thus, if a car in show or mint condition is advertised for $7,500 when average cars sell for, say, $5,000, the $7,500 car might well be looked at first. It may represent $4,000 worth of improvement over the $5,000 car, and $7,500 is the asking price, not the price the owner will take after negotiation.

After a while, a collector learns the approximate cost of restoring a car. A major restoration may well require 400 to 1,000 hours work, at an hourly labor rate of $10 to $15. A recent restoration of a Mercedes-Benz 300S convertible required about 1,000 hours of labor, plus hides for upholstery, material for the top, chrome parts, a few mechanical parts, a set of tires, carpeting, and new rubber for the bumpers. The labor cost was $3.50 an hour as the job was done by a small rural shop.

The experienced collector looks at a car in need of restoration and mentally estimates $600 for upholstery. He then figures $250 for a new top. Carpeting will cost $100. A set of tires will cost $90. A new clutch will run to about $400. A valve grind will cost $500 for a double-overhead-camshaft eight-cylinder engine with eight carburetors, or $200 for a flat-head four-cylinder engine. Chrome will cost about $1,000. It is surprising how close to actual costs a collector's estimates will often run.

Price trend of a collection

This is the price trend of an "ideal collection" of classic and antique cars:

Cars in Fine Condition	1970 Price	1973 Price
1913 Mercer Raceabout	$ 40,000	$ 45,000
1914 Stutz Bearcat	22,500	29,000
1938 Mercedes-Benz 540K roadster	25,000	35,000
1935 Mercedes-Benz 500K roadster	20,000	35,000
1902 Olds curved-dash roadster	3,500	5,000
1937 Duesenberg SJ convertible	42,000	72,000
1939 Bugatti SC drop-head coupe	8,750	20,000
1927 Rolls-Royce P1 Ascot convertible sedan	20,000	24,000
1930 Cadillac V16 roadster	35,000	40,000
Total	$216,750	$305,000

This "portfolio" of classic and antique cars increased in value in three years by at least $88,000—about 40 percent. If anything, the rate of increase errs on the conservative side. The Mercer Raceabout shows little increase in price, and the price increase of the Bugatti SC does not recognize the fact that one such car recently sold for $53,000.

The prices of these cars in the early 1950s show the twenty-year price trend. A Mercer Raceabout could be purchased for $25,000 then; a Stutz Bearcat, for $15,000; Mercedes-Benz 500K and 540K roadsters, $15,000 each; an Olds curved-dash roadster, $2,000; a Duesenberg SJ convertible, $3,000; a Bugatti SC convertible, $1,500; a Rolls-Royce Ascot convertible, $4,000; and a Cadillac V16 roadster, also $4,000. All of these nine cars could have been purchased for $84,500 in the 1950s. Early in World War II the entire collection might have been purchased for $8,400, and prices remained at this level until the beginning of the 1950s.

Most of the above list is comprised of "rich men's cars" and there may be other, better investments in the classic and antique car field than these cars which represent the best according to the prevailing taste.

Cars available at reasonable prices

The great cars, either in mint condition or unrestored, cannot be purchased at the present time for reasonable sums of money. The question is, therefore, what can be purchased. The answer is the earlier, simpler cars with one or two cylinders and some with four cylinders. In the present market the smaller and older cars are not preferred and generally do not bring high prices. They are considered to be "quaint little buggies" that are too slow and too impractical to merit serious collector interest. Still these cars have risen in price.

A 1909 Maxwell two-cylinder roadster was for sale in Darien, Connecticut, in 1967 for an asking price of $1,200. It was in very good condition, but had aluminum pistons instead of the original cast-iron ones. It had no windshield and no top. In late 1973 this same car sold at auction in the same area for $5,500—almost five times the 1967 price but still not a huge figure.

The famous 1902 curved-dash Olds may still be purchased for about $5,000 and the 1907 one-cylinder Brush can be purchased in fine condition for about $4,000. The 1901 Cadillac roadster can be acquired for about $6,000, and this same price applies up through the 1906 model year.

The 1909 and 1910 Hupmobile open cars can be purchased for about $4,000. Maxwell roadsters of the years 1902 to 1909 can often be purchased for similar sums. So can the Orient Buckboard of 1903. The one-cylinder Reo of 1904 to 1906 is in the same price class, as is the 1914 Saxon roadster.

A Ford made before the era of the Model T cannot be bought in this price range. The early Fords are much higher in value, and the 1905 Model F two-cylinder car sells for about $10,000.

To acquire a Ford for $4,000 or less, the collector should look at the early four-cylinder Model T cars of about the year 1917, not earlier. The 1917 Model T touring car sells for about $3,000, and for the same price a Ford touring car all the way up to the last model turned out in 1927 can be purchased. This is quite a price distance from the $30 to $35 that a good 1927 Model T touring car could be purchased for when it was in excellent condition and just two years old. Model A open cars bring much higher prices than the Model T.

In addition to these earlier and very much simpler cars which can still be purchased at reasonable prices, the collector can consider the later and more sophisticated classics and antiques, but among these the choice of good cars at moderate prices is very limited. These are a few of the finer cars now available at reasonable prices which may well rise in the near future:

- A Bentley convertible of the middle 1930s can be purchased for $6,000 to $7,500. This car is excellent in appearance and operation and well worth the price.
- BMW roadsters and convertibles of the years 1936 to 1939 can be purchased for sums between $4,000 and $5,000. These are as good as almost any sports cars of the period. Their body styling is first-rate.
- Cadillac V8 touring cars of the years 1917 to 1922—splendid, large, sophisticated automobiles—can be found in the price range of $5,000 to $6,000.
- Chryslers at prices from $5,500 to $6,500 include the 1924 to 1926 Chrysler 70 roadster, the 1928 Model 72 roadster, and the 1929 Model 75 roadster, which was known as the Chrysler Blue Boy when it was first produced for a price of $1,555.
- Packard six-cylinder roadsters or touring cars made in the early 1920s—good-looking, reliable cars—can be purchased for $6,000 to $7,000. The eight-cylinder, twelve-cylinder, and limited-edition models are sky-high in price.

If you plan to purchase an antique or prewar classic car:

1. Secure present and back issues of the *Old Car Value Guide,* published in Prescott, Arizona, to see market prices.
2. Check advertisements in newspapers, the *Bulb Horn* magazine, and other antique car magazines to see what is being offered and what prices are being asked.
3. Inspect cars in the category in which you are interested to see their condition in relation to price.

Postwar classic automobiles

Many cars produced in the post-World War II period are and will be in the investment category. The following cars are a selection of those which are most likely to reward the investor.

Rolls-Royce and Bentley

The Rolls-Royce Silver Cloud series—mainly five-passenger sedans—first appeared on the market in 1955. The chassis and engine
were very much like the preceding model, with a six-cylinder "F
head" engine. The first of the Silver Cloud models was called the
Silver Cloud I, and was as rugged as a truck. The car was totally
reliable and required little attention and little servicing.

The Silver Cloud I model was continued to the autumn of 1959,
when the Silver Cloud II was introduced. It had the same body as
the Silver Cloud I but was a much more sophisticated and complicated machine with a V8 of a design similar to the engine used in
the present Silver Shadow series.

The Silver Cloud III appeared in 1964 and was continued until
1966, in which year the Silver Shadow series of much smaller and
less impressive automobiles was introduced.

The Bentley SI corresponds to the Rolls-Royce Silver Cloud I.
The Bentley SII is the opposite number of the Silver Cloud II, and
the SIII corresponds to the Silver Cloud III.

The only difference between the Rolls-Royce and the Bentley are
the radiator, the bumper guards, and the name. The angular Rolls-
Royce radiator is more costly to make than the rounded Bentley
radiator, and the Rolls-Royce sold for about $250 more than the
Bentley when new. However, the Rolls-Royce is very much preferred
to the Bentley on the secondhand, or investment, market and car-
ries a much higher price tag.

The Silver Cloud III (the last of the big Rolls-Royce cars) is
greatly favored in the investment market, as is the Bentley SIII.
Both cars bring the highest prices of all of the Cloud I, II, and III
series and the Bentley SI, II, and III series. The outstanding features of the III models are that the hood line is a little lower
and there are four headlamps. The premium is vastly greater
than the difference in quality or specifications between the III
models and the II models.

It will pay a prospective investor in a Rolls-Royce or a Bentley to
travel to England in order to purchase the car he wants. There are
several reasons for considering such a time- and money-consuming
trip. In the first place, Rolls-Royce cars of the Cloud series and the
Bentley S series cars are plentiful all over England. One dealer in
London, Viceroy Carriage Company, at the present time is selling
eight to ten secondhand Rolls-Royce and Bentley cars a week at
both retail and wholesale.

Another reason is that prices of the Rolls-Royce Cloud series and
the Bentley S series are much lower in England than in the United
States, even after the cost of shipment to this country is added. In
addition, the Rolls-Royce Silver Shadow and Bentley T series, the

This 1924 Rolls-Royce Silver Ghost sports tourer was sold in Geneva in 1973 for $43,000.

latest models, are just as high in price in England as they are in the United States. So are the Rolls and Bentley cars earlier than the Cloud and S series.

The only possible disadvantage in purchasing these cars in England is that they are righthand-drive vehicles. For some people such cars are harder to drive in America than the normal lefthand-drive cars, although most drivers can quickly become accustomed to driving on the opposite side of the car. Nevertheless, righthand-drive cars are not easy to resell in this country, although the price of such cars is not distinctly below the price of lefthand-drive cars.

If any work has to be done on a Rolls or Bentley purchased in England, it is possible to have this work performed for less money in England than in America, and possibly the work will also be of a better quality. Thus, the investment in a Rolls or a Bentley may well pay for a trip to London and around England for the purchaser and his family, and there may still be a profit in the transaction when the car is finally sold in the United States.

On the early 1974 market the Silver Cloud I standard sedan could be purchased in England for about $6,000; the eight-cylinder Silver Cloud II for $8,000 to $9,000; and the Cloud III for $9,000 to $11,000. If the car is in absolutely mint condition, as much as $1,000 might be added to the above prices, but rarely more, unlike the great premiums that perfect cars bring in the United States.

All of these cars are originals. None is a conversion of a Bentley

Rolls-Royce Silver Cloud II with lefthand-drive was offered in London for $9,750 in early 1974, when the price in the United States was $15,000.

to a Rolls-Royce, which involves fitting a new radiator and a few other parts, and which can be done in England for about $750. Such a conversion cannot be sold as a Rolls-Royce to a knowledgeable prospective purchaser except at a discount as compared with an original Rolls, and a purist collector would not have one of them in his stable.

The Bentley SIII can be purchased in England for $4,300 to $5,000, and the Bentley SII for $3,000 to $4,000. An excellent six-cylinder Bentley SI was offered for sale recently for $2,750. The average Bentley SI sells for $1,750 to $2,200, a price which places this car within the means of the most modest automobile purchaser in the United States.

Between 1970 and late 1973, Rolls-Royce and Bentley cars of the above series increased over 50 percent in price, with the exception of the Bentley SI, which increased in price about 25 percent. Half of this three-year rise in price took place in 1973.

In early 1974 the Rolls-Royce Silver Cloud III sold in the United States for at least $20,000. The Silver Cloud II was priced at about $15,000, and the Silver Cloud I at around $10,000. The Bentley SIII sold for about $15,000; the SII for about $12,000; and the SI for about $7,500.

The unique feature of this entire series of automobiles is that they are standard sedans, reliable and maintainable, yet they have "negative depreciation," which the usual car does not have. It is unlikely that the present high market for these cars will slacken off except in the event of an economic slide.

Mercedes-Benz

Throughout most of the 1950s, Mercedes-Benz produced economical, highly reliable, and well-styled cars—the 220 and the 220S convertibles. These cars are not spectacular looking, nor do they give tremendous performance, but they are elegant. There has been a gradual price rise in these cars during the past three years, but they still can be purchased for relatively little money. A 220 or 220S in good condition can be purchased at the present time for about $3,000. The cars have a six-cylinder overhead-camshaft engine and require little maintenance if given ordinary servicing. Between 1971 and 1974 they rose perhaps $1,000 in value.

When the 300S first appeared in 1951, carrying a price tag of about $13,500, it was considered a competitor of the Rolls-Royce, although it was made only as a roadster, a coupe, and a cabriolet with double curved bars on the top. It had a six-cylinder overhead-camshaft engine, three carburetors, the finest leather and wood interior, and was altogether a most luxurious car. In a sense the car was a throwback to prewar styling. It had classic lines and was very much like the great 540K of the late 1930s, but far quieter and far more reliable.

The cabriolet is probably the most preferred 300S, followed by the rarer roadster and finally by the coupe. About ten years ago these cars reached their low point when a good 300S could be purchased for less than $2,500. The price has risen steadily since that time and at the end of 1973 one could be purchased for $10,000 to $15,000.

In 1966 a car collector bought a 300S roadster for $800. The car was in relatively good mechanical condition and the engine did not have to be taken apart. A new clutch was installed for about $150 and the differential was taken apart and adjusted. The body was in poor shape and required stripping of the paint and welding of pieces. The wood had to be refinished and new leather had to be provided. Chroming had to be done and new chrome parts installed. The restoration to near-perfect condition cost over $4,000, including a new top and new carpeting.

Ten years ago the Mercedes-Benz 300SL roadster, an extremely streamlined yet classic car, could have been purchased for under $2,500. Seven or eight years ago the price was no higher than $3,500 for a model in good condition. The price today is about $7,500 and it is rising.

The companion car to the 300SL roadster is the 300SL gullwing, in which the doors open upward instead of outward. This car has

A price of $37,500 was paid at auction in mid-1973 for this 1937 Mercedes-Benz drophead coupe.

always been preferred to the roadster because it is unique in appearance, because fewer of this model were made, and because it is generally considered to be superior in operation. This car was never in the bargain category and rarely sold under $5,000. Three years ago a good one would bring about $6,500. Recently 300SL roadsters have been advertised at over $12,000. There is a strong demand for these cars in Germany, where they originated, and Germans have been buying the cars in America and shipping them home at a cost of about $10,000 a car.

The finest Mercedes produced in the postwar period is the elegant 600, the great V8 sedan that appeared in 1966 and is still being made in virtually its original form. Ten years ago it sold for about $22,000. Now its price is about $36,000. It is a direct competitor of the Rolls-Royce, particularly the larger and rarer models.

The Mercedes 600 models include a five-passenger sedan, a seven-passenger sedan, and the pullman, a huge car with a very long wheelbase. The 600 is in some ways a nightmare of complexity, and the owner should be prepared to spend lavish sums on repair bills, including those for the fuel-injection and air-suspension systems. It is not at all unusual to see Mercedes 600s stalled on the highways of New York—and chauffeur-driven cars at that. Still, a second-hand 600 can sometimes be purchased for about $8,000, and the car in the past two years has risen in price in some instances by over 50 percent and will probably continue to rise.

Jaguar

The Jaguar XK120 of the early 1950s was far in advance of its time in performance and in appearance, and particularly in price. The Jaguar has remained more than competitive in price since that time. The XK120 is a classic car. Its handling qualities are beautiful. It is highly reliable and requires little maintenance. After the pound was devalued, the price in America dropped from about $4,700 to about $3,900, and at the latter price many of these cars were imported. Many of them are still in service and appear on the market regularly.

At the present time the Jaguar XK120 roadster is a great buy. It has hardly begun to rise along with other postwar classics. Three years ago an XK120 in fine condition brought $3,000. Today it brings $4,000 and even less at times. Parts are still available for the car and there are many repair shops that understand Jaguars. In the winter of 1973 there were several XK120 roadsters, advertised as being in good condition, offered for $2,000 and even a little less. Very often when these cars are seen, their condition is somewhat less than as described.

The XK150 is a more refined car and later than the XK120. The car is beautiful and possibly makes the best appearance on the road when compared with other sports cars in the same price range.

The XK150 is not in great demand and it does not sell for high prices as yet. In fact, the price of the car has risen little in three years. An XK150 three years ago might have been purchased for $3,000, and $3,000 may purchase a good one today. An unrestored one may bring as little as $1,000.

In the winter of 1973 a mint-condition 1958 XK150 roadster was on the market in the New York area. It had perfect leather, upholstery, and top. It had Pirelli tires and Borani chromed wheels. Every piece of chrome on the car was like new. The car was fitted with Lucas driving lights. The body was in perfect condition. The paint could possibly have been improved by compounding, which the garage selling the car agreed to do at no extra cost. The asking price for the car was $4,500. To get a $3,000 XK150 into the condition of this particular car, which had a new engine with only 6,000 miles on it, would cost well over $1,500.

M.G.

The M.G. is starkly simple in both appearance and mechanical design.

The Model T.C. was the first put out by M.G. after the war. It was a roadster with no windows. It seated two people and had a simple four-cylinder engine. It was by no means mechanically perfect, but it was a very sporty little car that cost about $1,600 in America.

The price paid at auction in March, 1974, for this 1939 S.S. 3½-liter two-seater was $20,000. This car is a forerunner of the Jaguar.

The Model T.D. appeared in 1950. It was essentially the same as the T.C. mechanically and in body style, but it had a few notable refinements, particularly better brakes.

In good condition these cars can now be bought for $3,000 and sometimes less. An unrestored car might be bought for half this figure. They have risen in price perhaps $500 in the past three years, and in the present market they are gaining favor rather rapidly.

The M.G. T.F. two-seater of 1954 and 1955 was a very much more refined, more streamlined car than the earlier models. The radiator was distinctly different. Three years ago a T.F. in excellent condition, with perfect body and paint, was offered for sale in Washington, D.C., for $750. Today the same car might bring $3,000, possibly a little more because of its condition.

The advantage of the earlier M.G.s is that, because they are so stark in appearance, they are timeless and never will go out of date. Also, since the horsepower is around fifty-five and the cars weigh little, they are highly economical to operate. They are so simple mechanically that they are both reliable and inexpensive to repair. In fact, almost any owner can learn to make many of the repairs on the car.

Ferrari

If a motorist has never driven a Ferrari, a good case can be made out that he has never experienced the ultimate in driving. The handling qualities of the Ferrari are hard to believe. In fact, the Ferrari makes a good driver out of almost anyone. So great is the driver's feeling of absolute control of the car that driving strain is reduced materially.

Strange as it may seem, most Ferraris on the market today are not good investments. Most of those for sale are the conservative two-passenger or four-passenger coupes put out in the early to middle 1960s. They are neither a sports car by design nor a particularly attractive coupe, being somewhat nondescript in appearance. In addition, they are not trouble-free and their repair costs are sometimes beyond human comprehension.

The ordinary coupe made in the middle 1960s can be purchased on the present market for about $4,000. The earlier coupes, back to perhaps 1958, can sometimes be purchased for as little as $3,000.

The special types of Ferrari are entirely another matter as far as cost goes, with the Ferrari America and the Ferrari Super America at the top of the preferred list and at the top of the price list too. The Ferrari America and Super America of the late 1950s and 1960s sell for upwards of $10,000, and a mint-condition coupe or convertible can reach $20,000.

The Berlinetta Lusso of 1964, a finely styled and mechanically fine car, is a great favorite. It sells for about $7,500. While it has not appreciated much in price recently, it has not declined in price since 1967 and may well go up in the future.

The Ferraris made earlier than 1955 are expensive cars which are rapidly becoming classics, no matter what the model. There is, however, buyer preference for the roadsters.

There is one Ferrari model that combines a great many desirable qualities, including beauty, reliability, low maintenance cost, and low price on the present market. This is the 250 G.T. convertible coupe with detachable hard top. It requires a minimum amount of maintenance and has almost a timeless streamlining, accomplished by body-designer Farina. Five years ago, this car could be bought for $3,000, and even as late as two years ago it had risen little from this low. Now it sells for $4,500 to $6,500 and is becoming more and more of a classic. It is not as popular on the West Coast as it is in the East, and may still be available in the West for about $3,000.

Ford's products

One of the more desirable of the postwar classics is the early Ford Thunderbird produced in the middle 1950s. It is a classically designed car with the reliability and repairability of Fords. It is rapidly becoming a true classic and may well rise in price. It seats two people and has something of a continental appearance. Three years ago a good early Thunderbird could be purchased for $1,500 or less. Now a good one costs over $3,000 and some cost as much as $4,500. Both the coupe and the convertible are sought by collectors and both models bring comparable prices.

An outstanding example of American workmanship in the postwar period is the Mark II Lincoln Continental of the middle 1950s. The mechanical design of the car was excellent. The paint was of the highest quality, and the leather was the finest hides imported from Scotland. These coupes sold for as little as $1,500 three years ago. Now an average price for a good Mark II Continental is $3,500, and occasionally one can be purchased for $2,500. For a reasonable price the buyer acquires an excellent, unique, impressive-looking car, which to a considerable extent was handmade. If a Mark II can be secured in good condition for $2,500, it is a good candidate for a price rise in the next year or two.

Collector's choice

The cars discussed in this chapter and the many other collectibles analyzed earlier in this book have been selected as being worthy of consideration as investment possibilities. However, they are not the only collectibles worth investigating, and the would-be collector may well find another field more to his liking. Whatever area of collecting is decided upon, there is a good chance that the collectibles will appreciate in the future as so many have done in the past and are doing today, to the delight of those who have invested in them and enjoyed living with them as their value increased.

Index